RELIGION AND ALIENATION

GREGORY BAUM

Religion and Alienation

A THEOLOGICAL READING OF SOCIOLOGY

PAULIST PRESS

New York / Paramus / Toronto

Library of Congress
Catalog Card Number: 75-28652

ISBN: 0-8091-1917-X (paper)
ISBN: 0-8091-0205-6 (cloth)

Published by Paulist Press
Editorial Office: 1865 Broadway, N.Y., N.Y. 10023
Business Office: 400 Sette Drive, Paramus, N.J. 07652

Printed and bound in the
United States of America

Contents

Contents

To
Rosemary and Philip

Preface

One of the best ideas I ever had was to take a two-year leave of absence from my university to study sociology at the New School for Social Research in New York. I was interested in sociology largely because I could not understand why the Catholic Church, despite the good will of clergy and laity and the extraordinary institutional event of Vatican II, had been unable to move and adopt the new style of Catholicism outlined in the conciliar documents. I thought that sociology, as the systematic inquiry into society, should be able to answer this question. But what I did not expect was the profound influence that the study of sociology would have on my entire theological thinking. I became convinced that the great sociological literature of the 19th and early 20th centuries records human insight and human wisdom as much as philosophical writings, and that it ought to have a special place in the education of philosophers and theologians. I found that the sociological tradition contains basic truth absent from philosophical and theological thought, truth that actually modifies the very meaning of philosophy and theology. I am thinking here especially of the relationship between mind and society. While sociologists may differ in their understanding of this relationship, all of them in one way or another acknowledge that society (the institutions in which we live) affects our consciousness (the way we perceive reality and think about it). Thought, in other words, is socially grounded. I began to feel that the exclusion of sociological literature from philosophical and theological education has been a misfortune. What I want to do in this book, therefore, is to introduce the student of theology to the sociological tradition. My hope is that more theologians will turn to the sociological literature and enter into conversation with it.

Among the many things that impressed me when I read

the classical sociological writings was the central place that the study of religion occupied in the work of the great thinkers. While theologians look upon the Christian religion mainly in terms of faith, hope and love and frequently become uneasy about the church's presence in the world, sociologists for the most part regard religion as a powerful factor without which it is impossible to account for the creation of culture and society. This certainly was the view of Max Weber and Emile Durkheim, even though neither of them regarded himself as a believer. Religion, however spiritual in appearance, has a social impact which may be hidden from the theologian but which sociologists make the special object of their attention. I cannot deny that the study of sociology gave me a new sense of the power and meaning of religion.

What also greatly impressed me in the sociological literature was the humanist perspective adopted by these great thinkers. They studied society to detect in the social institutions the trends that hurt and diminish human life, and they tried to create sociological theory that would actually promote the social processes that promised to make society more truly human. Beginning with Alexis de Tocqueville and Karl Marx, the great sociologists were moralists. Since they distinguished themselves from Christian thinkers and from historical scholars who examined society in an interested way, in defense of specific secular or religious institutions, the sociologists insisted that they studied society in an objective manner. Their approach was value-free and scientific. They wrestled against inherited prejudice and personal bias. At the same time, they were committed to values. They had a vision of what human life ought to be like, and it was this commitment to an anthropology that enabled them, each in his own way, to detect the alienating or dehumanizing aspects of society and look for social processes that promised to deliver people from their plight. The theological reader in particular is greatly impressed by the moral passion in the sociologists, despite their effort to be objective. This moral quality makes the classical sociological literature so different from most of the publications that emanate from the research institutes and sociology departments of our universities today.

This moral concern struck me as soon as I began my study

of sociology. In an article, "Personal Testimony to Sociology," which I wrote two months after my arrival at the New School and published in the fall of 1969 in *The Ecumenist*, I expressed my amazement at the great concern for human life found in classical sociology and suggested that this moral concern was in fact the perspective from which these thinkers examined society. I continued to read the sociological literature from this angle, and while my reading convinced me of the validity of my approach, I discovered that my interpretation of the classical authors was not shared by many commentators. Why were there so many interpretations? I eventually came to realize that the sociological literature is always read from particular hermeneutical presuppositions and that the interpretation of the great authors depends, in part at least, on the perspective of the commentator.

In the well-known work, *The Structure of Social Action*, Talcott Parsons presents the thought of the great sociologists of the 19th and early 20th centuries from his special viewpoint: he finds in them the sociological insights that have prepared, piece by piece, the vast sociological synthesis produced in the 20th century, in which the original insights are interrelated, adjusted and harmonized. Parsons rightly regarded himself as one of the principal architects of this synthesis. When we turn to Robert Nisbet's beautiful book, *The Sociological Tradition*, we are introduced to the same social thinkers from a slightly different perspective. Nisbet believes, as the title of his book indicates, that present among the various social thinkers was, despite their considerable differences, a basic agreement on the nature of society and the fundamental concepts, in terms of which the social reality must be analyzed. He therefore presented the sociological literature grouped around the fundamental concepts that emerged early in the tradition and were later modified and refined but never abandoned by it. If we then read Irving Zeitlin's interesting *Ideology and the Development of Social Theory*, we are again introduced to the classical sociological thinkers read from different hermeneutical presuppositions. For Zeitlin the development of social thought reached a high point, a watershed as he calls it, with the sociology of Karl Marx, and from that time on, every single sociologist worked out his theory of society with Karl Marx looking over his shoulder. Zeitlin persuasively argues that each social thinker has been, in one way or another, in conversation with Marx's ghost and that the stance he has adopted in this conversation determined the manner in which he analyzed society. While I do not compare myself with these learned professors of sociology, I did feel that it was reasonable for me to read the same sociological literature from another perspective, one that I had adopted quite spontaneously and tested and confirmed by subsequent studies. Ernest Becker, in his *The Structure of Evil*, has adopted a very similar focus for his reading of the social thinkers of the Enlightenment. While I do not claim that this is the only perspective from which these authors can be read authentically, I insist that the humanistic passion was a central dimension of their thought and that I am able to defend my interpretation of these authors against the commentators who come to very different conclusions. Since a vision of human life that includes its destiny has an implicit theological *a priori*, an implicit theodicy as Max Weber would say, I have decided to call my book *Religion and Alienation: A Theological Reading of Sociology*.

In the course of the book I move from sociology into theology properly so-called. I try to make use of sociological concepts and insights to understand more clearly what Christian practice should be in the present and how we can more adequately formulate the presence of the Holy Spirit in society.

I wish to thank my colleagues in two departments, religious studies and sociology, with whom I have engaged in lively dialogue over the years, especially Irving Zeitlin and Roger Hutchinson. I also wish to thank several of my students, in particular John Mitchel, Donna Geernaert, James Reimer and James Pambrun, for letting me use their research in the writing of this study. I dedicate this book to two close friends with contrasting yet converging interests, Rosemary Ruether and Philip McKenna, with whom I have been in constant dialogue for a long time.

Gregory Baum
St. Michael's College
University of Toronto

May 24, 1975

Introductory Readings

Raymond Aron, *Main Currents of Sociological Thought*, 2 vols., Doubleday, New York, 1970.

Ernest Becker, *The Structure of Evil*, George Braziller, New York, 1967.

Alvin Gouldner, *The Coming Crisis of Western Sociology*, Avon Books, New York, 1970.

C. Wright Mills, *The Sociological Imagination*, Oxford University Press, New York, 1959.

Robert Nisbet, *The Sociological Tradition*, Basic Books, New York, 1966.

Talcott Parsons, *The Structure of Social Action*, 2 vols., Free Press, New York, 1968.

Irving Zeitlin, *Ideology and the Development of Social Theory*, Prentice-Hall, Englewood Cliffs, N.J., 1968.

I
Religion as Source of Alienation: The Young Hegel

The young Hegel, writing at Frankfort, was greatly concerned with the relation of religion and alienation, and his thoughts, incomplete and fragmentary though they were, continue to appeal to contemporary religious thinkers. In his Frankfort manuscripts, published in English under the title of *Early Theological Writings*,[1] Hegel anticipated modern theological literature arguing against traditional theism, against the outsider God, the God over and above history, the God out there. At Frankfort, Hegel went through a phase in which he negated reason as the norm of human history. Reflection objectifies life and hence, according to Hegel at Frankfort, inevitably falsifies life and becomes estranged from it. Thinking severs us from the sources of life: life must be lived, not thought. Thinking negates life. The riddle of life and its apparent contradictions cannot be mastered conceptually and then reconciled in a rational synthesis—they can be resolved only through commitment and action. Human life is unified through loving. This phase of Hegel's biography is not well known, for in his later philosophical system, he regained confidence in the power of reflection and the role of reason in overcoming the contradictions of life.

Of special interest to us is the essay, "The Spirit of Christianity and Its Fate," in which the young Hegel, in an imaginative effort, presents the Old Testament as an example of alienating religion and the New as the religion that recreates humanity in love. It is not likely that Hegel regarded his theological essay as a reliable interpretation of the scriptures. It offered him, rather, a literary form for bringing out the alienat-

ing elements of religion and contrasting them with opposing
religious trends that reconcile and liberate men. Since we are
interested in the young Hegel's critique of religion, we shall
pay little attention to the absurd projection of the negative account on "Jewish religion" and instead, following contemporary studies on Hegel at Frankfort, offer a systematic presentation of religion as source of alienation.[2]

Let us follow the young Hegel in his analysis of the manifold alienations of human life. The supreme source of man's
multiple alienation, Hegel then thought, was the conceptualization of the divine in inherited religion. Attempting to think and
resolve by reflection the interrelation and co-existence of infinite and finite being, people have come to objectify the divine.
They have created the "bad infinity," an infinite being over and
above the finite world, extrinsic to and apart from human life
and history. Hegel supposes that this was the religion of the
Old Testament. Here God was the God over and above history,
the divine stranger in the heavens, who ruled the earth and its
peoples from above and only intervened in their history at certain moments. This view of God as stranger and object, Hegel
thinks, has been adopted by official Christianity. In the church,
God is preached as the almighty supreme being in heaven who,
while having no communion with the cosmos and human history, graciously enters the lives of men and women to help them
in their predicaments; yet even then, this God remains the totally other, the divine stranger, the infinite object. It is this bad
infinity, according to the young Hegel, that gives rise to the
manifold alienations of human life. Hegel held that the separa-
tions and cleavages that dominate modern life as he saw it de-
veloping before his eyes, were rooted in the inherited religion.

God as object and stranger does not exist. This was Hegel's solution. The bad infinity must be rejected. At the same
time Hegel did not fall into the atheistic language adopted by
some contemporary death-of-God theologians. There was indeed a good infinity. Hegel affirmed an infinity, not over and
against the finite world but in and through it, grounding it,
energizing it, orienting its unfolding. Yet, this good infinity
could not be conceptualized. It could never become the object
of the mind. The mediation between the finite and the infinite

was possible only in love, in action, in a life dedicated to over-coming the contradictions in human existence. For the young Hegel it was Jesus Christ who was the first to realize that the sky was empty, that the infinite was not a supreme being over and above him, to which he was asked to submit—but a su-preme mystery operative within him as source of his life, his love, and his forward movement. Yet this mystery could never be expressed as a truth of the mind. God reveals himself in rec-onciliation and in sacrifice. It is by loving that people solve the riddle of life and achieve the unity beyond all estrangement, separation and contradiction. While the inherited religion was the source of alienation in society, Hegel held that present in this religion, in the person of Jesus Christ, was available a breakthrough to a non-alienating human life and an under-standing of religion that saved people from the cleavages and contradictions of their society.

In the *Early Theological Writings* Hegel anticipates the radical rejection of extrinsicism in Christian theology in the Protestant and Catholic tradition. The infinite is immanent in the finite, not by absorbing or destroying it but by assuring and protecting its finitude and existence. The infinite is in and through the finite, but never identical with it, never absorbed by it, never exhausted by it. The infinite grounds the finite, orients it, and defines its ultimate future. The mode of God's immanence is, therefore, not identity but transcendence. Pan-theism is here clearly rejected. Following Hegel, Christian theo-logians, impatient with the extrinsicism of traditional theism, have been able to affirm God's immanence in human life and history without in any sense weakening the sense of God's tran-scendence. Transcendence is the mode of God's presence. Some theologians—I am thinking, for instance, of Maurice Blondel and Leslie Dewart—followed the lead of the young Hegel in as-serting that the divine mystery manifests itself only in and through human action and becomes available to the mind only as people reflect on what they are doing. God is the never ob-jectifiable mystery implicit in human love and commitment.

The young Hegel held that the inherited religion was the source of a threefold alienation, man's alienation from nature, from himself, and from his fellow man. But before we proceed, we must take a critical look at the strange vocabulary adopted by Hegel in contrasting alienating and reconciling religion. He identified alienating religion with Judaism. Following the dominant Christian tradition of projecting on Jewish religion all the antitheses of salvation—blindness, infidelity, legalism, etc.— Hegel read the Old Testament, in particular the story of Abraham, as the typical expression of bad religion; here God appeared as object and stranger in an unqualified way. None of Hegel's allegations were based on careful scriptural scholarship. His constant reference to Judaism in the *Early Theological Writings* was a literary device to describe the alienating religion of Christian orthodoxy. What Hegel did not realize— as no theologian did until fairly recently—was that by using Judaism as a symbol of unredemption, he perpetuated an image of a living people that created prejudice and contempt for this people and gave rise to the desire to see their religion suppressed. This is a significant instance where Hegel's insight into the alienating power of religion did not go far enough: he did not discern, in the Christian language that negates Jewish religion, the source of domination and the legitimation of violence. Hegel manifested the same blindness in regard to the subjugation of women in society and the contribution made to this by alienating religion.

Hegel's "The Spirit of Christianity and Its Fate" is a brilliant and imaginative *tour de force.* Our interest in this essay is quite limited here. We find throughout the essay descriptions of three distinct, though interrelated types of human alienation produced by religion. Through the worship of a God conceived as object and stranger, we read, people become estranged from the nature to which they belong, from themselves as persons, and from one another as friend and fellow human being.

Let us first look at men's estrangement from nature. If God is object and stranger, if he is conceived of as separated from men and their world, then men must turn away from their environment in order to find him. Then we no longer expect to find God in nature, but in separation from nature. We no longer reach out to discover an inner harmony between man and his natural environment; we no longer trust in a common light shining through human life and the cosmos. As people abandon this hope, they seek salvation from a God who is a stranger over a strange world. The world is no longer home. Nature becomes an object of fear and a source of danger. Instead of searching for the proportions in nature that are congenial to human life and exercising creativity in nature inspired by confidence, people begin to oscillate between the fear of nature and the desire to dominate it. People acquire fear of the foreign environment and a sense of impotence, the inability to transform this environment into a garden. Men's creative spirit no longer finds in nature the laws and purposes within which they can become active and through which they can elevate nature. This fear gives rise to the will to dominate nature and make it serve the independent purposes of men. The loss of creativity leads to the search for power. The rule for man's dominance over nature is not a measure within nature which is like unto him, but his own advantage, his profit, his strength against his enemies. The fear of nature thus gives rise to the exploitation of nature and its eventual destruction. Because he is unable to find God in nature, nature becomes purely and simply an object to man, a foreign object, to be ruled and conquered and eventually to be destroyed. Hegel foresaw what we have come to call the ecological crisis.

Hegel continues this analysis to show that the false self-elevation of man over nature actually makes him fall into nature and become almost indistinguishable from it. For as man separates himself more and more from nature, he begins to look upon nature as an enemy, as opposed to his own life purposes, and becomes obsessed with the quest for survival. Surrounded by a hostile environment, man defines himself in terms of conquest. Abandoning the spirit and adopting the struggle for survival as the principle of his life, man becomes in fact like an animal. Surrounded by his enemies, man eventually invokes the God who is object and stranger to him and his world, asking him to protect him from the onslaught of his enemies and to suppress their power. Man creates for himself a harsh divinity who curses his foes and crushes their strength. He inscribes in his God the image of all his hatreds and, by doing so, makes for himself a God who protects and promotes his wars, his dominations, his conquests. Falsely separating himself from nature, man unwittingly becomes assimilated to nature's destructive trends. Hegel describes here what in modern times has often been called the return of the repressed.

Since Hegel's day social thinkers have greatly extended the critique of people's alienation from nature, i.e., from their natural environment or from their body and sexuality. Sometimes these forms of alienation have been attributed to the practice of religion.

Closely related to man's alienation from nature is his alienation from himself. If God is object and stranger, Hegel proposes, then we do not look for an inner harmony in our existence; we expect no transcendent melody to sound in our heart nor a light to shine in our lives that gives meaning to our existence. If God is over and above human life and history, then the only light we expect comes from a foreign source. In this way people become estranged from their own depth. They no longer listen to the voice speaking within their lives. They turn to listen to the orders from a stranger who rules from afar —*ein Fremder über Fremdes*. People then no longer expect to discern in their own experience, their own consciences, their own sensitivities, the measure of life and a light which transcends their finitude and limitation; the light is then sought outside of themselves. The transcendent principle is then the object over against man, the external principle that governs man according to a wisdom foreign to him. Here man comes to look upon himself as empty, as being nothing at all, as having no certain ground within himself on which to stand and from which to face his life. People define themselves, rather, as servants of a foreign God, bent on obeying his law.

Here man loses his freedom. He becomes basically dependent and enslaved. Even the freedom he yearns for is in reality a false freedom of independence from others and even from God. Instead of discovering himself in the lives of others and in the mystery of life out of which he and these others draw their vitality, instead of enjoying a freedom that unites him with others and with the world and its infinite life, man finds a freedom of alienation that separates him from others and makes him secretly yearn to become independent from God. This resistance to God only strengthens the urge to create a divinity that is ever more lordly, more powerful, the stranger in heaven who forces him into submission. Soon man experiences himself as impatient, as obstinate, as the sinner before this God. Since his personal inclinations all go counter to the demands which the divine stranger makes on him, he is pushed into an abiding sense of guilt and a complete rejection of himself. The yearning for salvation before this all-powerful God only intensifies the destructive game of servile submission, secret protest and guilty self-repudiation.

What made men objectify the divine in the first place? Why did people create for themselves a foreign divinity in a distant heaven? The young Hegel thought that these projections were due to people's refusal to love and to live a reconciled life. The inability to love made them regard reason as the highest faculty and approach the divine mystery as an infinite object of the mind. This objectification of the divine gave rise to an ongoing destructive dialectics that enslaved man, estranged him from himself and from others. Hegel makes the biblical story of Abraham the proper parable of alienation. Abraham left his family and his country. His inability to love and live a life reconciled to friends and to the land impelled him to become a stranger in a strange land and there, out of his alienation, bring forth an objectified divinity, a strange God who was not present to the people and their land but who imposed his government on them from above. This God then imposed his rule on Abraham himself and made him the creator of a religion that has become a source of alienation in the world. The divinity worshiped by Abraham—and it is likely that the young Hegel at Frankfort here included the God worshiped by the Christian church—was an expression of man's self-rejection and his estrangement from humanity and the human environment.

In Hegel's *Early Theological Writings*, bad religion was a human projection compulsively produced out of man's inability to love. Man projects the worst of himself, his self-rejection, unto the cosmos. This theory of religion is much more subtle and profound than Feuerbach's theory, proposed four decades later,[3] according to which religion was man's projection unto the cosmos of what was best and highest in him. God, for Feuerbach, was the projection of man's greatest dreams and deepest aspirations; God represented man's unrealized possibilities in terms of love, goodness and beauty. Karl Marx refuted Feuerbach's cheerful and superficial atheism; he accused Feuerbach of not asking what evil operative in human life makes people create projections and prefer unrealities to the real. For Hegel, long before Marx, projections were always inversions. They turned the right order upside down and hence generated confusion and destruction. To the extent, therefore, that religion is a projection of human life, it is produced not by the noblest in people but by the worst in them, by their inability to love and the subsequent rejection of themselves. Since the divine stranger has to keep all of men's enemies in check, he becomes the symbol of all that men hate and at the same time the lord to which they desire to submit. God is produced out of the negation of the best in human life, and this God in turn intensifies this negation, strengthening people in their self-hatred and fostering the exploitation of the environment. The deliverance from this projection, as we shall see, is not offered by an effort of the mind and the advent of Enlightenment philosophy but by a life of love, sacrifice and reconciliation.

Finally, the bad infinity estranges man from his fellows; it undermines the unity of the human family. The refusal of love which generated the objectification of God as object and stranger perpetuates itself in the hostile camps which this refusal has created. The divine lord protects the failure of love that has produced his image in the continuity of antagonistic groups and classes. Men will then be unable to seek the mystery of life, operative in and through people, calling them to be friends and enabling them to bridge their differences. Men will then be unable to seek the divine mystery in the other person, friend or foe, enabling them to bring forth gestures of reconciliation over inherited differences and barriers. God as object and stranger is related to people only as master. He is the supreme lord, aloof, extrinsic to life, existing apart from man as an independent subject; and man can find him only by obeying him as a ruler. God is master, and man is his servant. The only unity which men in this situation can hope for is the unity of being ruled by this divinity, i.e., the common submission to a divine stranger. The structure of human life thus becomes one of domination.

Bad religion promotes the structures of domination in human history. Domination, not communion, is the key to human unity. The master-slave relationship which characterizes the divine-human encounter is projected upon the whole of humanity and people are made to define their relation to one another in terms of master and slave. Peoples and groups are related to one another through power imposed on them from above. Love becomes confined to fewer and fewer men and women, for on the larger scale people become imprisoned in unbridgeable relationships of unequal power. God as object and stranger becomes the legitimating symbol for all regimes of domination. The king of kings in his rule over the world establishes and sanctions the princes who exercise government and through their laws impose order on people estranged from one another, on people caught in their own selfish activity, doubtful of their power and mission. Alienating religion, according to Hegel, divides the human family into rulers and the ruled.

By way of summary we note that the three alienations produced by bad religion, alienation from nature, from oneself and from one's fellows, are profoundly interrelated. While they can be distinguished and described separately, they affect one another and intensify the burden of separation. In some way they are all due to the refusal to love and to the objectification of the divine as the stranger above history. Since God is no longer a mystery to be encountered in nature, in one's own depth, and in the human community, individuals begin to fear nature and seek to dominate it, mistrust their own experiences of life and seek security in submission, and perpetuate the divisions of mankind in abiding structures of domination. The three alienations feed upon one another. While for the sake of clarity one should never speak of alienation unless one specifies from what exactly people are being alienated, in view of the interrelationship of the various forms of alienation, it is also reasonable to speak of alienation without referent. Alienation then refers to the structures of separation which prevent people from enjoying their powers, from living up to their destiny, and from participating in the unitive forces of love and truth operative in their midst.

We note in passing that in his mature philosophical work, Hegel greatly extended his understanding of alienation.[4] In the perspective of history which he adopted in his mature work, the various forms of alienation from which men have suffered, and still suffer, are not simply understood as structures of domination to be overcome but also as stages, as counterweights to previous errors, as necessary evil, and as such as exercising a positive role in mankind's total evolution toward freedom. Alienation is not all bad; without it, people would not have become aware of the hidden contradictions in their lives and acquired a new consciousness transcending present errors without abandoning present truth. Yet the radicalism of the young Hegel, especially his analysis of religion and alienation, remains of lasting interest to contemporary theologians.

Contemporary theologians admire Hegel's openness to the negative critique of religion without fearing that authentic religion will thereby disappear. We have already indicated that the young Hegel recognized good religion, i.e., religion that was capable of de-alienating human life. For if the divine mystery is present in and through the finite reality—Hegel thought that this was in fact revealed by Jesus Christ—if, in other words, the divine is present in nature, present in one's own personal depth and in the community at large, then religious openness to God will lead to reconciliation. If people listen to the divine call and act in keeping with the divine impulse, they will discern the harmony between themselves and nature and thus create a garden in this world; they will get in touch with their own depth and be reconciled to the sources of their vitality; and finally they will learn to overcome the divisions of mankind and be reconciled to others through the common sharing of truth and love, marvelously operative in mankind.

We have already mentioned that Hegel's account of good religion in his early writings (as well as his reflection on religion in his mature work) has profoundly influenced modern theologians, Protestant and Catholic. A growing number of them have come to speak of God, and listen to God, as the non-objectified and non-objectifiable mystery present in people's lives, as ground out of which they come to be and as horizon toward which they move, as orientation operative in their lives and as vitality out of which they act. This has come to be the form of Christian piety for many believers today. This transformation of awareness is not due to the direct influence of Hegel. To explain this transformation we must turn to the sociology of culture. The new conditions of society, which Hegel foresaw and for which he worked out a new understanding of religion, have in the meantime exerted their influence over a century and produced a specific consciousness in which the meaning and power of religion has changed. Present religious experience, mediated by the gospel, often condemns the individualism and alienation of the dominant society and reveals God's presence in those dimensions of people's lives that reconcile them to one another, humanize their social existence, and anticipate the peace and justice of the promised age.

What may seem excessive in Hegel's analysis of bad religion, and here few contemporary theologians follow him, is his claim that religion has *caused* alienation in personal and social life. Does religion have so much power? Does religion actually influence the shape of culture and the form of society, or is it mainly a realm of spiritual contact between God and man without much influence on the concrete conditions of life? Can we attribute alienating effects to religion? Or would it not be more reasonable to say that, at the worst, bad religion confirms the alienation which society has generated?

Certainly, Karl Marx regarded Hegel as hopelessly "idealistic" when he attributed to the symbolic structure of the mind power over the concrete conditions of society. In the English-speaking world, philosophers and educated people in general have tended to follow Marx in his evaluation of German Idealism; they have regarded as outrageous and contrary to common sense the Idealist claim that the structure of the human mind enters into the production of the historical and cosmic reality. People tend to take for granted that the world is a given, a finished object confronting the human mind, and that true knowledge consists of the mind's conformity to the reality existing outside of itself. The mind reflects reality, it does not create it. Facts are facts, and it is the mind's task to discern and recognize them. German philosophers, perhaps more than others, have had great difficulty with this common sense approach.

Already Kant insisted that the experience of reality is always mediated through the human mind, that the world out there is never encountered in the raw, and that facts simply as facts are not accessible at all. Contrary to common sense, the reality we encounter, including the facts, is already ordered by the human mind, and the world to which we belong is in part the result of our creativity. The human mind enters into the creation of the world. What does this do to objectivity? Kant held that the categories of the human mind were the same everywhere and that the regularity and stability of the world were safely grounded in the mind's identical structure. It is well known that Hegel went much further; for him, the human mind itself was historically constituted. Man's mind was not a given, not identical throughout human history, not an absolute on which to ground the stability of the world. The way people saw the world depended on their social and cultural tradition, and even the structure of the mind, mediating the experience of the given, was inherited from the particular tradition to which they belonged. Hegel attributed great creativity to the mind—this is the meaning of Idealism—for not only did the individual mind mediate the experience of the world and make life meaningful for the person, but the individual mind also belonged to a collective mind, produced by a particular social and cultural tradition and hence was itself derived from the creativity of previous minds. For Hegel, mind was the creative principle in the world and its history. All this may sound rather strange to common sense. Yet this was the intellectual background from which Hegel attributed so much power to religion. Religion, as a special symbolic structure of the mind, had the power to produce alienation or, if faithful to divine revelation in Jesus Christ, to reconcile men to one another and to themselves.

Hegel's idealistic philosophy makes good, concrete sense, however, if it is read as a treatise in sociology. For sociologists, following Hegel, have attributed great power to the symbols of the mind. Sociologists had to acknowledge that the experience of the world is mediated through the symbolic structure of the imagination. By symbolic structure they mean the framework of the mind, through which people open themselves to the world and through which they respond to it. The symbolic structure of the mind makes people see the world in a particular way, orient their lives and act in it in a particular direction, and thus mediates the given present into the future yet to be made. Man's self-symbolization creates the reality in which he lives and which he is. We note that the symbolic structure of the mind is not freely chosen; it is inherited from a particular tradition and appropriated through participation in the community. Sociologists have no objection, therefore, to speaking of a collective mind. For the social and cultural conditions in which people live do indeed create among them a common consciousness or mind-set in which the individual participates, lives his life, and exercises his personal creativity. Sociologists, then, have no difficulty in accepting that the human mind is historically constituted. It is not simply a given; it is not identical in all ages and in all cultures. Mind has always been produced by a people and their history.

Sociologists also like to adopt a dialectical language when speaking of the interrelationship between personal consciousness and collective mind-set. On the one hand, the common mind-set is a given into which children are born and socialized by parents and school; and, on the other, sufficient freedom remains in persons to acquire a new self-understanding and, in conjunction with others who have undergone the same conversion, to transform society and eventually even modify the common mind-set. In this process, institutions play a powerful role. For institutions not only assure the physical survival of a people, they also embody their collective self-understanding and hence mediate the common consciousness to the next generation. Institutions create the continuity of a tradition. The power of religion operates through the institutionalization of symbols. We are here anticipating thoughts that shall be developed at greater length in subsequent chapters. Hegel's idea that religion as a form of consciousness is able to affect the social structure in which people live makes him a forerunner of the sociological tradition.

In this chapter we have looked at religion as cause of social pathologies. In the following chapter we want to look more closely at man's institutional life and ask the converse question: Can religion be an expression and consequence of social alienation?

Recommended Readings

Henry S. Harris, *Hegel's Development: Toward the Sunlight, 1790-1801*, Clarendon Press, London, 1972.

G. W. Hegel, *Early Theological Writings*, trans. T. M. Knox and R. Kroner, Harper & Row, New York, 1948.

Richard Schacht, *Alienation*, Doubleday, New York, 1971.

Notes

1. *Early Theological Writings*, trans. T. M. Knox and R. Kroner, Harper & Row, New York, 1948. Cf *Hegels Theologische Jugendschriften*, edit. Hermann Nohl, J. C. B. Mohr, Tübingen, 1907.

2. The interpretation of Hegel's early essay, presented in this chapter, has been derived in reliance on P. Asveld, *La pensée religieuse du jeune Hegel: liberté et aliénation*, Publ. universitaire de Louvain, Louvain, 1953, and B. Bourgeois, *Hegel à Francfort*, J. Vris, Paris, 1970.

3. Ludwig Feuerbach, *The Essence of Christianity* (1841), Harper & Row, New York, 1957.

4. Richard Schacht, *Alienation*, Doubleday, New York, 1971, analyzes the concept of alienation in the philosophical writings of the mature Hegel, especially in his *Phenomenology of the Spirit*. The author is curiously insensitive to Hegel's early theological writings.

II
Religion as Product of Alienation: The Young Marx

After looking at Hegel's analysis of religion as the source of alienation, we shall now turn to a very different sort of analysis, one made by the young Marx, which looks upon religion mainly as the product of alienation. Marx did not altogether neglect the dialectical relationship between mind and society, but against the intellectual trend of the young Hegelians of his day, he emphasized almost exclusively the role of institutions in the creation of man's self-awareness. The significant insight of Marx was that society produces human consciousness. "Consciousness can never be anything else than conscious existence, and the existence of men is their actual life-process. . . . Life is not determined by consciousness, but consciousness by life. . . . Consciousness is from the very beginning a social product, and remains so as long as men exist at all."[1] Yet according to the sociological reading of Hegel, presented in the preceding pages, it would be quite wrong to think of Marx as in direct opposition to Hegel. For both Hegel and Marx were concerned with the objective, social, institutional factors in the creation of culture and consciousness. What characterized Marx was simply his exclusive preoccupation with economic and political structures and his almost complete neglect of the cultural and symbolic factors.

The young Marx developed his idea of religion as a product of man's self-alienation when he responded to the religious atheism of Feuerbach. In this book *The Essence of Christianity*, Feuerbach had presented a theory according to which religion was the projection of man's highest aspirations

21

unto the cosmos. As a child still ignorant of his own powers projects his own unrealized potentialities unto his parents and invests them with the dreams of what he wants to do and be, so have people in the days of their immaturity projected their highest aspirations, their dreams, their potentialities, unto the cosmos and venerated as divine what was actually their own destiny as human persons. This, very briefly, was Feuerbach's theory. God was the symbolic language for expressing man's as yet unlived powers and talents, the great human future, the perfection of human life that was man's task to achieve. Feuerbach, we note, did not regard religion as an insignificant cluster of superstition; he attached great importance to it. It was for him the imaginative expression of man's glorious destiny. If understood correctly and divested of its theistic interpretation, it was a reliable account of the meaning and power hidden in human life. It was the task of Enlightenment to make people aware that the magnificent world of religion did not speak of God but of man. To the extent that people projected their highest aspirations unto the divinity, they emptied themselves of their own powers, regarded themselves as impotent and in need of help, and became estranged from their own life and destiny. Religion as understood in the days of man's immaturity was an alienating power. But through the conversion of the mind, produced by Enlightenment, religion could come to reveal its own power and initiate people into the greatness which was theirs to achieve in the world. From Feuerbach's viewpoint, traditional religion, by defending belief in God, was cause and promoter of man's alienation from his own depth and power.

Feuerbach's religious psychology is quite uninteresting in comparison with the Hegelian version we examined in the last chapter. For Feuerbach God is the projection of the highest in man, and the reason why man engages in projections is simply his immature state. Feuerbach's psychology was naive. There was for him nothing of the inversions and distortions associated with psychological projection that we find in the Hegelian theory. According to Hegel, we recall, people objectify the divine implicit in life itself as a divinity above and apart from life—that is, they project the divine as a stranger in heaven, who as the projection of the best in man becomes the worst for man. For this divinity transforms the universe into a world of fear and offers peace only to the extent that everything and everybody submit themselves to his domination. Born out of the refusal to love, God signifies everything of which man is afraid and guarantees a universe of order and punishment. Hegel anticipated depth psychology when he describes how these projections, inspired by self-centered wishes, actually achieve the very opposite of what was wished. While God appears as the projection of the highest, in actual fact he is the projection of the lowest, the most hateful in man, namely his refusal to love, the wish to stand alone, and the will to interrupt fellowship.

Karl Marx rejected the religious atheism of Feuerbach not because of its imperfect psychology but because of its lack of sociological understanding.[2] While Marx agreed with the atheistic option of Feuerbach, he complained that Feuerbach did not give adequate attention to the social reasons why people in fact project the best within themselves unto the cosmos. What are the social conditions that drive people to make projections? If these are not analyzed, if the cause of these compulsive dreams are not found in the social order, then the Enlightenment advocated by Feuerbach will inevitably be followed by other projections. It will not do to unmask the illusory character of religion, unless this is accompanied by changes in the social order, overcoming the frustrations that prompt people to create illusions. Feuerbach simply unmasked the symbolic world of the feudal order, but what he substituted in its place was the symbolic world of universal reason, characteristic of bourgeois society. It was an idealist illusion, Karl Marx held, to suppose that Enlightenment alone could achieve significant changes in people's lives. For religion and mental life in general are largely reflections of people's actual social and institutional realities, and hence man's consciousness is changed not so much by new arguments as by transforming the social institutions in which he lives. Feuerbach's atheism was not good enough. It was based on the idealistic illusion that intelligence alone can change the human reality, the illusion which Marx regarded as the ideology of the new ruling class. Atheism, for Marx, was acceptable only if it included a sociological analysis of the contradictions in society that made people create religious illusions. Atheism is acceptable only if it leads to a radical transformation of the social order. "The secular base (of religion) must be understood in its contradictions and revolutionized in practice."[3]

For Karl Marx, then, religion is the product of social alienation. The discrepancies in the social institutions inflict burdens on people, diminish their humanity, distort their self-understanding as human beings, and eventually create false consciousness in them. What takes place is a distortion of awareness, according to which the present social order becomes the measure of reality. People then generate ideals that protect this falsification of perception. First among these ideals is religion. Religion persuades people that the present ordering of society is the acceptable order, and it directs their yearning for happiness away from the human to the divine world. Religion becomes, therefore, the heavenly image of the society to which people belong, but it is an inverted image since society constitutes itself by domination and injustice and hence inverts the truly human values. "This state and this society," writes Marx, "produce religion which is an inverted world consciousness, because they are an inverted world."[4] Religion is thus the measure of society's social ills. Religion is the product of alienation and, once produced, protects and fosters this very alienation.

Man's self-alienation was a central topic for the young Marx. He analyzed it from various viewpoints, and to this day scholars are not agreed on how to combine the various lines of thought into a single theory. Added to this is the difficulty that the mature Marx no longer used the word "alienation," and it is not clear whether his later analysis of the contradictions in the social and economic institutions deals with the same dehumanizing effects that he had previously discussed under the title of alienation. It is not our purpose to enter into this discussion. In this context we are interested in Marx's analysis of labor as the source of man's multiple self-alienation.

In the "Economic and Philosophical Manuscripts,"[5] the young Marx analyzed the dehumanizing effect of modern industrial society, i.e., of labor in the factory, of external labor as opposed to creative work. His perceptive treatment of human alienation often anticipates, in a few insightful paragraphs, later sociological and anthropological theories dealing with the alienating effects of modern life. The anticipatory value of these early manuscripts recall the anticipatory power of Hegel's early theological writings on religion and alienation. While Marx analyzes alienation from the bottom up, and Hegel, in his early writings, mainly from the top down, both of them are quite ready to acknowledge the dialectical relationship between mind and society and hence there is no need to read one author as invalidating the other. It may very well be true that religion—bad religion, to use Hegel's term—is both the product and the source of alienation.

Marx begins his analysis with the denunciation of the factory system of his day. The industrial mode of production, operated for the sake of profit, is regarded by him as the source of a specific alienation that affects first of all the workers and is eventually communicated to the whole of society. In the factory system men, destined by nature to creative work, are convicted to dehumanizing labor, the nature of which Marx carefully analyzes. At the same time, the exploitation of the workers is the source of wealth for the owners of industry. Marx insists in his early writings that it is not private property that produces labor and its dehumanizing conditions but that alienating labor produces private property. The rightful gain of which the workers are deprived constitutes the wealth of the owning class. Property is defined by the young Marx as alienated labor. "Capital is not only accumulated labor. . . . Capital is power of command over labor and its products. . . . Capital is stored-up labor."[6] Private property, we note, does not refer to the possessions people have or should have to protect their independence and to enjoy themselves. This positive nature of property is affirmed in Marx's early writings. But private property understood in its negative sense is the product of labor imposed on men and women in the factory. This labor does not enhance the lives of those engaged in it, yet it produces power and wealth for those who own the means of production. Marx's critique of labor, then, applies to all industrial forms of production, operated for the profit of the owners, be they private persons, large corporations, or even the state itself. It also applies, therefore, to the state capitalism adopted in some communist countries. It is no wonder that Marx's early writings, so important for the New Left, are not appreciated in the communist world.

In his early writings Marx's analysis of alienated labor remains very close to the actual experience of workers. What he offers us is a perceptive anthropological study of how the human person is transformed by being a worker in the factory. Marx here anticipates the critical thought of subsequent social thinkers. Marx has the profound conviction that alienation is not natural to human life, that it is imposed by the institutions in which people live, and that human life is destined to be free and express itself in creative activity. Marx reasons here from an anthropological *a priori* that is ultimately, so it would seem, theological.

Marx's analysis on the alienation produced by labor includes the threefold alienation from nature, from personal life, and from human fellowship. Marx was surely aware that his analysis of man's productive life recalled Hegel's analysis of alienating religion. Marx specifically compares money to a powerful divinity operative in life, omnipotent, capable of transforming enemies into friends and reversing men's judgment on the significant issues of life. "The power to confuse and invert all human and natural qualities, to bring about fraternization of incompatibles. the divine power of money, resides in its character as the alienated and self-alienating communal life of man."[7]

Labor inflicted on people in the factory alienates them from nature. Their own body becomes a stranger to them. They become unable to experience their body as medium of participation in culture and enjoyment; the body becomes for them purely and simply an instrument for work. The mental life of the worker is wholly oriented toward moving his body in accordance with the strenuous pattern set by his mechanized tools. The labor devours his energies. The exhausting activity, regular and unrelenting, deadens his imagination and obscures his intelligence. Eventually his body itself comes to resemble a mechanical instrument. The perfect worker is the one who repeats the same motions, at the same intervals and at the same

speed, adapted to the rhythm of the machine. By avoiding useless gestures and free-floating thoughts the worker becomes
one with the machine he operates. The perfect worker shaped
by the industrial system is the one who resembles the machine.
"The more value he creates the more worthless the worker
becomes; the more refined his product the more crude and
misshapen the worker; the more civilized the product the more
barbarous the worker. . . . The more the work manifests intelligence the more the worker declines in intelligence and becomes a slave of nature."[8]

The worker finds it impossible to be at home in his place
of work. Work for him is not in any sense a fulfillment of his
desires; he works because he wants to survive. "The alien character of work is clearly shown by the fact that as soon as there
is no physical or other compulsion it is avoided like the
plague."[9] Yet so destroyed is the worker's capacity for enjoyment and his freedom of imagination that he is unable to feel at
home in life even when he returns from the factory. The worker
feels himself freely acting only in the basic functions of eating,
drinking and sexual intercourse, but since these activities are
genuinely human and sources of joy only in the context of a
fully human life, they only intensify his alienation from nature.
The natural activities which are meant to express human happiness easily deteriorate into frantic animal functions. The
worker has been made a stranger to his body and to the natural
environment in which he lives.

In a deeper sense, industrial labor alienates the worker
from himself because the product of his hands is removed from
him and made the source of wealth and power for the lords of
labor. Marx contrasts the creative work of the craftsman who
builds pieces of furniture with the labor of the industrial
worker whose work is largely mechanical and repetitive and
who never sees the product of his hands. The worker has no
claim on his own work. What he produces in no way belongs to
him. It is shipped away as commodity and enriches the masters
of industry. The worker sacrifices his body and his vitality in
the factory; he gives the best he has, yet all of his human
energy is stolen from him. When he goes home at night his
forces are gone. He has objectified himself, but the objects

have been removed from him. This situation differs from that of the tired craftsman who in the evening looks at the objects he has made. Factory work for the profit of another is alienating; it is, in Marx's terminology, "external work." The work is external to the worker because it does not flow from his own creativity and because it does not humanize the environment to which he belongs. External work or forced labor estranges the worker from his deepest self.

Marx's analysis, based on the inhuman conditions of industrial production in the 19th century, is still applicable to the conditions of work in the 20th century. For even if factory work has been lightened through a complex labor-saving technology, the great amount of work that is being done in industry and administration is still external labor, is still the source of personal frustration, a waste of human talent, and avoided like the plague except under pressure. The work of most people in modern society still contributes to the building up of wealth and power to which they have no access. Marx's analysis of the alienation due to external work has an abiding validity. Does work in the sweat of one's brow belong to man's natural condition on this earth? The biblical story did not think so; it regarded such work as a curse and a punishment. Nor did Karl Marx. Marx based his critique of society on a humanistic understanding of man's social existence and on the conviction that human fulfillment and happiness were in fact the destiny of humankind. Again it is hard to overlook the implicit theological *a priori*.

As the alienation of labor proceeds, according to the Marxian analysis, the laborer loses his personhood altogether; he becomes like the things he makes, a commodity. He becomes part of the factory system, including the raw materials, the products, the machinery. Management looks upon the workers as numbered items in the industrial process; they are evaluated in terms of costs and production. According to Marx, the worker himself eventually loses his sense of being a person. He accepts himself as being a thing, a priced object, a piece of equipment to be manipulated, a number in a ledger. Since the worker himself is bought and sold, he comes to regard as objects in the same industrial process his fellow workers who labor with him or compete with him, but who have ceased to be persons in their own right. The worker has becomes alienated from his fellow human beings. His relationship to others is completely determined by their place in the industrial process. Alienating labor thus reifies the worker's relationship to his fellow man. What takes place is the breakdown of friendship, of community, of common dreams and values. The worker finds himself in a universe of manipulation which destroys the common human fabric, out of which personal life is created. While they work, sweat, and suffer together, the workers are strangers to one another. Forced labor has removed them from their common humanity.

At this point Marx expands his analysis of alienation from the class of workers to the owners of industry. Their wealth, their form of life, is derived from the exploitation of the working class. Relying on Hegel's famous analysis of the master-slave relationship in his *Phenomenology of the Spirit*, Marx shows that the slavery of the slave is inevitably communicated to the master. By having power over the slave the master becomes slave himself. For by defining himself as master, and not just as person, the master links his self-understanding and his life-style to the slave; he makes himself dependent on the slave; he cannot affirm his life without the slave and thus he falls into the bondage which he imposed on the slave. Slavery enslaves the slave as well as the slave-holder. Thus for Marx, the labor which turns the workers into objects ruled by the laws of industry also affects the lords of industry, for they too define their lives in terms of objects, production, merchandise, and economic competition. The owning class also reify their personal relationships; they become slaves to their routine, they are devoured by their acquisitive preoccupations, they are estranged from their own depth and from their fellow men. Their lives are determined by profit. The masters of labor eventually come to share in the alienation which labor inflicts on the worker.

For Marx the symbol of the total reification of human life is money. This quantification of life begins with factory labor and culminates in a society wholly dominated by the quest for money. All values and all dreams are assigned a price. Money becomes the visible sign and seal of the manifold alienation due to labor. "Money, since it has the property of purchasing everything, of appropriating objects to itself, is, therefore, the object par excellence. The universal character of this property corresponds to the omnipotence of money, which is regarded as an omnipotent being. . . . Money is the pander between need and object, between human life and the means of subsistence. But that which mediates my life mediates also the existence of other men for me. It is for me the other person."[10]

Money, as object par excellence, transforms everything into itself. Since money assures my life, my independence, my power in the world, I tend to equate self-affirmation with the money I own. In my relationship to others I realize that they too have a price and that they can be manipulated like objects. Money can overcome division and strife, make ugliness attractive, and draw us to those whom we consider repulsive. We ourselves and those with whom we associate are equally subjected to the supreme value of money, which sums up in itself all the power and virtue in this world. Money is the omnipotent ground and source of human existence, bringing forth a multitude of beings and transforming all things into itself. "Since money, as the existing and active concept of value, confounds and exchanges everything, it is the universal confusion and transposition of all things, the inverted world, the confusion and transposition of all natural and human qualities."[11] Money as stored-up, depersonalized, alienated labor is the agent of universal alienation. It is the divinity of modern society.

Marx has described for us a threefold alienation of man due to labor: the alienation from nature, from oneself, and from human fellowship. He has shown that as this alienation becomes deeper, it is felt less. The first alienation induced by labor is painful. The body hurts. The laborer knows that his bodily condition frustrates his powers, his inclination, his very nature. The second level of alienation removes him so much from the core of his personal existence that he may become quite numb and unresponsive to the oppression inflicted on him. He retains little imagination to formulate for himself the conditions of his misery. At the final stage, when the workers—and with them the owning class—have become objects in the process of production, the alienation creates in them a false consciousness, in which life appears no longer as it is but inverted, ruled by the omnipotence of money. At this point, people may no longer be aware of their alienation. The truly alienated man may be quite cheerful. The person whose consciousness has been totally falsified will not experience his life as painful, he will not feel that his life ought to be different; on the contrary, he will accept the present conditions of existence as the measure of what life is meant to be. Precisely because the worker bears his pain in his body, he is less likely to be as alienated as the bourgeois who is physically comfortable. Middle class people are vulnerable to false but cheerful consciousness as workers are not. The beginning stage of alienation is painful, and for this reason enables people to discover the extent of their enslavement and possibly even to organize political forces to transform the conditions of life. In other words, the early stage of alienation has a positive role to play in the evolution of society. The complete alienation of the comfortable classes, made happy by money and security, blinds them to the truth and plays no positive role in the humanization of society.

Marx brings out an aspect of alienation that has influenced the thought of subsequent sociologists and psychologists, but has often been neglected by the more popular understanding of alienation. For Marx, alienation, or at least certain forms of it, is ambiguous. Alienation is not all bad. For while alienation expresses the loss of man's humanity and as such has negative effects on people's lives, it may at the same time have some positive effects. Since alienation excludes people from life, damages their powers, and pushes them to the margin of the dominant society, it often makes them more aware of the injustices of society. Alienation prevents people from being totally identified with their society; they are thus able to transcend the given social order and overcome the false consciousness the society induces in its members. Prophecy is possible only among the alienated. To be estranged, to be marginalized, to be deeply hurt by the system offers the possibility of analyzing more correctly the discrepancies and inequities of the social order.[12] For this reason, Marx held that the workers whose alienation was physically painful were able to come to true consciousness, while the comfortable classes whose false consciousness was more total, and who were situated at the center of society, were caught in their blindness, unless indeed they were willing to identify themselves with the working class and take upon themselves the pain of the deprived.

In Hegel's mature work, which we did not discuss in the preceding chapter, the ambiguous character of alienation is a central feature. For in Hegel's system every negation has a positive role, and out of human alienation is born a new form of reconciliation and unity. The mature Hegel was as much aware as Marx himself that complete alienation from nature, from oneself and from one's fellow men produces false consciousness which disguises the causes that have produced it. The truly alienated person becomes cheerful again. The more popular understanding of alienation has lost this dimension. When the contemporary social scientist studies alienated youth —that is, young people who have dropped out of school, refuse to participate in the social and economic life of society and are caught in the clutches of passivity—he often forgets that these young people may be much less alienated from human life than the cheerful suburbanites who try to enjoy their daily routine, dominated by money-making and the needs created by the market economy. In this context, then, it may be possible to recognize a positive meaning in certain forms of alienation.

We have mentioned several times that Karl Marx regarded religion as the product of the alienation inflicted on human life by the contradictions of the social order. We have analyzed in some detail the alienation due to the external labor imposed on men. Marx thought that people who are unable to find themselves and their happiness in the world to which they belong tend to create another world for themselves in which their true destiny appears. Religion is, therefore, man's self-awareness so long as he has not found himself. Religion is the measure of man's earthly misery. The alienation present in the social order produces religion as an inverted world consciousness, inverted because based on an inverted world. Religion tells the story of man's injustices to man, but tells it in such a way that it legitimates the present order and creates a hope for justice that remains forever illusory. "Religion is the general theory of the

world, its encyclopedic compendium, its logic in popular form
. . . its enthusiasm, its moral sanction . . . its general basis of
consolation and justification. It is the fantastic realization of
the human being inasmuch as the human being possesses no
true reality."[13] Religion is, therefore, always false consciousness, reflecting and protecting the injustices of the present social order. For Marx religion was the supreme legitimation of
the structures of domination in human society.

How can the alienation inflicted upon men by external
work be overcome? How can people free themselves from the
multiple alienation despite religious legitimation? The Marxian
reply to this is clear: only through radical social change. It is
not by new theories but by changing the social conditions of
life that human consciousness is transformed. Let us at least
hint at the kind of change which Marx advocated. The means
of production, Marx held, should not be in the hands of a few
wealthy people or powerful corporations, but should be transferred into public ownership. In modern, technological society,
industries are of course indispensable, and even with new and
imaginative labor-saving devices some heavy work will always
be necessary; yet if it were possible, through a social revolution, to democratize the economic and industrial life so that
workers would be able to participate in the management of industry, and, secondly, that their work would not contribute to
the profit of the few, or the government, but to the well-being
of the entire community, the nature of labor would undergo a
significant change. It would no longer be the foundation of
private or government wealth. If industries are no longer run in
order to maximize production and increase the profit of the
owner, and be this the state itself, but in order to provide
goods and services necessary for the well-being of the community, then the style of work will express the workers' care for
the people as a whole and assume a more humane character.
This was the ideal. Critical Marxists claim that despite the destruction of capitalism in Russia, the alienation of labor continues because a tight bureaucracy prevents the workers from
sharing in the management of their factories and because the
industries are owned and operated by the government, through
a managerial class, for the financial benefit of the state and its

international trade.[14] The nature of labor has not substantially changed.

Let us return to Marx's notion of religion. Religion is always and inevitably "ideological." What does this mean? Ideology, for Marx, does not refer to the symbolic framework of the mind as a neutral, value-free concept. In the Marxian terminology, ideology is always something false, a distortion of the truth for the sake of social interest, a symbolic framework of the mind that legitimates the power and privileges of the dominant groups and sanctions the social evils inflicted on the people without access to power. According to Marx, every community of men generates through a largely unconscious process a set of symbols that protects its position of power, affirms its identity over against its competitors, and makes it easier for the government to rule. For Marx, then, religion as well as culture is largely ideological in character. Even philosophy, at least the dominant philosophy, is a subtle defense of the dominant class.

Since Marx's day this concept of ideology has been detached from the doctrinaire Marxist background and become a central category of sociological analysis. It has become impossible to reflect on religion and culture without taking into account an ideological critique. Removing the notion of ideology from its Marxist background meant two things. First, while Marx restricted the source of alienation to the order of industrial production and hence understood ideology as a hidden defense of actual economic power relations, sociologists have become aware of ideological trends in culture and religion that legitimate other forms of power and sanction social evil not derived from the economic system. Secondly, while Marx held that the oppressed class alone was free of ideology, and that true consciousness was available only to the workers who had become aware of their exploitation (and to those members of the middle class who identified themselves actively with the workers), later sociologists regarded the formation of ideologies as a universal phenomenon and hence applicable to all groups, including the economically exploited. Ideology, in this modified Marxian sense, has become an important concept in the sociology of knowledge. It is generally recognized today that all manifestations of culture and religion contain in some way or other ideological trends, trends that approve the dominant values and protect the seats of power in society.

This modified Marxian concept of ideology has been adopted by Christian theologians in their effort to gain a critical understanding of the Christian religion and the development of Christian doctrine. It is the task of theology to discover in the actual, concrete proclamation and celebration of the Christian message the ideological trends that distort the truth for the sake of strengthening the church against its competitors, legitimating the dominant social and economic values of society, and promoting obedience to secular and ecclesiastical authorities.

The most startling example of ideological deformation in the history of Christian teaching, an example in no way derived from economic pressures but from purely religious sources, is the persistent anti-Jewish bias present in Christian teaching almost from the beginning. We shall deal with this ideology in greater detail further on.[15] Because of the church's conflict with the synagogue and because of the church's need continually to justify its messianic reading of the scriptures, Christian preachers and teachers accompanied the proclamation of the Christian gospel with a refutation of Jewish religion and the negation of Jewish existence before God. The church regarded itself as the true Israel, the chosen people of God, that had replaced the original, the unfaithful Israel. Christian writers tried to persuade their readers that the people of Israel had never understood the prophetic message, not even in the days of the prophets, that they had never known God, that they had always lived in blindness and infidelity, and that by refusing to believe in the Christian message they had doubly excluded themselves from salvation. According to the ideological framework of Christian preaching the Jews eventually came to symbolize the enemies of God and all that is unredeemed and inhuman in the world. This monstrous ideology, so closely associated with the Christian church, communicated a profound anti-semitic bias to the whole of Western culture, and while Nazi anti-semitism did not have religious roots and hence is not the product of Christianity, it did prolong the church's ancient symbolism. By linking itself to the ancient anti-Jewish tradition, Hitler was able to make the Jews the scapegoat for the troubles of his country and rally a good deal of Christian support for his cause, at least in the early years of his political power. Only since the extermination of European Jewry have Christian theologians been willing to submit the Christian tradition to an ideological critique, discover in it the many-leveled anti-Jewish trends and attempt to formulate the Christian message freed from distortions and false negations. It is the task of theology, as we shall see later on, to liberate the church's life from the various ideologies that distort the Christian message.

Karl Marx, let it be said, restricted his understanding of ideology to the legitimation of political and economic power so that he remained quite unaware of other ideological trends. In particular, he never confronted the anti-Jewish ideology present in Christian tradition and Western culture. Even though he himself came from a Jewish family and knew of the hundred ways in which institutions and individuals excluded Jews from participating in society, he refused to analyze this form of injustice. When he was asked, in the forties of the last century, to defend the emancipation of the Jews in Germany against the arguments of Bruno Bauer, Marx wrote two papers, published under the title *On the Jewish Question*,[16] in which he supported the political emancipation of the Jews on the one hand, and on the other projected a human emancipation for them that would destroy their religion as well as their identity. Since Marx reduced the religious and the human question of Jewish identity to economics and assimilated it to the universal emancipation from capitalism, he was unable to confront the anti-semitic ideology that pervaded his environment and deal with his own prejudices acquired from his identification with the dominant society. In the second part of *On the Jewish Question*, Marx draws a picture of "the Jews" according to the hostile stereotypes of his day.[17] In all of his writings, it must be added, he never mentioned that he himself came from a Jewish family. It is hard to avoid the impression that Marx's insensitivity to religion was connected with his refusal to face the Jewish question in a more honest way.

Karl Marx, as we have seen, saw in religion only economic

and political ideology. The religion he encountered in his day was almost totally identified with the social and political order and served as the sacred guarantor of the *ancien régime*. Marx never made a careful study of the history of religion. He never asked himself the question whether religion had always and everywhere exercised the same legitimating function. Two generations later, another German sociologist, Max Weber, made a detailed study of the social role of religion and discovered that while in most ages the successful religions offered an ideological defense of the existing order, there were also periods when religious trends were a source of social criticism and, by offering a new vision of human life, actually affected the transformation of culture and society. Max Weber demonstrated that religion is not only a dependent but also an independent variable. It is never purely and simply the reflection of society; it also contains within its traditions critical and creative elements. In a set of important essays,[18] Max Weber has shown that even in the same religion and the same period of history, religious commitment has quite different political meanings depending in part on the social class of the believers. Since the social classes—the peasants, craftsmen, small business people, the bourgeoisie, the aristocracy, etc.—have their own characteristic piety and adapt the symbolic meaning of the common religion to their collective aspirations, it is impossible to come to quick generalizations about the social function of religion. In each case, a careful study is required. Karl Marx failed to do this. He only saw the ideological element in religion.

There is, however, a beautiful passage in one of Marx's early essays which recognizes that something is operative in the religion of the oppressed classes that goes beyond ideology. "Religious suffering," Marx writes, "is at the same time an expression of real suffering and a protest against real suffering. Religion is the sigh of the oppressed creature, the heart of a heartless world, and the soul of soulless conditions."[19] Then follow the oft-repeated words that do not live up to the description of religion that preceded them: "Religion is the opium of the people." Opium is the expression of real suffering, it is a consolation sought because of frustrations imposed by the social order, but opium is not a protest against suffering. Opium may be the sigh of the oppressed creature but it is not the heart and soul which intuit, in the midst of an unjust and exploitative world, what human life is meant to be like. Marx admitted that in religion is preserved the conviction that human life is meant to be different from its actual oppressed condition. Man's destiny is to be fulfilled in happy community.

Marx himself was gripped by a profound faith in the destiny of man. This was the source of his social passion. The analysis of man's self-alienation in his early writings was inspired by this humanistic vision of the future. The preceding pages have shown that his analysis transcended the conditions of politics and economic life; it had a more universal human meaning, based on the anthropological distinction between external labor and creative work and on the implicitly theological conviction that humanity is destined to be free.

In our first two chapters we have chosen limited, but significant sections from the work of Hegel and Marx to study the relation of religion and alienation. Each author has made us sensitive to opposing viewpoints; each author has anticipated future developments in social science. While Hegel concentrated on religion as the cause of alienation and Marx on religion as the product of alienation, there was no need to read the two thinkers in an antithetical way, for both authors readily acknowledge the dialectical character of human history, where mind and society interact in a complex manner not reducible to a simple cause-and-effect chain. We also note that neither the young Hegel nor Marx ever regarded alienation as an anthropological necessity. For them human life in society was not necessarily alienating; alienation was always the product of disabling factors, and it was man's destiny to free himself from these oppressive forces. This view differs from the position taken by some 20th century thinkers that human life in virtue of its social character is inevitably alienating. We find this position in existentialist philosophers and in social thinkers as far apart as Sigmund Freud and Peter Berger.

In this chapter we have taken grave exception only to the reductionism of the young Marx, i.e., to the reduction of human consciousness to its political and economic base and the consequent neglect of cultural and symbolic factors in the constitution of human history. Yet we saw that even Marx alluded to the prophetic or critical role of religion, a phenomenon we shall examine more carefully in a later chapter. Religion, we conclude, is always and inevitably ambiguous. Since Hegel and Marx, this has been amply demonstrated by sociologists. There are many trends and layers in one and the same religion. It may be possible for the student of religion to discern the alienating trends—the trends which produce alienation (alienation from above) and interacting with them the trends produced by socially-induced alienation (alienation from below)—but it may also be possible to discern in religion, and this is what we hope to do in this study, creative, de-alienating trends that initiate men and women more deeply into their humanity and nourish the dream of a more humane social order.

Recommended Readings

Herbert Aptheker, edit., *Marxism and Alienation*, Humanist Press, New York, 1965.

Joachim Israel, *Alienation: From Marx to Modern Sociology*, Allyn and Bacon, Boston, 1971.

Ernest Mandel *et al., The Marxist Theory of Alienation*, Pathfinder Press, New York, 1970.

Karl Marx: Early Writings, trans. T. B. Bottomore, McGraw-Hill, New York, 1964.

Karl Marx: Selected Writings in Sociology and Social Philosophy, trans. and edit. T. B. Bottomore, McGraw-Hill, New York, 1964.

István Mészáros, *Marx's Theory of Alienation*, Merlin Press, London, 1970.

Notes

1. Karl Marx and Friedrich Engels, *The German Ideology*, International Publishers, New York, 1947, pp. 14, 15, 19.

2. The first section of *The German Ideology, op. cit.*, pp. 3-79, deals with Marx and Engel's response to Feuerbach. More especially, confer Marx's famous "Theses on Feuerbach," *op. cit.*, pp. 197-199. The Theses are also found in *Karl Marx: Selected Writings in Sociology and Social Philosophy*, trans. and edit. T. B. Bottomore, McGraw-Hill, New York, 1964, pp. 67-69.

3. From the 3rd thesis on Feuerbach. Cf. preceding note.

4. "Contribution to the Critique of Hegel's Philosophy of Right, Introduction," *Karl Marx: Early Writings*, trans. T. B. Bottomore, McGraw-Hill, New York, 1964, p. 43.

5. These manuscripts are available in *Karl Marx: Early Writings, op. cit.*, pp. 61-221.

6. *Ibid.*, pp. 75, 85.

7. *Ibid.*, p. 192.

8. *Ibid.*, p. 124.

9. *Ibid.*, p. 125.

10. *Ibid.*, pp. 189-190.

11. *Ibid.*, p. 193.

12. Cf. Max Weber's remarks on marginal intellectuals, *The Sociology of Religion*, trans. E. Fischoff, Beacon Press, Boston, 1968, pp. 124-126.

13. *Karl Marx: Early Writings*, p. 43.

14. Cf. Ernest Mandel, *The Marxist Theory of Alienation*, Pathfinder Press, New York, 1970, pp. 38-42, and Antonio Carlo, "The Socio-Economic Nature of the USSR," *Telos*, 21 (Fall 1974), pp. 2-86.

15. See pp. 77-83.

16. *Karl Marx: Early Writings*, pp. 3-33.

17. For a discussion of Marx's *On the Jewish Question*, see Emil Fackenheim, *Encounters Between Judaism and Modern Philosophy*, Basic Books, New York, 1973, pp. 145-148. Also confer Edmund Silberer, "Was Marx an Antisemite?" *Historia Judaica*, Vol. XI, 1949, pp. 3-52, and Shlomo Avineri, "Marx and Jewish Emancipation," *Journal of the History of Ideas*, 1964, pp. 445-450.

18. Max Weber, *The Sociology of Religion*, trans. E. Fischoff, Beacon Press, Boston, 1968, pp. 80-137.

19. "Contribution to the Critique of Hegel's Philosophy of Right, Introduction," *Karl Marx: Early Writings*, pp. 43-44.

III
Alienation in Industrial Society:
Ferdinand Toennies

At the end of the 18th century a new world came into being. The movements associated with the Industrial Revolution and the French Revolution translated the rational ideals of the Enlightenment into social institutions. The application of science and technology to the processes of production created a complex factory system and, with it, a new successful class, built on industry and commerce, and a new servant class, the workers, drawn into the urban centers from various parts of the country. The Industrial Revolution changed the conditions of life for large sections of the population. The middle class began to desire an ever greater extension of their power and their enterprises. They sought to improve the conditions of life in terms of comfort and efficiency, aspired to an ever higher standard of living, sought to maximize the role of science and technology in society, and tried to expand their markets at home and in distant lands. At the same time, the working class, unprotected by social legislation, entered a world of exploitation and powerlessness.

The democratic revolution, with its ideals of equality and freedom, made people realize that society itself was not a given, that it was man-made, that it could be subjected to criticism, reorganized, and planned in accordance with the wishes of its citizens. All inherited institutions became problematic. What appeared was the vision of a new world, rationally constructed, made to correspond to the well-being of the citizens and their ever growing expectation of life. What this democratic revolution did not criticize was the free enterprise economy.

41

Yet the dream emerged among the champions of the new society that through science, technology and democratization, man would eventually gain control over the world, solve the problems that inflict misery on people, and create a realm of freedom and happiness on earth.

This modern society, created at first in certain parts of Europe and America, spread through these continents in the 19th and 20th centuries and still is the Western world to which we belong, even if the original confidence regarding it has been shaken. In the 19th century the new world created an optimism which supposed that the further application of utilitarian reason to the processes of production and political organization would improve the conditions of life and lead along the road of unlimited progress. This society regarded itself as the high point of world history, as the enlightened age, in comparison with which the preceding ages were primitive and undeveloped and had value only as preparations for the modern world.The dominant attitude of the successful class, the bourgeoisie, and of the intellectuals who represented and spoke for them, was the enthusiastic endorsement of the new world in the making. Liberalism was a way of progress.

There were, however, the great critics of society. We have mentioned Hegel and after him Marx, both of whom were critical of the individualism and the conditions of life produced by the new society. There was, moreover, a group of thinkers, later called "sociologists," who were sensitive to dangerous and destructive trends in modern society. In his *The Sociological Tradition*,[1] Robert Nisbet has presented the thought of these men and shown that it was precisely by comparing and contrasting the new society with the traditional one that these thinkers devised concepts for analyzing social action. This comparative method generated sociology. Sociology was created by thinkers who asked themselves how the new industrial society affected the people who were part of it and how this differed from the human condition in the older societies. It was precisely because of a malaise with the new industrial society that these thinkers began to analyze the effect of institutions on human life and made themselves sensitive to the dehumanizing trend implicit in the conditions of the new urban centers. The sociologists represented a countervailing trend in the intellectual life of the 19th century. While the temper of the age rejoiced in the achievements of the scientific age and the liberal society, the sociologists produced careful analyses of culture and society which, because they were critical, have retained their validity till today. The sociologists tended to reject the highly rational view of life and the attempt to construct a society based on scientific principles; they recognized, with Hegel and the Romantic reaction against the Enlightenment, that there are values, dreams, symbols and deep wishes, woven into the human community, without which society will eventually disintegrate.

In the 19th century, the critical approach to liberal society gave rise to two different political orientations. Some men, critical of the emerging culture, tried to defend the old order from breaking up and adopted a conservative outlook, while others, equally critical of the present, repudiated also the inherited forms of life and looked to the future for the creation of a more humane society. These latter were the radicals. But whatever the political orientation, the sociological literature of the 19th and early 20th centuries remains a source of critical insights into industrial society, and contemporary radical criticism is often simply an expansion and adaptation of these earlier perceptions.

Auguste Comte, the social philosopher of France who invented the term "sociology" and who is sometimes regarded, unjustifiably so, as the father of sociology, was rather untypical for the sociological traditon. Comte, writing in the first half of the 19th century, was imbued with the spirit of rationalism, at least in certain fundamental respects. It was he who proposed the famous law of the three stages, the evolutionary principle, according to which culture and society move away from religion and the non-rational aspects of life to the rational and demonstrable. He tried to show that there were three ages or stages of this evolution,[2] the religious age when people accepted religious explanations of life's unsolved problems, the philosophical age when people sought purely rational and speculative explanations of life, and finally the scientific age when people were able to demonstrate the laws operative in society and recreate society according to human needs. Comte called this doctrine of progress "Positivism." He repudiated religion and philosophy as shadows belonging to a former period of history and trusted that science, empirical social science, would lead the modern world into freedom and true community.

At the same time, while Comte identified himself with the rational and scientific Enlightenment, he did have, as a sociologist, a deeper insight into the nature of society, an insight that was in fact in contradiction with his scientific emphasis. He came to the view, very influential in subsequent social thought, that society needs symbols to assure its cohesion and strengthen its will to live. People form a stable society only if they have a symbolic language in which they celebrate their common values and dreams. Since the new social order, based on reason, would have to deal with the non-rational factors of social life, Comte created a new religion, the worship of future humanity, which was to express in symbolic form the orientation of society and inspire the citizens in their common effort. Comte combined in a curious and inconsistent way the rationalist approach of the Enlightenment, which held that religion would wane under the impact of modern science, and the sociological approach, critical of the Enlightenment, which attributed to religion a significant function in creating and maintaining society.

Auguste Comte, as we said, was not typical for the group of men who engaged in sociological analysis. On the whole, the sociologists, beginning with Alexis de Tocqueville writing at the same time as Comte, severely criticized, for its harmful effect on human life, the rationalism, scientism, utiliarianism and individualism of bourgeois society. They did not share the fashionable philosophies of progress. They made themselves sensitive to the forces in the new society that impoverished human existence. Even though they used different vocabularies, they tended to agree in the comparison between the old, aristocratic society that had been challenged and in principle overcome by democracy and industrialization, and the new, liberal society that was in the making at the important centers of Europe and America. They agreed that the new mobility of life —the horizontal mobility of people who move from one place to another following work opportunity and commercial interests, and the vertical mobility of those who move upward and downward on the social scale—was undermining the cohesiveness of the social order and destroying the authoritative traditions of the past. They feared the disappearance of values. Even Karl Marx, who regarded the bourgeois age as a necessary step on the way to the emancipation of the people, thought that the new, free enterprise society destroyed all traditional values; the one value that remains, he wrote, is the cash-value.[3]

The social critics of the 19th and 20th centuries tended to agree in their comparison between the old order and the new society. They tried to find concepts that typified life in these two diverse environments. What they searched for were not detailed descriptions but useful models that would enable them to contrast the old order and the new society and gain insight into basic effects which these social orders had on human life. While the sociologists opted for a different vocabulary, they constructed their models of comparison in very similar fashion. The terminology of the German sociologist, Ferdinand Toennies, has become classical and is still used in sociological literature. Toennies called what was most typical of the old order *Gemeinschaft* (community) and what was most typical of the new order *Gesellschaft* (society).[4] How did he describe these two typical societies?

Toennies understood *Gemeinschaft* in terms derived from family life; it is natural, inherited, received. It precedes deliberation and choice. One is born in the community and accepted it as part of the order of nature. *Gemeinschaft* is the human community where people grow up and live in reliance on one another, where they are more aware of their common bond than of their own individuality. They experience the "we," the common identity more strongly than their own "I," their personal identity. People know themselves to be a community where each has a place of honor, where authority and inequality are accepted, and where each is deeply identified with the entire social order. We think of communities in the feudal age which have existed for centuries, where each family has its place, where the families together constitute a closely knit unity, even though they belong to different levels of authority and prestige.

People are bound by common values, a common vision and a common religion. They live out of a spiritual and intellectual tradition they hold in common, hand on by their mutual interaction, and protect by a common vigilance.

Toennies understands *Gesellschaft* in terms derived from free associations. Here the individuals precede the group. Here persons, after deliberation and free choice, have determined to form a society, have decided what laws should rule their interaction and what function the society is to fulfill. *Gesellschaft* is not natural but artificial. It is a rational construction. Here each member is aware of his own individuality and group-consciousness is relatively weak. It is possible to say "we" only in certain clearly defined circumstances. Since the association is based on the equality of members, the inevitable differences in power and prestige give rise to envy and strife. Persons not bound in a close community are concerned with their own advancement and success. *Gesellschaft* is inevitably a place of competition where each, by balancing rights, seeks to promote his own cause. The social bond existing among the citizens of society is not a communal one of shared values; the bond is purely legal. Sociologists often refer to it as an associative bond. It remains external to the personality, it is experienced as a necessary burden; it is in no way an integral, taken-for-granted part of personal life.

A society of the *Gesellschaft*-type, of necessity, undermines the inherited values, dreams and religious ideals. The liberal society, created at the great industrialized urban centers, drew people away from the social matrix of their origin, the village or the small town. They became socially isolated, one competing with the other, each concerned to promote his own well-being. The bond that unites them is contractual. Apart from these various contractual links the citizens have nothing in common. Severed from the richness of an ancient tradition, they become increasingly preoccupied with pragmatic purposes and the immediate tasks of daily life. The new urban population, while striving for a more comfortable life, actually suffers the loss of great riches. Cut off from the social matrix, people become alienated from their own humanity.

Toennies' book *Gemeinschaft und Gesellschaft*, in English

translation *Community and Society*, written during the eighties of the last century, presented a detailed analysis of two types of society, the traditional, closely-knit and the liberal, contractual one, and constructed a social psychology which showed the effect of the institutions, in which people live, on their own self-understanding. How do the structures in which we live affect our awareness, our values, our feelings? Typifications of this kind can be found in writers who preceded Toennies. Hegel himself foresaw the disappearance of what he called "ethical society" in which we-consciousness predominated, and the emergence of an individualistic social order in which the citizen acquires a strong I-consciousness and experiences himself over against society and possibly even over against himself. Toennies builds on his predecessors. In his book, which has become a classic, he creates a socio-psychological typology which to this day remains an arsenal for critics of modern society. Most of the accusations leveled against modern industrial, capitalistic society by contemporary radicals can be found in Toennies' *Community and Society.*

Strangely enough, the value-free style of Toennies' book did not reveal to the reader whether his critical analysis of liberal society was made from a conservative or a radical viewpoint. In fact his criticism of the impoverishment of life induced by the modern, industrial society became a source for both conservative and radical critics. Many people read the book as if the author yearned for the old feudal order and wanted to persuade his contemporaries to resist the spread of modernity. In this century, Toennies' book has even been accused of providing the Nazi movement with good arguments and legitimating its return to tribalism. This ambiguity, we might mention, is found in a good deal of the early sociological literature that revealed the ill effects on human culture of individualism, rationalism, and the money- and profit-orientation of modern society. This is true above all in German social thought, since, from the end of the 18th century on into the early 19th century, Germany produced an important intellectual reaction to the rationalistic Enlightenment and created a cast of mind among the intellectuals that was to last right into the 20th century. It is quite true that Toennies drew an idyllic picture of *Gemeinschaft* and fostered conservative sentiments; in actual fact, however, he was a socialist (not a Marxist!) who hoped that from the seeds of *Gemeinschaft* which survive in modern society would be created a new form of social life— fraternal, communal and liberating.

Before we give a more detailed account of Toennies' social psychology, we recall that the distinction between *Gemeinschaft* and *Gesellschaft* is not presented as an historical description of two contrasting, actually existing communities. There are no human groups that are purely and simply "community" and others that are purely and simply "society." We always find some contractual elements in "communities" and some communal elements in "societies." What Toennies did—and here he followed the example of previous writers—was to construct social models that brought out the essential nature of two contrasting types of society and directed the student to the significant observations he might otherwise miss. Already, fifty years earlier, Alexis de Tocqueville had written that in his studies he was looking for "the image" of society, the picture of its basic inclinations and its character to learn "what we have to fear or to hope from its progress."[5] Later, toward the end of the 19th century, Max Weber was to call these models "ideal types."[6] Ideal types are intellectual structures produced by the mind by exaggerating certain significant characteristics of a social group and creating a model that is useful for the observation and the analysis of actually existing societies. Ideal types are heuristic devices. Their usefulness must again and again be demonstrated. It must be shown by looking at actual societies that the ideal types adopted make the observer concentrate on the most typical and most significant elements of that society and thus gain important knowledge about its life, its development and its interaction with others. The typification of *Gemeinschaft* and *Gesellschaft*, we note, has never been abandoned by sociologists.

In his *Community and Society*, Ferdinand Toennies tried to show that to the two social forms of life correspond two distinct anthropological principles. The personal principle of life and action operative in people living in "community" he called "natural will," and the corresponding principle of life and action of people living in "society" he called "rational will." In a detailed analysis stretching over several chapters, Toennies showed that the coming to be of people in traditional communities follows the organic model of nature. People grow. Their natural inclinations are extended by sharing in the common life. Participation in custom, in common memories, and in religion creates in them feelings and inclinations that become second nature to them. These socially induced inclinations are grafted onto people's personal nature and give rise to spontaneous actions that are in harmony with their own personal nature as well as the well-being of the community. Personal inclination and common good move in the same direction.

By contrast, what is operative in the self-constitution of people in a society is rational will. "The theory of *Gesellschaft* deals with the artificial construction of an aggregate of human beings which superficially resembles a *Gemeinschaft* insofar as the individuals live and dwell together peacefully. However, in the *Gemeinschaft* they remain essentially united in spite of all separating factors, whereas in the *Gesellschaft* they remain essentially separated in spite of all uniting factors. In the *Gesellschaft*, as contrasted with the *Gemeinschaft*, we find no actions that can be derived from an a priori and necessarily existing unity; no actions, therefore, which manifest the spirit and the will of the unity even if performed by the individual; no actions which, insofar as they are performed by individuals, take place on behalf of those united with him. In the *Gesellschaft* such actions do not exist. On the contrary, here everybody is by himself and isolated, and there exists a condition of tension against all nature."[7]

In *Gesellschaft* the basic anthropological principle is rational will. Actions are not spontaneous; they are based on deliberation and discrimination. They are freely chosen and endorsed because they seem useful and important in regard to the elected end. Since action takes place subsequent to critical judgment, there develops a tendency to interpret and understand the situations of life in a way that judgments can be made easily and correctly. People desire that life be measurable. In *Gesellschaft* there is thus an inevitable trend to translate quality into quantity and the manifold values handed on by tradition into measurable unities that can be easily evaluated and judged. While in *Gemeinschaft* the natural will was operative within the activity of people, in *Gesellschaft* the rational will precedes the action, keeps itself apart from action, and retains an ever critical distance. What emerges in *Gesellschaft* is, therefore, a different type of human awareness. The "I" emerges out of the "we." More than that, the ego-consciousness separates itself from life and action; it is stripped of all feelings and spontaneous reactions and becomes an empty, critical thinking mind. The thinking that defines this personal identity, according to Toennies' analysis, is not contemplative reason, the reason that seeks to be in touch with the whole of reality, but purely pragmatic reason, the reason that imagines the outcome of the action taken and compares it with the end and purpose that are regarded as useful and important.

In *Gesellschaft* the relationship between people becomes quantified. Trust and mutuality gradually disappear. What takes over in these relationships can be defined in terms of money. What is important in the life of society can be bought. "Every man becomes in some measure a merchant."[8] The market becomes the perfect image of contractual, liberal society. "In *Gesellschaft* every person strives for that which is to his own advantage, and he affirms the actions of others only insofar and as long as they can further his interest. Before and outside of convention, and also before and outside of each special contract, the relation of all to all may therefore be conceived as potential hostility or latent war."[9] This war of all against all is restrained by the market conventions and contractual arrangements and tamed into a system of general competition. Competition becomes a vague symbol of unity, but by an inevitable logic the contractual bond as signified by money is increasingly weakened by the hostility of all against all, and open war is never far below the surface.

By the same principle, moreover, mastery and slavery will be determined in this system by those who hold the money—the industrialists and the merchants associated with them. Toennies was not a Marxist—besides he wrote at a time when Marxism had not presented itself to the world as a system—and yet he came to the conclusion that the modern, liberal society would, according to a logic built into its basic structure, eventually divide the population into two classes of masters and servants.[10] While Toennies did not advocate class conflict as a weapon, he agreed that the logic of *Gesellschaft* would eventually turn the state into an instrument protecting the masters in society and perpetuating the oppression of the slaves, i.e., those who have no access to power. In *Gesellschaft* it was ultimately domination that would constitute the unity of the people.

Toennies saw here a parallel between the personal and the social. Just as in *Gesellschaft* a man's personal life is brought under the domination of a separated, critical ego that is incapable of identifying itself with personal life and making decisions that spring from life itself, so would the human community be eventually ruled by a separated power, foreign to the innate forces of social life, imposing decisions that did not emerge from the common life but were derived from interests inevitably at odds with the life of the whole. What Toennies describes in his *Community and Society* is the gradual alienation of man, inflicted on him by modern, capitalist society, an alienation from his own depth, from his feelings, his nature, his spontaneity, his truly human pains and joys as well as his alienation from his brother and from the community.

What is the effect of *Gesellschaft* on religion? Religion, for Toennies, was the celebration of the common values and sacred laws that constitute the community. Religion, he writes, "even in the state of highest development, retains its hold and influence over the mind, heart and conscience of men by hallowing the events of family life: marriage, birth, veneration of elders, death. And in the same way religion hallows the commonwealth, increases and strengthens the authority of the laws."[11] Many years prior to Emile Durkheim's work, Toennies came to the conclusion that "the religious realm especially represents the original unity and equality of a whole people, the people as one family which by common ceremonies and places of worship keeps up the memory of its kinship."[12]

What, then, was the effect of *Gesellschaft* on religion? Toennies tried to show that the separating or alienating factor operative in modern, contractual society destroys the common bond that holds people together and therefore inevitably undermines religion. In *Gesellschaft* the minds of people are united simply by public opinion, by norms and rules that emerge from science and good sense and from reflections that intend to promote the well-being of society. Yet the logic operative in *Gesellschaft*, which transforms the contractual society into a group defined by general competition and a thinly disguised state of war, also transforms public opinion as embodiment of rational intelligence into a set of rules and conventions that protect the market, private property, and the power of those in charge of industry and commerce. Public opinion, in Toennies' analysis, remains perpetually external to people. It cannot become part of them as religion had been in the *Gemeinschaft*. Public opinion promotes alienation. It separates people from their life energies, from the bonds of friendship and love, from the values inherited from *Gemeinschaft*, and it undermines the sway of religion in their hearts.

To avoid misunderstanding it is good to recall at this point that these reflections on *Gemeinschaft* and *Gesellschaft* are not descriptions of actually existing societies; they deal with ideal types. Thus, while Toennies shows that *Gesellschaft* tends to eliminate religion and replace it with public opinion, he admits at the same time, in a language that anticipates the work of Durkheim a decade later, that even in modern contractual societies "all regulations and norms . . . retain a certain semblance to the commands of religion, for, like those, they originate from the mental . . . expression of the spirit of the totality."[13] In particular, Toennies notes that "the 'binding force' of contracts does not detach itself easily from trust and faithfulness in the consciousness of men." This phenomenon was also observed by Durkheim: from it, the French sociologist came to the conclusion that even modern, individualistic society remains grounded in a set of shared values.[14] Toennies did not go quite that far. Yet Toennies admitted that certain elements of *Gemeinschaft* actually remain operative in societies dominated by *Gesellschaft* trends, and he regarded these seeds as source of inspiration for the creation of a more humane society. The ongoing transformation into *Gesellschaft*, he wrote, "means the doom of culture itself if none of its scattered seeds remain alive and again bring forth the essence and the idea of

Gemeinschaft, thus secretly fostering a new culture amidst the decaying one."[15] Toennies held that the traditional religions would not survive in modern society and could not deal with its alienating trends, but he never discussed the future of the religious seeds. Like most sociologists after him, he had little trust in the innovative power of religion.

It should be added that Toennies also saw a more positive side in the *Gesellschaft* trend. He held that man's separation or alienation from his humanity, induced by modern institutions, was not without some positive aspects. Toennies showed that the two types of social groups, *Gemeinschaft* and *Gesellschaft*, produce two different states of human interiority and self-awareness. The inwardness of people living in *Gemeinschaft* is "conscience": they are profoundly identified with a tradition and its values, they share a common perspective, and they are able, being rooted in a common life, to distinguish between good and evil and engage themselves in selfless actions that serve the community. The inwardness of people living in *Gesellschaft* is "consciousness": here the thinking self, separated from others and from its own vital functions, experiences itself as standing over against the world, other people, and even its own bodily presence, and is capable of submitting all of these to a critique. Toennies writes: "Consciousness is the freedom of the rational will in its highest expression."[16] "Consciousness implies self-criticism, and this self-criticism turns as much against one's own practical blunders as conscience against one's imagined wickedness. Self-criticism is the highest or most intellectual form of rational will, conscience the highest or most intellectual form of natural will."[17] What Toennies describes as the uniquely modern consciousness, namely man's self-definition as a thinking self over against the rest of reality, is the consciousness already anticipated by Descartes in his *cogito*-argument and analyzed by Hegel in its relationship to modern rational institutions. Toennies did not deny the achievement of this typically modern consciousness, which is even able to bend back over itself and make its own life and development the object of its reflection. Toennies' own sociological work, his self-critical analysis of the culture to which he belonged, was after all a product of this very consciousness, and he had no intention of abandoning it. What he wanted to show, however, was that this new consciousness had been acquired at a great price. A certain alienation was the condition for the rise of man's critical self-awareness. A degree of alienation, then, has positive meaning. While it separates people from the sources of their humanity, it also enables them to see more clearly what goes on in the world and in themselves. This possibility of self-criticism Toennies had no intention of giving up.

We have treated Toennies' thought at some length, since his theory of alienation was adopted by many sociologists, especially in Germany. Toennies did not in fact use the word "alienation"—he preferred to speak of man's "separation" from his own depth and from his fellow man. Nor did Toennies use the word "secularization," even though his analysis of the inevitable waning of religion in a *Gesellschaft*-type society constitutes a theory of secularization that was to become quite common among sociologists. Max Weber, while making Toennies' analysis of society more nuanced, essentially followed him in his evaluation of the modern world. For Weber, the critical, rational trend, expressed in varying degrees in the institutions of modern life, leads to a growing "rationalization" of culture and to a consequent "disenchantment of life."[18]

Max Weber's analysis, we note, concentrated on the effects of the ever growing bureaucracy.[19] He showed that the modern search for more coordinated, efficient and controlled social processes tends to expand the bureaucracies, create new hierarchies, demand ever larger numbers of staff members, multiply the rules and legal requirements, and create more careful division of competences and the corresponding delineation of powers. Weber thought that the drift toward rational authority, observable in industrial society, would lead to the extension of bureaucracy to all areas of social and political life: it would create institutions in which very few independent decisions are made, except at the very top, where all transactions are carried out according to written instructions, and where the employed staff members have hardly any personal contact with one another or with their clients. The reform movements in society, which seek to submit the life of society to more rational standards, would inevitably increase the extension and weight of bureaucracy and hence create organizational patterns more rigid and depersonalizing than the preceding. Weber's study of bureaucracy over a wide variety of cultures convinced him that the instrumental rationality that dominates the industrialized world would transform the whole of life into "an iron cage":[20] human life will become dreary, flat and unimaginative, with no room for passion, prophecy or religion. No inspiration, Weber feared, would survive in modern society. He anticipated much of what Herbert Marcuse was to say fifty years later regarding "one-dimensional man."[21] Even though Toennies was an atheist and Weber an agnostic who claimed to be religiously un-musical, both interpreted the waning of religion as a sign of cultural decadence.

We note that Toennies' and Weber's theory of seculariza-tion is quite different from the theories of Comte and Marx. Comte, we recall, held that the truth of science would deliver society from the primitive explanations of religion and philo-sophy. Comte rejoiced in the power of scientific reason and trusted that it would be the great instrument of humanization. He looked forward to the disappearance of religion. For both Comte and Toennies there was an inner contradiction between religion and modernity, but while Comte saw the advent of the scientific age as the fulfillment of man's ancient hopes, Toen-nies feared that the spirit of the modern world would estrange man from his happiness and destroy his inherited culture. Both expected the decline of religion, but they interpreted the mean-ing of this decline in opposite ways.

Marx's analysis of the modern world resembles Toennies' in many ways: both were critical of liberal society, both de-scribe the alienating and oppressive effects of individualism, competition, the profit system and the market economy, both foresee class conflict, both interpret civil or bourgeois society as a system of domination. Yet on a more basic issue Marx and Toennies were far apart. For Marx looked upon history as directed toward man's liberation—in this he resembled Comte —while Toennies tried as far as possible to be a value-free sociologist who studied the development of societies without in-voking any over-all purposes and trends in world history. Marx, moreover, thought that his analysis of modern society pro-

duced scientific concepts that enabled him to render an account
of the actually existing society and thus determine the laws according to which its history will proceed, while Toennies presented his analysis as ideal types, did not pretend that they
were adequate accounts of the actual society, and hence came
to more modest scientific conclusions. Toennies could agree
with Marx's multiple analysis of alienation (in the previous
chapter we have looked at one analysis, the alienation of labor),
but Toennies also took into account the cultural factors operating in society. Toennies did not restrict his analysis to economic
life and the processes of production; he included in it other factors of institutional and symbolic life. While he holds with
Marx that institutions create consciousness, he does not use
this principle to reduce the independent role of cultural factors.
For Toennies history is more open in the sense that its future is
undefined and at the same time more caught in the present
since he did not share with Marx the evolutionary vision. Finally Toennies repudiated the class struggle as a tactics of reform:
he held that the class struggle was ultimately based on
Gesellschaft ideals and that it would generate a mind-set not of
brotherhood but of domination. One has the impression that
Toennies is a communitarian socialist who hopes that out of
the return to small communities and other forms of shared life
a new culture will be created.

As far as religion is concerned Toennies does not follow
Marx at all. While he alludes to the fact that religion exercises
a legitimating role in society, he never reduces it to ideology in
the Marxian sense. Toennies anticipates Durkheim; he sees
religion as the symbolic celebration of the social ideals and
common values, and even though, as an atheist, he does not accept its ontological reality, he still regrets the waning of religion as a sign of increasing alienation and the breakdown of
culture. While Marx's great spiritual anguish was the oppression of the lower classes, which he made the starting point of
his reflections, Toennies' main concern and fear were the decline of culture and the alienation of human life, on all levels of
society, from its essential sources.

In the judgment of Toennies and the German sociologists
after him, modern industrial society leads inevitably to the

secularization of life. This view is even shared by many sociologists in England and North America who otherwise do not follow the peculiarly German intellectual trend to regard technology, capitalism and utilitarian democracy as a system leading to cultural decline and the loss of human values. We shall discuss these theories of secularization further on. At this time we must make a few observations to place into historical perspective the pessimistic view of modern liberal society found in Hegel, Marx, Toennies and Weber. This consistent negation of modernity is characteristically German. What are the reasons for this?

There was first of all the German reaction to the French Enlightenment, constituting a cultural and intellectual movement at the beginning of the 19th century, curiously linked with the national struggle for liberation from the Napoleonic victories. The German lands were more traditional than Western Europe; they were less industrialized; they were divided into small dukedoms and principalities, still firmly set in the aristocratic age, with the hereditary strata of peasants, craftsmen, small merchants, the clergy, the princes—and working for them the bureaucrats in their chanceries—and of course the professors and students at the various universities. Apart from a few cities, there was no strong bourgeoisie in Germany. There was no social base for liberalism. The new ideas coming from France undermined the German tradition; they appeared foreign to the Germans of all estates. The Germans did not believe in reason unless feeling was taken seriously as well; they did not believe in the individual unless he was understood as embedded in a living tradition and community; they did not accept that all men were equal unless room was left for the recognition of particular traditions and cultural pluralism; they did not believe that collectivities were constructed out of isolated individuals but strongly held that groups of people were organic unities, alive by a common spirit, having a history of their own and a destiny to which to respond. In a famous article, "Conservative Thought,"[22] Karl Mannheim has shown how this conservative response of the German people to the rationalist Enlightenment and its creative expression in the writings of their thinkers actually produced a new mind-set or consciousness with a dynamic understanding of history, of reason and of human community, an understanding that generated a critical intellectual movement of its own, sometimes called the German Enlightenment. Hegel and Marx belonged to this movement but so did, generations later, Nietzsche and Freud. Conservative and radical thinkers agreed in their critical evaluation of modern, liberal bourgeois society. It is within this trend that the German sociologists were situated.

The German intellectual life at the end of the last century and the beginning of the present century was a vigorous, creative movement of scholars, in line with the German Enlightenment, who strongly reacted against the scientific Positivism that had been influential in Germany in the second part of the 19th century and more especially against the empirical, naturalistic, utilitarian thought associated, by the Germans at least, with Anglo-Saxon culture. This brilliant period of German scholarship has been looked upon by some historians as an intellectual turning point which might have given European society a new direction and a chance to overcome the forces that were pulling it apart.[23] Other scholars, without denying the extraordinary creativity of these German thinkers, have tried to situate their work in its social environment and concentrated on the social implications of their intellectual achievements.[24] The theory has been proposed that the great contempt of these scholars for modern society, for the scientific-technological as well as the commercial-industrial developments, was connected with the rise of industrialism in Germany, beginning in the eighties of the last century, and the creation of a new, successful class that threatened the power and prestige of the traditional intellectual leadership. The scholars saw the inherited values endangered, and with it the social order in which they held authority. In line with Toennies' analysis, German scholars, and with them the educated German public, distinguished between *Kultur* and *Zivilisation*, i.e., between a (superior) culture that stresses the spiritual, literary, and aesthetic aspects of life and an (inferior) culture that is dominated by science, technology, commerce and democratic politics. The Germans at this period proudly looked upon themselves as the bearers of *Kultur* and saw in this vocation the origin and justification of their political destiny. The distinction between *Kultur* and *Zivilisation* became an ideological instrument; for, with it, the dominant groups in Germany fought the entry of democratic forms into social life and defended the authority of the traditional orders against the pressure of the rising classes. The same distinction also served as a defense of the political aspiration of the imperial government against Western Europe, especially against England. The outspoken contempt of the German sociological authors for modern society, echoed by the philosophers, pervaded the whole of German cultural life at the turn of the century. Max Scheler, in an angry outburst against the bourgeoisie, wrote the not quite believable tour de force, *Ressentiment*,[25] in which he interpreted the irreligious temper of his day as an act of resentment on the part of the bourgeoisie: the middle class, entrapped in its utilitarian world and deprived of higher values and ideals, was envious of the flights of the spirit and begrudged the passion and surrender experienced by religious people. It is impossible not to see in the German literature on the inevitable secularization of modern life a certain ideology of decline.

Recommended Readings

Jack D. Douglas, edit., *The Technological Threat*, Prentice-Hall, Englewood Cliffs, N.J., 1971.

Jacques Ellul, *The Technological Society*, Vintage Books, New York, 1967.

Victor Ferkiss, *Technological Man*, New American Library, New York, 1969.

Herbert Marcuse, *One-Dimensional Man*, Beacon Press, Boston, 1964.

Arthur Mitzman, *The Iron Cage: An Historical Interpretation of Max Weber*, Alfred Knopf, New York, 1970.

Fritz Pappenheim, *The Alienation of Modern Man*, Monthly Review Press, New York and London, 1959.

David Riesman, *The Lonely Crowd*, Doubleday, New York, 1953.

Ferdinand Toennies, *Community and Society*, Harper & Row, New York, 1957.

Notes

1. Robert Nisbet, *The Sociological Tradition*, Basic Books, New York, 1966.
2. Auguste Comte, *Cours de Philosophie Positive*, Vol. I, La Societé Positiviste, Paris, 1892, p. 243.
3. Karl Marx, *The Communist Manifesto*, Appleton-Century-Crofts, New York, 1955, p. 12.
4. Ferdinand Toennies, *Community and Society* (1887), trans. C. P. Loomis, Harper & Row, New York, 1963.
5. Alexis de Tocqueville, *Democracy in America*, edit. Phillip Bradley, Vintage Books, New York, no date, Vol. I, p. 15.
6. Max Weber, *Basic Concepts in Sociology*, trans. H. P. Secher, The Citadel Press, New York, 1969, pp. 51-55. Cf. also Talcott Parsons, *The Structure of Social Action*, Vol. II, Free Press, New York, 1968, pp. 601-610, and Julien Freund, *The Sociology of Max Weber*, Vintage Books, New York, 1969, pp. 59-70.
7. F. Toennies, *Community and Society*, p. 65.
8. *Ibid.*, p. 76.
9. *Ibid.*, p. 77.
10. *Ibid.*, p. 83.
11. *Ibid.*, p. 219.
12. *Ibid.*
13. *Ibid.*, p. 222.
14. "Contract of any type could not be sustained for a moment, Durkheim argues (in his *The Division of Labor*), unless it was based on conventions, traditions, codes in which the idea of an authority higher than contract was clearly resident": R. Nisbet, *The Sociological Tradition*, Basic Books, New York, 1966, p. 91.
15. F. Toennies, *Community and Society*, p. 231.
16. *Ibid.*, p. 159.
17. *Ibid.*, p. 125.
18. Cf "Science as a Vocation," *From Max Weber*, edit. Gerth and Mills, Oxford University Press, New York, 1958, p. 155.
19. For Max Weber on bureaucracy see especially *From Max Weber*, pp. 196-244.

20. The term "iron cage" is from M. Weber's *The Protestant Ethic and the Spirit of Capitalism*, Charles Scribner's Sons, New York, 1958, p. 181.

21. Herbert Marcuse, *One-Dimensional Man*, Beacon Press, Boston, 1964.

22. Karl Mannheim, "Conservative Thought," *Essays on Sociology and Social Psychology*, edit. Paul Kecskemeti, Routledge & Kegan Paul, London, 1953, pp. 74-164.

23. Stewart Hughes, *Consciousness and Society: The Reorientation of European Social Thought, 1890-1930*, Vintage Books, New York, 1961.

24. Fritz Ringer, *The Decline of the German Mandarins, The German Academic Community, 1890-1933*, Harvard University Press, Cambridge, Mass., 1969.

25. Max Scheler, *Ressentiment*, Free Press, New York, 1961.

IV
The Ambiguity of Religion:
A Biblical Account

In the preceding chapters we have been introduced to the complex relationship of religion to society and culture. While we may not wish to follow the one-sidedness of the authors cited, we suspect that all their diverse viewpoints contain a good deal of truth. Much of what they have written corresponds to our own experience of religion and society. There are indeed alienating elements in religion; there are ideological trends in religion legitimating the existing power relations; and finally religion is often the glue, the common bond, that keeps a community together and inspires its cultural self-expression. If all these things are true, then religion must be a many-leveled, complex and ambiguous reality.

Before we deal with the ways in which social thinkers have tried to analyze the ambiguity of religion, we want to turn to the biblical account of good and evil in religion. This chapter will be mainly theological.

The Bible paints a highly ambivalent picture of religion. The faith of the people is ever threatened by various religious trends that undermine their openness to divine truth and falsify their understanding of the human world. It is possible to read the Scriptures as a textbook on the pathology of religion. The prophets of Israel offer us a detailed critical description of the corrupting religious trends; we learn from them to distinguish idolatrous religion, superstition, hypocrisy, legalistic religion, and finally religion as source of group-egotism and collective blindness. So vulnerable is the religion of God's people that it is in constant need of redemption; the believing community remains in need of the divine Word which continues to judge its religion and renew it in terms of greater trust, surrender and fidelity.

While the ambiguity of religion and its ongoing need for redemption is a commonplace for biblical scholars, this need has been minimized or even forgotten by Christian teachers and theologians. The claim that in Jesus Christ the ancient promises have been fulfilled and the final age of the world has arrived has led the Church to look upon itself too uncritically as God's holy people and become insensitive to the ambiguity of its piety, its teaching, its life and practice, in short its religion.

First and foremost are the repeated prophetic warnings against idolatrous religion. This warning belongs to the core of biblical teaching; it is summarized in the first commandment that God alone is to be worshiped.[1]

The very creation of Israel had been an act whereby the people were separated from the surrounding tribes involved in the worship of false gods. And yet the people remained vulnerable to idolatrous trends. The prophets continually reminded them to renew their dedication to the Holy One of Israel and to abandon their attachment to other gods, to idols and images, and to the worthlessness surrounding them. "Hear the word of the Lord, O house of Jacob. . . . 'What wrong did your fathers find in me that they went far from me, and went after worthlessness, and became worthless?' " (Jer. 2:4-5). The prophetic preaching against the idolatrous trends in the religion of Israel was not simply aimed at the worship of idols; it also included the repudiation of world views that were incompatible with faith in the true God. At the time of the Maccabees, the temptation of idol worship was present in the surrender to the pagan humanism of the dominant culture that undermined the faith of Israel (1 Mc. 1:43). In the New Testament the warning against idolatry continues. The condemnation of idol worship was then aimed not so much at the veneration of false gods and demons as against the universal tendency in humanity to forget the creator who revealed himself in works of his creation, and instead to elevate a part of this created order and worship it as if it were divine (cf. Rom. 1:18-32). The apostle Paul regarded this idolatrous trend as so powerful and central in human history that he derived from it the fall of culture and society into sin, violence, and the estrangement from all that is good and holy. Idolatry in this wider sense remained a constant temptation in the church. Either Christians serve the Lord, or they become slaves and venerators of created realities such as money (Mt. 6:24), personal gain (Col. 3:5; Eph. 5:5), political power (Rv. 13:8), envy and hatred (Ti. 3:3). Faith in the true God implied the radical repudiation of the divinizing trends operative in culture and religion. To believe that Jesus is Lord meant that nothing in the created order, neither people nor ideas, can ever lay claim to be an absolute and demand unconditional loyalty.

While the warning against idolatry holds a central place in the scriptures, it has not been central at all in Catholic preaching and teaching. In the Church's teaching, idolatry tended to be equated with the worship of false gods and hence did not refer to a sin commonly committed in monotheistic religion. There was no reason, then, why the Church should warn people of the idolatrous trends in their piety. This neglect of the biblical perspective was largely due to the Church's institutional self-interest. For if idolatry be understood as the absolutizing of the finite and the elevating of a part to be the ultimate measure of the whole, then the Church's unmitigated claim to absolute truth and ultimate authority becomes problematic. From the biblical point of view, the Church itself could become an idol. Church doctrine and ecclesiastical authority promote idolatrous trends in religion whenever these institutions no longer present themselves as serving the divine Word and as mediating a divine mystery that transcends them; the Church becomes an idol whenever it identifies itself with the kingdom of God. The Church is tempted by idolatry when it wants to multiply the absolutes and regard its teaching and its hierarchy as the ultimate norms for judging all forms of Christian life and faith. It is no wonder, therefore, that the Protestant Reformation in its struggle against the medieval Church made the biblical warning against idolatry central in the proclamation of the gospel. To this day, one of the most admirable characteristics of Protestantism is the ardent desire to discern the idolatrous trends in culture and ecclesiastical life. Yet even in the

Protestant Churches there is no structural guarantee against idolatry. Religion remains forever vulnerable to idolatrous trends. In the Catholic Church it was Vatican Council II that clearly distinguished between the Church and the promised kingdom of God and thus encouraged a critical trend among Catholics to discern the idolatrous elements in the life of their own Church.

Second, we find in the scriptures the denunciation of superstitions that distort the true faith of Israel. The scriptures repudiate astrology (Jer. 10:2; Is. 47:13), necromancy (1 Sm. 28:7-25), soothsaying (Ez. 21:21, 23; Zech. 10:2), and magical practices of all sorts (Ex. 22:18; Lv. 20:6, 27; Dt. 18:10). Even the wearing of amulets, a superstitious practice to ward off evil spirits, was strictly forbidden (Gn. 35:4; Jgs. 8:24; Is. 3:20; 2 Mc. 12:40). The reason why these practices were so vehemently repudiated was that they were a sign of fear and hence symbolized the waning of faith. These practices, moreover, recalled the ways of idolatrous religions; they invested with saving power the coincidental and the worthless. The New Testament continues to warn the faithful against magical rites of any kind (Acts 13:6-10; 19:13-19; Gal. 5:20; Rv. 21:27). Superstition is here regarded as the breakdown of truth. It is inspired by fear of the unknown and the suspicion that the universe is hostile and malevolent. According to the scriptures, the universe belongs to God and was created for humanity.

The ambiguity of religion, however, makes superstitious practices almost inevitable. Superstition is present in the transition from faith to credulity. The manifestations of the sacred in history have always inspired people to surround them with protective ritual separating them from the profane aspects of life, and, following a tendency that is hard to resist, the very gestures that were intended to serve the holy and keep it unalloyed acquire sacred authority themselves and become the object of veneration. The ambiguity of religion is such that the celebration of the sacred is never wholly free from superstitious trends. Faith in God's power is only too easily accompanied by a credulity that sees divine guidance behind coincidences. In Christianity it is in fact not always easy to decide whether a certain practice or a certain belief is based on God's self-manifestation in history or whether it is simply the product of human credulity. To most contemporary Christians the widespread belief in the verbal inspiration of the scriptures and hence in the inerrancy of the biblical books appears like superstition; for here, faith in God's Word recorded in the scriptures is transmuted into credulity in regard to the written text. Today Catholics have begun to ask themselves whether the belief in the infallibility of the Church and its hierarchy is part of their faith grounded in God's self-revelation, or whether it is the fading away of faith into an all too human credulity. Catholic theologians seek criteria for distinguishing between the authentic response of faith to God's Word and the superstitious extension of faith into wishful thinking.

On the other hand, the ambiguity of religion is such that the radical efforts on the part of religious leaders to root out all forms of superstition have usually led to such a rational and critical approach to life that religion itself began to decline. For when people can no longer accept the religious community and its liturgical gestures as bearers of divine grace, they fall into individualism and separate themselves from the sources of faith. There is then no pure religion. It remains ambiguous and hence in need of an ongoing critique.

A *third* corrupting trend present in religion is hypocrisy. The ancient prophets and Jesus himself revealed the nature of hypocrisy and denounced its destructive effect on the believers, individually and collectively (Is. 29:13; Eccl. 1:29-30; 32:15; 36:18-19; Mt. 6:2, 5, 16; 23:5-12). Believers are hypocritical to the extent that their religious words and gestures do not correspond to their hearts. Hypocritical religion is play-acting. We assume a role to which we are faithful, but we separate ourselves inwardly from the meaning of this role. We go through the motions of religion in order to deceive the public. The hypocrite undertakes public penances and assumes gestures of faith in order to be seen by people. In other words, hypocrisy is an attempt to use religion to advance one's position in life: it is a manipulative abuse of religion. It is easy for people to recite religious creeds and join in religious celebrations to protect their role in the community, enhance their authority, and derive the benefits which the community bestows on its dedicated members. Jesus recalled the preaching of Isaiah: "They have honored me with their lips, but their heart is far away from me" (Mt. 15:7; cf Is. 29:13). According to the biblical account, this self-serving use of religion may be due to purely personal ambition or, more often, to the interests of a particular class. The preaching of Jesus stressed that hypocritical behavior protects the power of the dominant groups and enhances the respect in which ordinary people hold them. Hypocrisy is a particular temptation for those who exercise authority in religion.

Again we notice the inevitable ambiguity of religion. The practice of religion itself produces the occasion for hypocrisy. Since religion is a communal activity, since in religion people are responsible for one another, it may at times be necessary for a person, especially if he exercises a position of leadership, to give witness to the common faith and celebrate the common hope, even if he is unable at the time to endorse these interiorly. This sort of fidelity to the community, disregarding personal doubts and hesitations, could become the source of new religious experience and nourish personal faith. At the same time, public witness of this kind could also lead ecclesiastical leaders into hypocrisy. For while the intention behind their testimony may at first be simply to strengthen the community of faith, the fact that their words also enhance their authority in the community may in the long run become important to them and affect their interest as a group. Even here an ongoing critique is necessary.

The *fourth* corrupting trend in religion, carefully analyzed in the scriptures, is legalistic religion. The prophets of Israel and Jesus himself provided us with a detailed critique of legalism. Legalism, we note, cannot be equated with fidelity to a way of life, to liturgical rules, and to the norms in which a religious community embodies its ideals. The fidelity of the believing Jew to Torah does not represent what the Bible means by legalism, no more than does the loyalty of the Christian to the ethos of the apostolic community. Legalism is, rather, the religious attitude that makes observance the end of religion. Legalism substitutes observance for holiness (Am. 4:4-5; Is. 1:11-16; Lk. 18:9-14; Mt. 20:1-11; Lk. 15:25-30; Rom. 2:17-

24). For the legalist the laws and rites of religion are the ultimate norms of life; what he forgets is that laws and rites are meant to be symbols mediating inward transformation and new life. The legal structure of biblical religion was to establish people in a way that would deliver them from selfishness and group-egotism and lead them to communion with the divine mystery. The legalist deformation of religion concerns itself with the outside, the surface, of human existence. It concentrates on observance. It makes obedience to the law the ultimate sign of religious surrender and remains unconcerned and insensitive to the inward meaning of the law. Legalism creates a mask of conformity which makes the believer holy in his eyes and thus prevents him from coming to self-knowledge. Legalistic religion stresses will-power, and it is this very stress on personal effort that makes the legalist unaware of his real feelings, of his own brokenness, and hence of his need for redemption. The legalist tends to think that it is possible for people to make themselves holy if they only try hard enough. He has little appreciation for God's gratuitous presence to human life, bringing people to critical awareness and supporting their faithful action. And because the legalist thinks that holiness is within people's grasp, he tends to despise the men and women who are not as observant as he. Thus he elevates himself above the sinner, the outsider, the non-conformist. Because of this self-elevation, this reliance on himself, coupled with lack of self-knowledge, the legalist renders himself incapable of receiving divine grace; he does not live by faith.

The legalist, in the perspective of the scriptures, entertains a false understanding of God. God, for him, is an exacting lawgiver, a stern master who confronts his people with a set of laws, expects them to live up to them, and promises to reward them if they are obedient and to punish them if they disobey. But this is a caricature of biblical religion. For the message of both Old and New Testament is that God is the redeemer of his people, that God has taken the initiative in a covenant of mercy, and that the way of life divinely revealed—first Torah and then, from the Christian viewpoint, the new way—is the road that leads to fidelity and abundant life. The God of the scriptures has power over the human heart, and hence along with the commandments he offers the inward help enabling people to respond to them in faith. In the New Testament in particular we hear the good news that God is present and active in our history, that the divine mystery reveals to us the sin of the world and undergirds our actions of hope and love, that we are alive by a principle that transcends our own, limited powers, and that we have access to the life of holiness by relying on the divine grace operative within us.

Legalistic religion, we should add immediately, remains a dimension of the Christian life. While the great theologians of the Church, St. Augustine and St. Thomas in particular, have stressed the radical difference between holiness and observance, and while even the teaching of the Council of Trent, especially in the session on justification, tried to remove the suspicion of legalism from Catholic teaching, the ordinary preaching and the official teaching in the Catholic Church do not pay much attention to the critique of legalism so central in the scriptures. Even in Protestantism, which began as a vehement protest against the hypocrisy and legalism of the medieval Church, there is an ever-present need to be delivered from the ambiguity of religion and the legalist mentality. The roots of legalism are situated in the human psyche; for the legalist mentality is even found in people who have little to do with religion. Unfortunately religion readily lends itself to a legalist misunderstanding. The reliance on ceremonies and commandments only too easily leads to a false trust in the legal elements of religion, even when they are meant to proclaim and protect God's liberating presence in the religious community.

There is, however, a factor intrinsic to New Testament preaching that has prevented the Churches from making the struggle against legalism as central as it was for the prophets. We shall look at this factor more closely further on. It is worth mentioning at this point that the vehement preaching of the early Church against hypocrisy and legalism, following the preaching of Jesus himself, was usually presented as a polemic against the group of people called the Pharisees. The books of the New Testament, confessional documents with a strong polemical edge, describe the Pharisees as hypocritical and legalistic men with so much eloquence that to this day hypocritical and legalistic religion is called "pharisaism" in the language of Christians.

Modern scholarship has demonstrated that the New Testament has drawn a caricature of the Pharisees.[2] The Pharisees were in fact a radical party of reformers in Israel that made Torah and the faithful life the center of religion and the primary locus where people encountered their God as a living reality. This new spirituality made the Jewish community independent of the temple worship in Jerusalem and undermined the authority of the hierarchical priesthood; it also gave the people a sense of peace and self-possession in an age of oppression and delivered them from the feverish messianic expectations that pervaded occupied Israel in the century before the Christian era until the destruction of Jerusalem. The Pharisees had created a Judaism centered on daily practices, the study of Torah, and peaceful community life. It was the Pharisees' rejection of the apocalyptical mood and eager messianic hopes that made them impatient with the claims of Jesus. The Pharisees were the most powerful movement in Israel, and after the destruction of the temple and the waning of apocalypticism, they represented the sole spiritual force in Judaism. Rabbinical Judaism is derived from the Pharisees. The Church's conflict with the Synagogue was, therefore, mainly with the heirs of the Pharisees, and it was for these polemical reasons that the early Christian writers projected onto the Pharisees the various corrupting religious trends Jesus had denounced in his preaching. This polemical caricature of the Pharisees has had tragic consequences for the image of Judaism in the Christian tradition; it has also had damaging consequences for the Christian Church, which was led to believe quite falsely that Jesus' preaching against hypocrisy and legalism was not a message addressed to the community acknowledging his name, but a denunciation of Jewish religion. It was this false identification of "Pharisaism" that prevented the churches from submitting their life and practice to the preaching of Jesus against hypocrisy and legalism. As we shall see further on, it was the unwillingness of the Church to come to self-knowledge and confront the ambiguity of its religion that made it project the repressed elements of its own life onto the community of Israel which preceded and accompanied it.

The *fifth* corrupting trend of religion, recorded in Old and New Testament, is the falsification of people's self-understanding which is designated by the biblical words of "blindness," "deafness," or "the hardening of hearts." The ancient prophets and Jesus himself repeatedly revealed to people that they no longer saw themselves as they were: they had blinded themselves to reality, they clung to illusions that flattered them and protected the worst tendencies in their social life. The ironic phrase of Isaiah, repeated by Jesus, depicts the prophet as the one who drives the people's false consciousness to the breaking point: "Hear and hear, but do not understand; see and see, but do not perceive. Make the heart of this people fat, and their ears heavy, and shut their eyes, lest they see with their eyes, hear with their ears, and understand with their hearts, and turn and be healed" (Is. 6:9-10; Mt. 13:14-15). The people, we are told, made false use of the signs of election in their midst, the temple and the symbols of the covenant (cf. Jer. 7:4), to persuade themselves that they were indeed God's chosen people and to remain ignorant of what was actually going on among them. This notion of "blindness" remained central in Jesus' preaching. The self-interest of groups, classes, and peoples, we are made to understand, can be accompanied by so much self-delusion that they remain wholly unaware of the purposes, the motives and even the actions that determine their collective existence. The Bible describes here what Karl Marx was later to call false consciousness.

The people are blind when they misinterpret divine election as a guarantee that they are superior to others, have an elevated place in history, and are destined to triumph over their enemies. This misinterpretation prevents them from being aware of the actual danger in which they live and of their own infidelity to the divine promises. The divine election, commissioning the people to be a special witness of God's truth and generosity in history, becomes in the minds of stubborn and hardened men an election to a privileged status which grants them power over the destiny of others. This deafness leaves the religious community vulnerable, for it is no longer able to listen to God's Word, nor is it open to conversion and renewal. The people then regard themselves as a holy community, and their ministers as a holy priesthood. Their basic concern has become the protection of their privileges. They have so falsified their self-understanding that they do not see the games of power and the structures of domination at work in their community; and they do not notice how much these alienate ordinary men and women from the freedom and power to which they have been called.

Again, we notice the inevitable ambiguity of religion. For while religious people, following the scriptures, desire to be seeing and recognize the structures of evil present in their midst, they also want to praise the special mercy, of which they are the recipients. They do experience themselves as guided, as having a light available in their lives, as being in the truth. But as soon as they express these convictions and lay claim to a truth that transcends the confusion generated by society, they create a language that easily gives rise to an exaggerated belief in divine guidance and hence to false consciousness. Contemporary Catholics, to give an example, who no longer accept papal and ecclesiastical infallibility, are searching nonetheless for a language that expresses their faith in the Spirit guiding the believing community and making life-giving truth available to those who seek God's Word. There is no safe language in religion. The inevitable ambiguity of religion demands that it remain ever open to an ongoing critique.

The preceding remarks on idolatry, superstition, hypocrisy, legalism and collective blindness offer a summary—a partial one—of the pathology of religion revealed in the scriptures. What is the response of the faithful to these corrupting trends in their religion? The biblical key word is here "conversion." From the beginning of the prophetic literature through the entire Bible God calls his people to return to him, to seek his face, to repent of their sins, to be converted anew, and to enter into the peace and reconciliation to which they have been called. "Cast away from you all the transgressions which you have committed against me; and get yourselves a new heart and a new spirit. Why should you die, O house of Israel? For I

have no pleasure in the death of anyone who dies. Be converted, then, and live" (Ez. 18:31-32). This conversion to which the
people were called demanded a recognition of what they were
doing, an acknowledgment of how far they had removed themselves from the will of God, and a willingness to return to
greater fidelity to the divine promises. The prophets of Israel
addressed the people as if they were involved in collective sin
and suffered from communal blindness; the prophetic message
was meant to raise their common consciousness, to make them
aware of what they refused to look at, and to open them to the
summons of the divine Word. The prophetic call to conversion
was to make Israel aware of the corrupting trends in their
religious life and enable them, if they so wanted, to return to
the authentic religion revealed by God.

This call for conversion remains central in the New Testament. In the preaching of John the Baptist and that of Jesus
himself, the message of repentance and forgiveness was aimed
more directly at individual believers, even though the social
dimension of conversion was not entirely overlooked. Personally and collectively, people were called upon to recognize the
truth about themselves, which their self-delusion had hidden
from them, and to open themselves to the imminent coming of
God's kingdom. In the apostolic preaching, conversion (repentance, *metanoia*) remained a central theme. Since the ambiguity of life marked the Christian community as much as any
other, the faithful would remain in need of conversion until the
day of God's final victory. They were to listen to God's word
and submit to his judgment so that they be converted anew to
the source of life. Conversion here means a change of heart or
a raising of awareness.

It is curious and yet characteristic that, until recently,
"conversion" in the language of Christians usually referred to
the conversion of people to the Christian faith or even to the
Catholic Church. While in the New Testament conversion and
baptism were indeed the door by which people entered the
Christian community, it was never supposed that conversion
took place only once in the Christian life. Because of the ambiguity of religion, conversion remains a dimension of the Chris-
tain faith. By confining the meaning of conversion to the accep-

tance of the gospel faith, the Christian community forgot that
the call to conversion was addressed to its own members. In
this context, the word "repentance" acquired a purely moral
meaning; people were asked to repent of their sins, that is, of
their immoral actions. What was forgotten was that repentance
referred to much more than that; repentance, the equivalent of
conversion, included critical awareness, the acknowledgment of
the repressed, and a new openness to the hidden truth. It was
above all the biblical renewal of the 20th century that restored
to the Christian churches a deeper sense of conversion. Today
Christians are beginning to be aware that the call to *metanoia*
is to make them see more clearly the ambiguity of life and
religion and become open to God's healing and elevating grace.

We have suggested that the Church as a whole has not
made the religious pathology indicated in the scriptures central
in its own preaching. There are many sermons against superstition and hypocrisy, but very few dealing with idolatry, legalism, and false consciousness. The Church has tended to look
upon itself as the redeemed community, as the holy church in
which the messianic promises have been fulfilled, as the very
plenitude and embodiment of Christ extended through space
and time. If a community identifies itself as Christ's mystical
body, how much self-knowledge is available to it? Understanding its own life exclusively in terms of the redemption offered in Jesus Christ, the Church has largely lost the sense of
the ambiguity of religion.

Protestants have taken the biblical teaching on the ambiguity of religion more seriously than Catholics. Yet when contemporary Protestant theologians, following the lead of Barth
and Bonhoeffer, make a radical distinction between faith and
religion and pretend that the Christian gospel creates faith but
not religion, they also evade the challenge raised by the biblical
teaching. Christianity is community, worship, way of life, religion. It may be useful, at certain moments, to deny that Christianity is a religion. One may wish to stress the divine initiative
operative in men's conversion to God and denounce the emptiness of self-willed religious ceremonies; or one may wish to
emphasize that God is present in day-to-day secular life and
not confined to specifically religious moments. But it is quite

unacceptable to deny altogether that Christianity is a religion. Whether we follow the sociologists who understand religion mainly in terms of worship and the worshiping community or ⨯ those who prefer to define religion in terms of symbol systems directing people's lives and giving meaning to their existence, Christianity in whatever form is a visible religion. Theologians who insist that Christianity is only God-inspired faith, hope and love, and that the visible, social expression of these attitudes is always and inevitably a betrayal of the gospel, prevent Christians from coming to a critical self-understanding and in the long run weaken in them the sense of responsibility for their own communities. The ready acknowledgment that the Church is sinful through and through, characteristic of certain Protestant currents, is as unhelpful for the emergence of self-knowledge as the corresponding Catholic trend to deny altogether the sinfulness of the Church.

To understand why the Christian Church has not given more weight to the biblical critique of idolatry, legalism, and collective blindness, we must again refer to the Marxian notion of "ideology." Ideology, we recall, is the deformation of the truth for the sake of social interest. For Marx, this social interest was always and inevitably economic power. But this is far too narrow a view. Collectivities defend powers and privileges apart from the economic order, and by doing so distort their vision of reality. Needless to say, these distortions take place through mental processes that remain largely unconscious. When the scriptures speak of collective blindness—we recall our preceding analysis—they refer to a social phenomenon that may be properly called ideology. According to the biblical account, the social sources of the corrupting religious trends (abstracting for the moment from the psychic sources) are the protection of the community against hostile forces and the defense of its power elites. The corrupting trends tend to attach ⨯ people uncritically to their tradition, protect them from coming to self-knowledge, defend the authority of the dominant classes, create a false sense of superiority over others, and produce dreams of victory over outsiders. It is easy to see that this biblical critique of ideology made the Christian church uncomfortable, especially since it regarded itself as the messianic community. For ideological reasons, then, the Church did not integrate the biblical critique into its preaching. In fact, the Christian church created a special myth that protected it from confronting Jesus' critical preaching; this myth was the repudiation of the Jews. Since this myth has been so important in the Christian tradition we must deal with it at this point.

*   *   *

Almost from the beginning, the Christian church projected the critical preaching of Jesus, especially his denunciation of hypocrisy, legalism, and collective blindness, unto the scribes and Pharisees, the temple priests, and the undefined collectivity called the Jews. Thus the 23rd chapter of Matthew, which offers a brilliant analysis of ideological religion, is an accusation almost exclusively addressed to the Pharisees. It is they who preach, but do not practice; they who bind heavy burdens, hard to bear, and lay them on men's shoulders; they who do their good deeds in public to be seen by men; they who wear clerical stoles and fringes; they who love the places of honor at feasts and public celebrations; they who like to be called by high titles; they who traverse the sea to make a single convert and introduce him to their own oppressive religion; they who keep people from the kingdom of God; they who attach so much importance to legal and canonical regulations that they neglect the weightier matters of the law, namely justice, mercy and faith; they who are blind guides, straining out a gnat and swallowing a camel; they who cleanse the outside of the cup while inside they are full of uncleanliness; they who are like whitewashed tombs, beautiful outside but dead within. Chapter 23 then draws a line of continuity from the Pharisees to the disobedient sons of Israel who opposed and killed the prophets in the past. The Pharisees are heirs of unfaithful Israel: they now fill up the measure of their fathers. The chapter ends in the final condemnation of the generation of Jerusalem: upon them will come all the righteous blood spilled on earth. Their house, the house of Israel, will be forsaken and desolate.

There is, however, one section in chapter 23 that reminds the reader that the critical preaching of Jesus was originally applied by the early Christian community to its own self-understanding, in particular to the form that leadership should take in the church. How should the leaders in the new community be called? "You are not to be called teacher (rabbi), for you have one teacher and you are all brethren. And call no man your father on earth, for you have one Father who is in heaven. Neither be called masters, for you have one master, the Christ. He who is great among you shall be called your servant" (Mt. 23:8-11). This text fits obviously into a discussion within the Christian community, but by making it part of a sermon that is almost exclusively addressed to the Pharisees, the original meaning is almost completely concealed. Jesus' preaching against the pathological effects of legalism, clericalism and group-egotism was projected onto the Jewish community, and the Christian church, deprived of these principles of self-criticism, left itself unprotected against the ambiguity of religion.

We have already mentioned that the polemics of the New Testament against the Pharisees distorts the nature and function of this group of men in the history of Israel. Recent scholarship has brought out the spiritual and humanistic character of the Pharisaic revolution. While Jesus himself and possibly his early disciples used harsh, prophetic language to denounce the corrupting trends in the religion of their own people, later Christian preachers, speaking no longer out of an identification with Israel but out of a situation of conflict with the Synagogue, repeated the same words as a judgment pronounced by outsiders on the religion of Israel. In this manner, Jesus' prophetic exhortations acquired a different meaning: they were used as a weapon against the Pharisees and eventually against the entire Jewish people.

Why this polemic against the Jews? Since the Christian community saw in Jesus the fulfillment of the divine promises made to Israel and hence read the Hebrew scriptures from the viewpoint of the new covenant, it was necessary for them to argue against the Jewish reading of the same scriptures, especially against the interpretation of the Pharisees, based on the ongoing validity of the old covenant and the continuity of the Jewish tradition. In her book *Faith and Fratricide*,[3] Rosemary

Ruether has shown that from the very beginning the church had to accompany the proclamation of Jesus as the promised Christ with arguments invalidating the Jewish reading of the scriptures; she has called this refutation "the left hand of christology." It was this left hand that generated the anti-Jewish polemics. For the refutation of the Jewish reading was not restricted to exegetical and hermeneutical arguments; it included attacks upon the Pharisees, the most influential of the Jewish interpreters. Early Christian preaching presented the Jewish teachers as blind guides who had never understood the scriptures. And as it became increasingly clear that the Synagogue as a whole would not follow the Christian interpretation, Christian preachers began to claim that Jewish religion had never understood the scriptures, that the Jews had read them according to the letter, that their view of the ancient covenant had been carnal, that they had always been unfaithful, and that they had never known God. Only in Jesus did the scriptures reveal their spiritual meaning. The Jews, on the other hand, were a blind people, hard-hearted, legalistic, carnal, and devoid of spiritual insight.

Let us take a brief look at how this polemics progressed in the early church. The continuity between the contemporary Jewish opposition to the gospel and the ancient religion of Israel, already alluded to in the 23rd chapter of Matthew, became a fully developed theme. St. Paul split the entire history of salvation down the middle by distinguishing between the history of the divine promises and the human response to them in faith and the history of the law and man's servile obedience: Paul then identified the Christian church with the tradition of promise and the Jewish religion with the law devoid of divine grace. In chapters 3 and 4 of Galatians, he developed the dichotomy between the spirit of faith and the works of the law, between the spiritual and the fleshly understanding of the scriptures. Abraham, we read, was saved by the divine promises and by his trust in God's word, and he was told that the nations would be blessed in him since it was by faith in the divine promises, extended through Jesus, that the Gentiles were to be saved. Torah was introduced as a prison to heighten the sin in Israel. Those who live under the law, therefore, are estranged from the divine promises. Paul recalls the story of Abraham's two sons, one born from a slave woman, born according to the flesh, the other born from a free woman, born according to the promise. Now "these women are the two covenants" (Gal. 4:24). Mount Sinai bearing children for slavery corresponds to the present Jerusalem, the Jewish religion, "for she is in slavery with her children," while the spiritual Jerusalem is free, she is the mother of Christians. For purely polemical purposes the biblical critique of legalism has here been projected onto the Jewish religion. What Paul forgets is that in Jewish religion Torah had not been separated from the divine promises at all and that the obedience to the common law of life was understood by the best Jewish teachers as a personal response to God's covenantal love. Again, by applying Jesus' critique of legalism to the understanding of Judaism, the church deprived itself of the critical principles for dealing with its own structures of authority.

The picture becomes complete in John's gospel. The fourth gospel was written long after the devastation of Jerusalem when the surviving religion of Israel had become almost exclusively identified with pharisaic Judaism. For this reason, one must suppose, the author of the fourth gospel transforms Jesus' preaching against ideological religion into a polemics against the Jews, against the entire Jewish people. The Pharisees are hardly mentioned as a special group. The opponents of Jesus are simply the Jews, and this identification is so complete that the author almost forgets that Jesus himself and his disciples were members of the same Jewish people. In the fourth gospel, Jesus speaks to "the Jews" about "their law," as if he did not belong to them (cf. Jn. 8:17).

In the 5th and 8th chapters of John's gospel we find the negation of the entire Jewish religion. Here Jesus addresses the Jews in the following way: You have never heard God's voice, you do not have his word abiding in you (cf. 5:37-38); you search the scriptures because you think that in them you have eternal life (cf. 5:39), but you do not have the love of God within you (cf. 5:42); if you believed Moses you would also believe me, but you do not believe his writings (cf. 5:46-47); you judge according to the flesh (cf. 8:15); you know neither me nor my Father (cf. 8:19); you will die in your sins (cf. 8:21, 24); you are from below, you belong to the evil world (cf. 8:23); if you were Abraham's children, you would do what Abraham did (cf. 8:39); and if God were your father, you would love me (cf. 8:42), but you belong to your father, the devil, and your will is to do your father's desires (cf. 8:44); the devil has nothing to do with the truth, he is a liar and the father of lies (cf. 8:44); you have never known God and hence you do not recognize God's voice addressing you at this time (cf. 8:47, 55).

This polemics against the Jews was vastly expanded by the church fathers in an extensive *adversus Judaeos* literature. This literature depicted the fall of the synagogue into blindness and the history of Israel as a succession of infidelities. There was no room for Jewish religion before God. They no longer worshiped the true God; they had become idolaters. In her *Faith and Fratricide*, Rosemary Ruether has shown how the church's preaching split apart the antitheses of salvation—darkness and light, falsehood and truth, blindness and seeing, carnal and spiritual, damnation and redemption, reprobation and adoption —and applied the negative side to the Jewish people and the positive side to the Christian church. In ecclesiastical preaching the Jews became an inverted church, the people excluded from grace, reprobated, condemned, and preserved in history as a sign of God's wrath. Even the Pauline hope that before the end of time the Jews would be converted to Christ (cf. Rom. 11:26) was largely forgotten in the *adversus Judaeos* literature.

The negation of Jewish existence was translated into social and political terms when Christianity became the official religion of the Roman Empire. Through the Constantinian peace the Jews were pushed to the margin of society; they lived on as a pariah people, as social outcasts. And yet, even though they were a people without power, the Christian polemics against the Jews became even worse in the middle ages and the baroque age. What took place was a symbolic demonization of the Jews; the Jews were identified with the powers of darkness and all that was hostile to human life and to God. The legal oppression of the Jewish people lasted until the advent of modern, liberal society. But would the symbolism of negation and the language of contempt really disappear in the secular age? Many Jews in the 19th century entertained this hope.

After the extermination of six million Jews at the center of the European civilization a generation ago, the surviving Jews and the Christian community were shocked into a new awareness. While Nazi anti-semitism had no Christian roots—German Nazism was in radical opposition to biblical religion—it is alas true that the demonization of the Jews, inherited from the Christian tradition, helped Hitler to make the Jews the scapegoat of his political paranoia and gained him wide support among unreflective, traditionally-minded people. The negation of Jewish existence, which the church had symbolized in its doctrine, its sermons and its liturgy, and which had produced an endless series of pogroms and persecutions, but which the church had never translated into the final solution, was executed in a technologically perfected genocide by insane men who did not know the sources of their own compulsive hatred.

Auschwitz was a turning point.[4] The extermination of six million by a party of criminal men, accompanied by the silence of the churches and the passivity of the nations, was a singular event, transcending the human imagination of the awful, revealing the sickness at the heart of the Western tradition and the pathology of the Christian religion. The Holocaust is not an unfortunate, regrettable incident in Western history, to be blamed on the Nazis and German complicity and then to be forgotten. The Holocaust spells out a judgment on the spiritual tradition of the West. I do not mean, of course, that Christians should assume the guilt for the extermination of the Jews; no, this guilt is present in those who conceived, planned and executed the giant operation of horror. Yet the Holocaust is a significant, never-to-be-overlooked revelation of social pathology and the ambiguity of religion. It sheds light on the dark side of Western history. It reveals the anti-Jewish tradition within Christianity as the source of many forms of personal blindness and the focus of several social pathologies. Through the Holocaust the Christian churches are called to a new and unprecedented critical awareness of the ambiguity of their religion.

What nourished this unrelenting Christian hatred and contempt for the Jews? The original polemics began as the left hand of the christological proclamation; but it is impossible to account for the demonization of the Jews, taking place in subsequent centuries, simply with reference to the conflict between two communities, the winning church and the struggling synagogue. A sociological analysis alone will not do, for the anti-Jewish polemics continued and grew even worse at times when the Jewish community was very weak or even totally absent. What was operative in the anti-Jewish tradition was the convergence of several pathological trends connected with the exercise of religion. First, Christianity was the daughter religion dependent on and yet struggling against its parent religion, caught in a curious love-hate relationship; the church desired the humiliation and even the death of Israel, and at the same time it could not forget Israel. Israel became the necessary parent that had to be put down in every generation. Second, the Jewish people became "the shadow" of the Christian church, if I may use this Jungian expression; they were the people on which the church projected its own repressed destructive side. Calling itself holy and regarding itself as the messianic community, the church became unable to look at itself realistically; the church then denied the ambiguity of its religion, its infidelities, its betrayals, its legalism, its hypocrisy, and its blindness, and projected these onto the Jewish people. Hatred and contempt for the Jews serves as the Christians' defense against self-knowledge. Third, since the Christian people found it difficult to lose their own resentment against a strict religion and the negative feelings they entertained against God and Jesus Christ, they shifted these hostile feelings unto the Jewish people who had brought Jesus Christ to them. Hating Jews was the sublimation of hatred for God and Jesus. Fourth, we must recall that the Platonic trend in Christianity made people understand the spirit in opposition to the bodily dimension of life, especially sexuality, and this collective repression created the image of a carnal people, the Jews, which embodied the disguised underside of the Christian community. Finally, we call to mind the social pathology that makes society inflict wounds on a conquered people and then, ironically, regard these

wounds as justification for renewed contempt for the conquered. Thus the marginalization of the Jews pushed them into
certain sections of social life, for which they were later despised; the Christians hated the Jews for bearing some features
of the caricature, which they, the Christians, had created and
transferred on them. The church's myth that the Jews were a
reprobated people mystified these pathological trends and often
prevented Christian people from opposing injustices inflicted
on Jews by secular forces.

Auschwitz should be a turning point for Christian self-understanding. It reveals to us the power of social and religious
pathologies. It brings to light the dreadful consequences of the
destructive trends in religion. *Corruptio optimi pessima.* What
Christians are summoned to do—and this is part of the purpose of this book—is to confront the structures of oppression
and the symbols legitimating injustices in the Christian tradition. This means not only a radical confrontation with the anti-
Jewish trends in Christian preaching and teaching; it also
means the wrestling against the anti-feminist trends and the
suppression of women mediated by the Christian tradition; it
includes the overcoming of the church-centered understanding
of world history, which served as the legitimation of the white
man's hegemony in the world; it means the painful confrontation of all the ideological elements in the Christian religion.

Recommended Readings

Jean-Jacques von Allmen, *A Companion to the Bible*, Oxford University Press, New York, 1958.

Johannes B. Bauer, *Encyclopedia of Biblical Theology*, 3 vols., Sheed
& Ward, London, 1970.

Xavier Léon-Dufour, *Dictionary of Biblical Theology*, Chapman,
London, 1967.

Rosemary Ruether, *Faith and Fratricide: The Theological Roots of
Antisemitism*, Seabury Press, New York, 1974.

Notes

1. The presentation of biblical themes in this chapter relies heavily on Xavier Léon-Dufour's *Vocabulaire de théologie biblique*, Jean-Jacques von Allmen's *Vocabulaire biblique*, and on the notes and comments of *La Bible de Jérusalem*.

2. Rosemary Ruether, "The Pharisees in First-Century Judaism," *The Ecumenist*, 11, Nov.-Dec. 1972, pp. 1-7; Jacob Neusner, *From Politics to Piety: The Emergence of Pharisaic Judaism*, Prentice-Hall, Englewood, N.J., 1973.

3. Rosemary Ruether, *Faith and Fratricide*, Seabury Press, New York, 1974.

4. Cf Gregory Baum, "Theology After Auschwitz: A Conference Report," *The Ecumenist*, 12, July-August 1974, pp. 65-80.

V
The Ambiguity of Religion:
A Social Science Account

In the first three chapters we have examined different theories relating religion and alienation. While we were unable to follow the one-sidedness of these theories, we saw that they contained a great deal of truth. The young Hegel presented religion as source of human alienation, the young Marx saw in religion the symptoms of the alienation inflicted on people by economic institutions, and Toennies, speaking for a wide group of sociologists, regarded religion as the celebration of the common values and ideals grounding traditional society and hence foretold that the individualism and utilitarianism of modern life would undermine the common social bond and hence destroy religion altogether. There is no reason why these different theories could not all be true at the same time. Religion is a highly complex, many-leveled, ambivalent phenomenon; and even if these theories offer mutually exclusive explanations, they may well refer to diverse layers and trends in religion, each with different characteristics and different social effects. In the last chapter we have seen that the scriptures present religion as an ambiguous reality. In the present chapter we shall turn to the social critics of modern times to study in greater detail the ambiguity of religion. We want to examine the distinction between religion and magic introduced by Emile Durkheim and Max Weber, the distinction between authoritarian and humanistic religion made by Erich Fromm in reliance on Sigmund Freud, and finally the distinction between ideological and utopian religion derived from Karl Mannheim's sociology of knowledge.

85

It is easy to understand why theologians should be interested in the ambiguity of religion. Since they accept an ideal of genuine religion derived from the scriptures, they want to examine the existing religious practices to distinguish in them authentic religion from inauthentic trends. It is, however, surprising, at least at first glance, that sociologists and social critics engaged in a more objective study of religion (men who were mostly agnostics or atheists in their private lives) should also have tried to distinguish within religion authentic and inauthentic trends. We saw something of this in the young Hegel who distinguished between good and bad religion. While Marx and Toennies regarded religion as a much less differentiated social reality, subsequent social thinkers, making use of the ideas of Marx and Toennies, have studied the phenomenon of religion more carefully and come to distinguish in it divergent trends, trends that alienate people from their human resources and others that reconcile them with, and confirm them in, their full human potiential.

*   *   *

Durkheim and Weber made a clearly defined, ideal-typical distinction between religion and magic. While they were very much aware that the various religions studied by the social scientist, including the monotheistic religions, were never totally free of magical trends, they regarded the distinction as useful precisely because it enabled them to gain a more nuanced and critical understanding of religious practice and its effect on social life.

For Durkheim society began with religion. Religion was the primary reality. He argued against the anthropologists of his day who regarded magic as primary and religion as a later development derived from magic. In his famous study, *The Elementary Form of Religious Life*,[1] Durkheim tried to demonstrate that religion was the symbolic celebration of the values, ideals and hopes that bound a society together. This, we recall, corresponds to the sociological intuition of Toennies. Religion is society becoming conscious of itself. "For a society to become conscious of itself and maintain at the necessary degree of intensity the sentiments which it thus attains, it must assemble and concentrate itself. . . . A society can neither create itself nor recreate itself without at the same time creating an ideal."[2] Religion is the encounter of society with the ideal on which it is based. For Durkheim, then, religion is at one and the same time created by, and creating, society, even though he does not sufficiently clarify this dialectical interrelation. Religion is created by the community as the symbolic self-manifestation of its own depth; and in turn religion creates the community, that is, it confirms the members in the common values, initiates the new generation into the living tradition, and finally confronts the entire community with the highest ideals present in its history and thus acts as an impetus for social change and renewal. For Durkheim, then, religion is connatural to social life. While he himelf was an atheist, and while he observed the decline of religion in modern society, at least among the urban population of France, he felt that if modern society survives it will inevitably generate a new worship expressing its social bond in symbolic form. For Durkheim, "there is something eternal in religion."[3]

Religion then is primary. Arguing against Frazer who thought that religion had developed from magic and that there was really no difference between the two, Durkheim insisted that religion was the primary element of the earliest human communities and the source of their social and mental life and that magical rites, found everywhere in and through religion, were expressions of the decline and decay of religion.[4] There was an inner antagonism between religion and magic. How did Durkheim define the difference between them? Religion, for the French sociologist, is always and inevitably associated with a community. The priest serves within a community, and the sacred rites create a special bond between the people and their priest as well as among the people themselves. Religion expresses itself in a worship that constitutes the many into a single church—Durkheim used this word in regard to all religions![5] Religion is always social, serves the common good, saves men from egotistical preoccupations, and nourishes in them the power to love others and to surrender themselves to the social reality that embraces and transcends them. From this point of view, magic is the decay of religion. For while the magician may use the same rites as the priest and relate himself to the same gods and spirits, his magic does not create a bond between himself and his clients nor among the clients themselves. Magic does not create a church. Magicians do not belong to a community; they simply have a clientele. Magical rites, therefore, are not social, do not serve the common good, and do not facilitate surrender to the transcendent. On the contrary, magical rites seek power over the gods to make them serve the personal interest and advantage of the petitioner. Magic makes the petitioner selfish and undermines his religious dedication; and while magic is never wholly absent from the historical religions, and may sometimes even be practiced by priests, it is intrinsically opposed to the true nature of religion.

Max Weber's approach to the study of religion was quite different from Durkheim's, but he too made a clear distinction between religion and magic.[6] Weber did not follow Durkheim's holistic, social understanding of religion; he studied religious phenomena in a more evolutionary perspective and hence he shared the view of the anthropologists who claimed that religion developed out of magic. But Weber thought that the transition from magic to religion had an important social meaning.

Magical rites—here Weber agreed with Durkheim—seek power over the gods to make them solve the problems of the people who invoke them. Magic is concerned with particular, localized problems. In his interpretation of Weber's sociology of religion, Talcott Parsons says that magic deals with "*ad hoc* interests and tensions."[7] By contrast, religion expresses itself in ordered worship and in surrender to the gods. Religion is a principle that creates a believing community. It does not seek power over the gods to make them solve the problems of the people who invoke them. Magic is concerned with particular, basically irreligious. Max Weber contrasts the priest with the magician. The priest as guardian of religion speaks in the name of the community; the magician speaks in his own name and is a man of great personal power. People trust the priest because they believe in the divine power residing in the community; people trust the magician because of his special, inexplicable power.

What is important for Weber is that the passage from magic to religion is due to the application of "reason" to man's social life. Since the human being, according to Weber, is a meaning-making animal, he holds that significant changes take place in culture and society when men achieve greater unification of the various aspects of their lives, combine more successfully personal needs with the needs of the community, and acquire a more unified world view. This trend—called "rationalization" by Weber[8]—is a principle of social evolution. The religious breakthrough, overcoming the inherited magical trends, is part of a movement that creates a more complex, ordered, differentiated society which demands the transcendence of private wishes and family interests for the sake of a wider common good. In this perspective, religion is a principle of socialization. It detaches people from the fulfillment of their personal needs, and by investing with sacred importance the destiny of the entire community, in this world or in the next, religion generates what magic is unable to do, a selfless, sacrificial, communal way of life.

Weber clarified the contrast between magic and religion in his distinction between taboos and religious ethics.[9] Taboos correspond to magic: they regulate behavior according to purely ritual demands, they have only particular applications, they cannot be generalized, they appear arbitrary from the viewpoint of the totality of people's needs and purposes. Religious ethics, on the other hand, corresponds to religion. Religious ethics operates at a higher level of generalization, it is concerned with the well-being of the community and provides norms of behavior that enable people to participate in building the common life. Weber realizes, of course, that present in priestly religion are many elements of taboo; nonetheless, he thought that the ideal-typical distinction between magic (or taboo) and religion was useful for a clearer understanding of actually existing religions.

For Max Weber, the evolution from magician to priests, due to a wider application of "reason," continued to a third type of religious leader, the prophet.[10] The prophet is a man invested with extraordinary power who has a special message or recalls a forgotten teaching. He resembles the magician because like him he acts out of a power that resides in himself, but he differs from the magician inasmuch as his prophetic task is to preach a message that has meaning for the entire community. Both priests and prophets, then, are concerned with the community and its well-being, but the priest acts as a member of a priestly caste, exercises a power that resides in the community, and hence speaks largely as the protector of the existing social order, while the prophet speaks at a distance from the religious institution and traditional society. In Weber's view, the prophet is the important agent of "rationalization." We shall examine this sociological theory further on in connection with the creativity of religion.

We note in passing that Durkheim also noted the role of prophets in the history of religions. But for him it was religion, as the primary reality, that generated prophecy. For even the most critical prophet who condemns the practices and institutions of his religious community receives his vision and his values from this very community; the prophet criticizes the present state of the community in the light of its highest ideals.[11] Thus a prophet, exiled or even executed by his community, may in a deeper sense embody, more than any other person, the spirit of his community. What is involved in prophecy then is not the application of "reason" to religion but an act of fidelity to the genius of the inherited religion. Yet this difference between Weber and Durkheim is more apparent than real, since for Durkheim a certain society-building rationale is part and parcel of religion, thus making religion the source of logic and critique.

Both Durkheim and Weber, we conclude, despite their differences, distinguish in the historical religions disparate tendencies, which they call magic and religion, with different social and personal effects. Since the magical trend goes against the wider common good, it separates people from the full human potential that is present in the community. This is certainly Durkheim's view. Magical trends alienate people from the religious community and the development of their full human stature; religion, on the other hand, integrates people into social life and brings them in touch with the sources of creativity. Weber uses a more value-free language, but he also regards magic as a principle of separation and an expression of *ad hoc* concerns, while religion produces a more comprehensive vision of life, reconciling personal interests and aspirations with the destiny of a whole community.

It is worth mentioning in this context that under the influence of the sociological theory called Functionalism,[12] the distinction between magic and religion has tended to disappear in sociological research.[13] For Functionalists, the elements of social life must be understood in terms of the contributions they make to the stability of the whole. Functionalists regard as given the equilibrium of the existing social order, and all phenomena within this order are looked upon as contributing agents. Research carried out from this point of view has shown that magical rites, even though on the surface concerned with private interests and tensions, have nonetheless a social function in protecting the well-being and equilibrium of society. Magic has a "latent" social function—one that is hidden from the practitioners. In some cases magical rites dispel the fears in a certain section of the population and hence make them more peaceful workers; in other cases magic causes anxieties in people and hence generates energy for special tasks in society. In this perspective, magic and religion become indistinguishable.

The distinction between magic and religion, made by Emile Durkheim, is a sign that he may not be regarded as the father of Functionalism as it is sometimes supposed.[14] Durkheim did not look upon society as the ongoing equilibrium of social forces; he had a great sense of the vitality, the creative dynamism of society and its historical evolution. He did not try to find in the anti-social trends of magical religion latent functions, unknown to the practitioners, that made significant contributions to the maintenance of the social system. Despite his attempt to produce objective science, he did not hesitate to speak of "pathological religion," that is, of religion that works against the common good of the community, destroys dedication and concern, and is the bearer of magical trends.

* * *

We now turn to a second distinction, found in social

studies, between divergent trends in religion. In his book, *Psychoanalysis and Religion*,[15] Erich Fromm distinguishes between authoritarian and humanistic religion. Fromm, we note, does not speak as a believer. He regards himself as an atheist, but his study of religion comes to the conclusion that the negative critique offered by Freud, while true and valid, does not exhaust the reality of religion, and that in addition to the sick-making trends of religion there are others that are healing and humanizing. Fromm acknowledges the epochal breakthrough of Freud's negative critique of religion. Freud, as we shall see, extended the kind of thinking we encountered in the young Hegel's account of alienating religion. As a projection born out of the inability to be fully human, religion has the power to lock people more tightly into their impotence and intensify their estrangement from their human environment and their human resources. Yet—Fromm follows here the young Hegel —there are other religious trends, trends that communicate the ability to be more fully human.

Let me summarize two central Freudian critiques exposing religion as projection. The first is expressed in a little book, *The Future of an Illusion*, written late in his life, and corresponds to the general orientation of his psychoanalytical research. Here religion is understood as a compulsively extended infantilism, religion as "baby-trip"—if I may use this colloquial expression. Little children enjoy the protection of the parents who appear all-powerful and wise to them, the embodiment of warmth and care; and as the children grow up to face a complex and hostile world, fear is engendered, a fear of the threats and burdens confronting them, a fear that makes them cling to their childhood memories. They choose to remain passive, they refuse to grow up; and instead of breaking the desire for security and parental warmth, they project the paternal figure onto the cosmos, believe in a god with paternal or maternal features, and then experience the warmth and care for which they have longed. This is the illusion of religion: it is a projection founded on wishful thinking. But once this parental figure has been successfully located in the sky, it becomes a dangerous obstacle to growth and freedom. For this parent, invoked in prayer, now prevents the believers from leaving their childhood behind. Religion makes people dependent, it encourages their passive trends, it makes them uncritical, gullible, and immature, it nourishes their need for protection. People kept immature by a successful religious projection feel safe only in social, political and ecclesiastical institutions where few decisions are demanded of them, where they are led by strong authority figures, and where they can fit themselves into a rigid structure of law and order. Authority and obedience, which define the believer's relationship to the divinity, also determine the forms of his participation in church and society. What emerges is authoritarian religion.

This theme can be further developed by applying to the religious projection the Freudian discovery of the Oedipal complex. If the projected divinity is father, as it is in biblical religion, then the dependence on and veneration of this father figure are accompanied, at least unconsciously, by hostility against him, by a desire to remove him from his place, by a revolt against religion. Authoritarian religion, then, is not simply the promotion of a harmless infantilism; it also evokes in religious people strange and unaccountable feelings of anger, hatred and revolt, and because these cannot be given public expression nor even be inwardly acknowledged, they are shifted away from the divine object to another and find expression in a hidden self-hatred and/or in the hostility toward people who do not accept the same religion. Authoritarian religion, twisted through the unresolved Oedipal complex, becomes the source of self-punishing behavior and of collective hatred toward outsiders and non-conformists. This pathological development explains the extraordinary cruelty which authoritarian religion has produced in history. Let me add that theologians too readily pass off these organized expressions of cruelty as sins and failures, as unfortunate accidents, related to the inherited religion in a purely extrinsic way. This is too easy. The great advantage of the Freudian critique is that it enables us to explain how religions that make love and mercy central in their preaching become, nonetheless, the sources of organized and rationally-planned cruelty toward outsiders and non-conformists.

A second critique of religion, supplementing the first, is found in another one of Freud's small books, *Civilization and*

Its Discontents, which combines somewhat vague sociological speculations with the major themes drawn from his psycho-analytical studies. Here religion is understood as a projection induced by guilt-feelings—religion as "guilt-trip." In his conservative and pessimistic little book, Freud describes the pressures which modern, industrialized society exerts on individuals by increasing the demands made on them in terms of hard work, conformity, achievement, and obedience. The more complex the organization of society, the less the personal freedom of the individual. While individual people still dream of happiness, free self-expression, and the satisfaction of the instincts, they are made to feel guilty about their dreams by the imperious demands of industrial society. Modern civilization accuses them in a strong voice: You are guilty because of your deep wishes and desires. Freud held that contemporary society drives people into neurotic guilt-feelings with devastating consequences for their personal lives. This critique, we might add, fits well into the conservative sociological critique of modern society—we recall the work of Toennies—according to which industrialization severs people from the depth of their own humanity. However, the book also reveals Freud's lack of sociological sophistication. The great psychologist always sees the individual as a person over against a hostile and impersonal society; sociologists, on the other hand, recognize that the individual person comes to be by participating in a social process and that society is therefore never purely external to him but enters into the very constitution of his personal consciousness. We shall have occasion to return to this highly individualistic and politically conservative trend in Freud's psychoanalysis.

Society, then, makes people feel guilty. But who are the mediators of this judgment? According to Freud's more basic psychoanalytical research, the parents are the ones who communicate to the child the harsh demands of society. It is the voice of parents, internalized as the so-called super-ego or infantile conscience, that exercises the rule over the child, covers him with guilt, and executes society's harsh judgment on him. Morality, in this Freudian perspective, is nothing else than the voice of super-ego. Created through the internalization of the parents' demands, super-ego becomes the organ for receiving orders from teachers in school, priests in church, and authoritative persons in society. Our own rational sense of what is right and good remains weak and ineffectual before the voice of super-ego. Thus we are easily overwhelmed with guilt feelings without having a clear sense that we have done something wrong. Neurotic guilt feelings of this kind lead to many forms of irrational behavior. One of them is religion.

Overwhelming guilt feelings may give rise to a religious projection of a divine law-giver as lord of history. The accusation and condemnation addressed to us by our infantile conscience are so powerful that we cannot attribute them to mother and father nor to the social order to which we belong; they must come from a transcendent lord in whose debt we shall always be and before whom we can be at ease only if he is merciful and does not count our transgressions against us. If this projection is successful, people will remain in their guilt-prison, punish themselves except for occasional experiences of release, mistrust their own deep wishes, and lose confidence in their own powers.

Yet there are in religion significant moments of relief and forgiveness. Freud readily acknowledged this. Since the scientific spirit inevitably undermined religion—Freud follows here Comte's Positivistic thesis—he felt that people today are deprived of the occasional ecstatic release from guilt feelings, formerly offered by religion. The strict demands of modern society, therefore, drive people into oppressive guilt feelings of an intensity unknown in a previous, more religious age. Religion as a collective neurosis was then able to heal people from debilitating symptoms of their private neuroses. For Freud, then, unrelieved guilt is the typical illness of the modern age.

The religion created by guilt projections is complicated by the unresolved Oedipal complex operative in it. For the super-ego is often linked to the image of the father, whose power is the source of anger and resentment. While on the conscious level people are eager to obey, on the unconscious level they resent his authority and yearn for independence. We know from our own experience how easily this super-ego can be projected on authority figures of various kinds, on policemen or superiors, with the result that we feel restless in their presence, have strong feelings of resentment against them, entertain compulsive fantasies about them, and are unable to find the inner freedom to carry on an adult conversation with them. Such a projection makes people both servile and touchy; they seek the superior's approval with a smile and yet resent his very acts of kindness. By the same sort of unconscious process, the super-ego with Oedipal charge can be projected onto the church and its priests, and even unto the divinity.

This is the perspective from which Freud read the entire biblical story. God appeared to him like a supreme yet arbitrary ruler, handing his people a set of laws, punishing them for their transgressions and demanding worship and loyalty. Read from this perspective, the Christian story leads this development to its climax, for here the divine father is so displeased with his children that he desires the punishment of his favorite son. God derives great satisfaction from the crucifixion of his son. Once his justice and honor have been restored, he bestows his favor on the rest of his children. In Christianity, the believer approaches the divine father by pointing and referring himself to the sacrificed son and the cross on which he died. This authoritarian religion creates an imagination of law and punishment, offense and satisfaction, bloody sacrifice and cruel retribution. Freud is so pleased with his analysis of religion in terms of guilt and repentance that he creates his own imaginative myth, countering the biblical story, according to which belief in God originated in the Oedipal murder of the powerful father: the men of the earliest tribe, in an Oedipal frenzy, murdered the father who had access to all the women, and since they were unable to forget him in their guilt, they projected him as the heavenly avenger of their crime and the supreme guardian of law and order in the community. We recall here the young Hegel's analysis of bad religion. Following this line of thought, God becomes the symbol of everything men hate.

Erich Fromm accepted this radical, twofold critique of religion as a significant breakthrough on the way to human liberation. Yet he does not believe that the Freudian critique exhausts the reality of religion. What arguments does Fromm offer in favor of life-giving adult religious movements? Fromm combines a perceptive reading of Freud with a sympathetic understanding of the world religions. In the first place, then, Fromm does not interpret Freud as an enemy of religion purely and simply. He recognizes that Freud himself was dedicated to human development defined in terms of knowledge, brotherly love, reduction of human suffering, independence and responsibility, and he sees in this dedication "the ethic core of all great religions."[16] It is true that Freud himself did not explicitly recognize this humanizing trend in the world religions, but at least, so Fromm thinks, the Freudian critique of religion in no way undermines and invalidates this religious dedication to human growth. "The statement that Freud is against 'religion' therefore is misleading unless we define sharply what religion or what aspects of religion he is critical of and what aspects he speaks for."[17] It is at this point that Erich Fromm introduces his distinction between authoritarian and humanistic religion. Freud's critique revealed the alienating nature of authoritarian religion but left room for another kind of religious orientation, one that promotes human self-discovery and self-expression.

Fromm understands religion as any style of thought and action, shared by a group, which gives the individual a frame of orientation and an object of devotion.[18] From his study of the world religions he comes to the conclusion—we call this his sympathetic reading of religion—that all of them contain elements that further man's development and the unfolding of his specifically human powers, even if they also contain elements that paralyze these powers. Religion is ambiguous: it is both alienating and life-giving. Fromm's definition of the humanistic trend remains somewhat vague, but he does make one remark that moves his reflections into the field of theology and enables us to clarify his underlying thought. He writes, "Inasmuch as humanistic religions are theistic, God is a symbol of man's own power which he tries to realize in his own life, and is not a symbol of force and domination having power over man."[19] This sentence can be read as a formal definition of how humanistic religion differs from authoritarian religion: the former conceives of the divine in terms of participation and communion and the latter in terms of power and domination. There exists then, in the eyes of Erich Fromm, within human history a vast movement toward freedom, development and the transformation of life, which unites religious and non-religious people, which cuts right through the existing religions and communities of other kinds, be they political, scientific, or whatever, a movement that allows believers and atheists to work together for human liberation and resist together the forces that enslave men and inhibit human life.

How does a theologian evaluate Fromm's distinction between authoritarian and humanistic religion? Since Fromm remains vague in regard to his understanding of humanistic religion and tends to restrict it to purely ethical aspects, one possible interpretation is to deny that what Fromm calls humanistic religion is religion in any true sense. At the same time, another possible interpretation is to fill out the vagueness in Fromm's description and then relate his concept of humanistic religion to the religious and theological developments going on in the churches at this time. Since Fromm himself repeatedly mentions that contemporary theologians have given a humanistic understanding of religion, it is quite likely that his own thought has been influenced by the religious development in the churches. In particular, his sentence that in humanistic religion "God is not a symbol of power over man but of man's power"[20] recalls the effort of Protestant and Catholic theologians in this century to interpret God not as a supreme being over and above the world but as the mystery of life in and through human existence, delivering man from his brokenness and orienting him toward a redeemed future. For these theologians—we have referred to them in our first chapter—God is not the symbol of power over man but rather a symbol of power in and through man, that is, the symbol of the release of man's own power and its orientation toward growth and liberation.

Since, in a previous paragraph, we have presented a reading of the biblical and Christian story from the perspective of authoritarian religion, we must at least mention, however briefly, how this story is read from the viewpoint of humanizing or redemptive religion. Here God is not the supreme ruler or master. What the scriptures call God is the Truth, the Love and the Life, operative in human history as its deepest dimension, hidden from human eyes, especially because of man's sins; this divine mystery, hidden from the beginning, has manifested itself in significant events, in the history of Israel, in the history of other peoples, and in a special way in the life and victory of Jesus Christ. It is possible to formulate the church's traditional christology in this way.[21] The church holds that in Jesus is made manifest the divine truth or *logos* that is working in a hidden way in all of history. In Jesus the Christian encounters the living God. In Jesus is revealed and communicated the triune mystery of God, as truth or *logos* addressing people everywhere, as spirit empowering people wherever they are to follow the call of truth, and as love defining the ground out of which people come and the horizon toward which they move. It has been the effort of contemporary theologians to proclaim the Christian creed as the revelation of God's presence in the humanization and liberation of mankind.

We conclude, then, with Erich Fromm that religion is both pathogenic and therapeutic. This includes the Christian religion. We are now able to appreciate the new sensitivity Sigmund Freud's work has created among us. Theologians should no longer reflect on the teaching and practice of the Christian religion without asking themselves to what extent the inherited symbols initiate people into dependencies, guilt and blindness, and to what extent these same symbols, read out of different presuppositions, deliver people from dependencies, guilt and blindness. In a book called *Man Becoming*, I have tried to show that the gospel is in fact a healing message and that to remain faithful to this gospel it is necessary to submit the teaching and the practice of the Christian church to an ongoing therapeutic critique. There are indeed ways of speaking about God and praying to God that alienate people from their depth and their destiny and yet there are others that reconcile people with life and free them for a new future.

* * *

We now come to a third distinction between contrasting trends in religion. Following the sociology of Karl Mannheim, especially the articles collected in his *Ideology and Utopia*, I wish to distinguish between ideological and utopian religion.

Mannheim extended and modified the Marxian concept of ideology. We recall that for Marx religion was always and inevitably idcological in the sense that it was an expression of false consciousness, legitimating the power of the dominant class and hence defending the existing order of society. We noted that Marx had also spoken of religion as "the sigh of the oppressed creature" and acknowledged that religion may record the dreams of an oppressed group convinced that human destiny transcends the present state of misery. Later Marxist thinkers made use of this idea to interpret certain trends in Christian history, in particular the rise of early Christianity and the Anabaptist movement of the 16th century. Under certain political circumstances and the influence of revolutionary leaders, the religion of the oppressed may spell out a judgment on the powerful in society, summon people to a realistic awareness of their misery, and mobilize forces among the people that lead to radical social change.

The careful study of religion made it increasingly difficult for sociologists to look upon religion purely and simply as the sacred legitimation of the existing social order. Max Weber himself, in a series of three brilliant articles, published in English in *The Sociology of Religion*, examined the relation between religion and various classes in society.[22] He studied the religious trends among peasants, warrior nobles, the aristocracy, merchants, craftsmen, the dispossessed groups, and finally the various strata of intellectuals—and found that the kind of religion practiced by each of these groups was related to their real and concrete interests in society. At the same time, prophecy or critical religion was not confined to any one group or class. Weber concluded that the most oppressed classes had never been the bearers of new religious impulses. Innovative religion is found in those sections of society for whom a rational ethics is of great importance, such as craftsmen, merchants, and skilled workers. Needless to say, Weber did not deny the phenomenon of ideological religion which served the dominant class as a defense of its privileges and consoled the dominated classes with promises of heavenly rewards. Yet the conclusion of his essays was that an easy generalization of the relation between class and religion is not possible; in every case the concrete, historical situation must be studied.

Karl Mannheim, building on the sociologists who preceded him, extended and modified the Marxian notion of ideology and integrated it into sociological theory. For Marx, the concept of ideology had been a weapon for wrestling against bourgeois science and bourgeois ideals; he tried to defeat the arguments of the liberal philosophers by showing that their positions served the interests of the middle class. But Marx had not applied an ideological critique to the ideas of revolutionary movements; the most oppressed classes, Marx held, were not vulnerable to ideology, or at least, by becoming aware of their actual situation, they could acquire true consciousness. Consequently the Marxists themselves did not examine how their own movement made ideas serve revolutionary interests and hence to what extent it produced distortions of the truth. Karl Mannheim insisted that all groups, in virtue of their concrete place in society, look upon reality from a certain angle and entertain certain political aspirations; they consequently acquire a definite mind-set or mental horizon which defines the framework of their thought, their cultural life and their religion.

The study of these mind-sets became a central concern of Mannheim's sociology of knowledge. Each mind-set is associated with a particular group of people—a social carrier (Träger) in Mannheim's terminology—and dependent on the socio-political situation of this group in society. One of Mannheim's most important contributions to sociology was the discovery that the ideas and ideals of people develop as the group to which these people belong undergoes significant social changes. The development of ideas, of art and of religion cannot be understood apart from the mind-set to which they belong and apart from the socio-political changes taking place in their social carrier (Träger). Ideas, in Mannheim's terminology, are *seinsgebunden*,[23] i.e., are grounded in social reality. This sociological principle has far reaching implications for the study of religion.

Religious ideas are socially grounded; their meaning and power cannot be understood without taking into consideration the historical situation of the believing community. Applying this to Christianity we have to say that creeds have different meanings depending on the mental horizon with which they are associated and on the historical situation of the community in which this mind-set resides.

That the meaning of religious statements is *seinsgebunden* is not foreign to contemporary theology. For from the field of hermeneutics and the study of texts it has become clear to many theologians that the meaning of a religious statement is not only dependent on the social context in which it was first uttered but also on the presuppositions brought to it by the interpreter; these presuppositions in turn depend on the historical experience of the community to which the interpreter belongs. The Christian gospel gives rise to many meanings. What counts today is to find a formulation of the gospel that is appropriate to the church's present historical experience.

While surprising at first, the emergence of the same insight in various disciplines can be explained by the very sociology of knowledge we are here discussing. Mannheim himself often made the point that the emergence of the sociology of knowledge and the awareness of several mind-sets or mental horizons became possible and inevitable after the breakdown of the homogeneous strata in society, the intermingling of people with diverse backgrounds and social interests, and the social transformations that led some persons to conversion from one mental horizon to another.[24] Only in modern times, especially after World War I, has it been possible for people to compare and contrast various mind-sets either because they had passed from one to another in their personal history or because they daily associated with people who belonged to different mental universes. It was thus the new social conditions that led to the discovery of the socio-historical nature of truth in several academic disciplines.

In this context Karl Mannheim examined what he called the utopian mind-set and related it to the study of religion. I wish to extend his account to the distinction between utopian and ideological religion. Let me define ideological religion first. Religion (or any symbolic language) is ideological if it legitimates the existing social order, defends the dominant values, enhances the authority of the dominant class, and creates an imagination suggesting that society is stable and perdures. By contrast, religion is utopian if it reveals the ills of the present social order, inverts the dominant values of society, undermines the authority of the ruling groups, and makes people expect the downfall of the present system. Mannheim, let me add, does not always follow this narrow definition of utopia. Not all utopias are revolutionary. He often uses utopia in a wider sense as referring to visions of a new society that evokes criticism of the present order and releases energy for social change. Utopias envisage a qualitative transformation of the conditions of human life. Such utopias may be revolutionary or evolutionary.

An ambivalence in the definition of utopia pervades Mannheim's entire book. At first he offers a radical definition of the utopian imagination and presents it as a mind-set which, like ideology, distorts the perception of reality and leads to false and dangerous political judgments.[24] However, in the course of his book he widens his understanding of utopia. He begins to recognize that without an utopian imagination no new thought and no new action occur in society. He examines the various forms of utopian consciousness that have been important in Western history, and while he identifies himself with none of these, he comes to the conclusion that the disappearance of utopias leads to a static society and the reification of human life.[25] When, at another place in his book, Mannheim proves that a vision of the future is operative in sociological and historical research, he abandons as illusory the ideal of objectivity and value-neutral research.[26] Truth is not available from any standpoint whatever. Mannheim searches for a new definition of objectivity which includes the scholars' commitment to totality and social transformation. When Mannheim tries to define this commitment, he remains rather vague: he speaks of a commitment to "an ethical position," "a political élan," and "a total view," which expresses the scholars' readiness to regard their own perspectives as partial, to situate them in ever wider spheres of reference, to remain open to other people's perception of reality, and to reach out for a conception of humanity and the historical process that leads to ever greater human liberation.[27] Through research carried out from such an orientation, scholars are able to overcome the distortions of ideology and utopia in a new objectivity, and yet—and here is the ambivalence—it is only through a commitment to a certain utopia that historical truth becomes available.

Historical religion, to return to our topic, can be both ideological and utopian, depending on the historical age, the political situation of the religious community, and the form of people's religious experience. Looked upon from this viewpoint, religious symbols are inevitably a hidden political language. Social scientists are not justified in reducing religion to its political dimension. On the other hand, the student of religion must admit that no matter how spiritual and how private a religious concern may be, it always has a political implication; it is never socially neutral. Mannheim's distinction between ideological and utopian religion has opened up a new field of research for the student of religion.

Theologians engaged in inquiries of this kind are surprised to find that Christian spiritualities that are God-centered and recommend the contempt of the world may in actual fact be subtle legitimations of worldly powers. Even the great saints were often so identified with their culture that without knowing it, and despite their other-worldliness, they unconsciously sanctioned the injustices of their society. Reading, for instance, the letters of Thérèse of Lisieux and Père Charles de Foucault, both remarkable religious figures and prophetic in the context of the ecclesiastical tradition, we discover that they provided religious legitimation for the colonial expansion of France and its claim of cultural superiority. Karl Mannheim's sociological approach has shown that a religious attitude that encourages contempt for the world may in actual fact go hand in hand with an uncritical identification with this world and its power structures.

Since the word "utopia" is used by Mannheim in a special sense, distinct from ordinary usage, it is important to point out that not every dream of a perfect future is, in Mannheim's terms, utopian. Hopes of future happiness that are based on the prolongation of present values and strengthen the dominant institutions are in fact ideological. The perfect world painted in television advertising where beautiful people living in beautiful

houses solve their daily problems by buying appropriate com-
modities is a highly ideological imagination, for it is nothing
but the extension into unreality of the values and institutions
basic to the present consumer society. Was the picture of the
future painted in *The Greening of America*,[28] a book widely
read in the sixties, a utopian or an ideological imagination? Did
it shake people loose from the inherited values, make them
critical, and summon them to action? Or did it persuade people
that a new culture was in the process of creating itself, blind
them to the real holders of power, and thus encourage a political passivity that left the established order without chal-
lengers? These questions are not always easy to answer. In a
later chapter we shall see that the Christian preaching of future
hope, the coming of God's kingdom and the creation of a new
heaven and a new earth, bears within the same ambiguity.

Many scholars have simply ignored that religion has ever
been utopian. Marx himself did not recognize this. The later
Marxists, as we mentioned earlier, were aware of the radical
character of the apocalyptical elements in early Christianity
and recognized the theory and practice of revolution in the 16th
century Anabaptist movements. In his *Ideology and Utopia*,
Mannheim devotes a section to the study of "chiliastic religion,"[29] that is, the radical religious movements of the late
middle ages which expected the coming of the new age of the
Spirit, an ecstatic age in which the contradictions of life, imposed mainly by domination and institution, would be overcome. These movements created great unrest among the population; sometimes they encouraged people to revolt. Because
of their utopian orientation, these groups suffered persecution
and death at the hands of the established authorities, secular
and religious. In her book, *The Radical Kingdom*, Rosemary
Ruether has shown that the revolutionary mind-set had its
origin in Jewish apocalypticism in the centuries preceding the
Christian era and that it has been mediated to Western culture
through the apocalyptical elements in New Testament literature.[30]

The radical consciousness of Jewish apocalypticism was
created among the faithful believers who read the ancient messianic promises made to Israel under the pressure of political

occupation and cultural oppression. Since the prolonged occupation of Israel threatened the survival of Jewish independence and the cosmopolitan culture of the Empire tended to
undermine the traditional faith, at least among the upper
classes, some Jews began to form resistance groups. Some of
these moved into the mountains. They regarded themselves as
enemies of the Empire and sometimes even repudiated the official Judaism. Their precarious existence was nourished by the
hope that the messianic promises were about to be fulfilled.
The injustices of the present order cried to heaven for ven-
geance. God could not remain silent. These radical groups
created a new kind of religious literature which revealed that
God's judgment was upon the present order, that the seats of
power were about to be overthrown, that God's victory was
near, and that he, the Lord, would create a new society where
his faithful people would live in justice and peace. Some of
these apocalypticists acted as erratic freedom fighters. This
apocalyptical mood lasted into the first century of the Christian era. We mentioned before that Jesus preached his gospel
in such an environment and occasionally adopted the apocalyptical theme, even if he never identified himself with the radicals. The early Christian communities caught the apocalyptical
fever and many of them expected the coming of God's victory
in their own generation (cf. Mt. 10:23; 16:28; 24:34). Some of
them even produced their own apocalyptical literature. The last
book of the New Testament belongs to this. While the gospel is
not identical with these apocalyptical trends, they are so closely
connected with it that Christian preaching has again and again,
under certain social and political conditions, created a radical
mind-set.

How can we define this apocalyptical consciousness? First,
it regarded society as evil. Human sin and oppression had pen-
etrated to the very fibers of the institutions so that social reform had become impossible. Second, society must be destroyed. In fact, this destruction was already beginning; the evil
operative in it was already tearing it apart. God's judgment on
it was definite. Third, a new society was about to be created,
free from the injustices of the old. This new order would be
God's work, and for this reason no one knew exactly what it
would be like. It would embody the divine promises of justice,

love and peace, but it could be spoken of only in figurative and symbolic language. This consciousness, mediated through the apocalyptical biblical passages and the radical Christian groups, is the source of the Western revolutionary tradition, for political radicalism to this day has the identical threefold structure. The radicals hold that their society is so rotten that it cannot be reformed; they hold that the society must be destroyed, and since its inner contradictions are already tearing it apart, its future is doomed; and finally they hold that the new society to be created after the destruction of the old will be qualitatively different from it, cannot be described in detail by people caught in pre-revolutionary consciousness, and must be spoken of, for the time being, in the symbolic language of justice and peace.

In his *Ideology and Utopia*, Karl Mannheim does not recognize the connection of the chiliastic-utopian consciousness with ancient Jewish apocalypticism. What interests him more is the need to distinguish the chiliastic-utopian consciousness present in the early socialist movements from the more deterministic and scientific form of consciousness that emerged in the Marxist movement and found expression in official Marxist doctrine. The critical Marxists of the 20th century and the social thinkers of the New Left, however, have recovered some of the chiliastic elements and regard their political movement as bearer of utopia.

Revolution is not the only form of utopia. Karl Mannheim presented other forms of utopian consciousness that have been effective in Western history. Unfortunately, since he was not primarily interested in religion, he did not link the other utopias to religious ideas and developments as he did in the case of revolution and chiliasm. But the close connection between the radical tradition of Western society and expressions of biblical religion is sufficient evidence to repudiate the idea that religion is always and inevitably ideological. Religion is ambiguous; it is the bearer of diverse and sometimes contradictory trends; it is both the creator of ideologies and the bearer of utopias.

* * *

A weakness of the Functionalist approach to the study of religion—we referred to this previously[31]—is the one-sided emphasis on those elements of religion that contribute to the creation and maintenance of the social equilibrium and hence the insufficient recognition of the utopian religious trends. Peter Berger and Thomas Luckmann are no Functionalists, far from it; society for them is not a self-stabilizing system but a precarious creation ever in need of props and defenses. And yet they understand religion in largely Functionalist terms as the sacred canopy or ultimate sacred legitimation of the social reality and man's ever-threatened self-definition. True, in his *The Sacred Canopy*, Peter Berger acknowledges that religion, in particular biblical religion, has often played a world-shaking role and questioned the taken-for-granted character of the inherited institutions. He concludes that "religion appears in history as both a world-maintaining and a world-shaking force."[32] Still, by adopting a systematic sociological approach which defines religion in terms of its world-constructing and world-maintaining function, he does not leave adequate room for exploring the aspects of religion that go counter to his principal definition.

We find the same Functionalist trend in Berger and Luckmann's understanding of science, including sociological science. In their book, *The Social Construction of Reality*, they classify science with theology and philosophy as a conceptual machinery of universe-maintenance.[33] Science produces a symbolic universe legitimating the precarious social reality. While science, including sociology, undermines the sacred symbolic universes that have been created and removes universe-maintaining knowledge from the man in the street—thus appearing radical and critical—in the mind of the scientists science continues to fulfill the task of world-maintenance. But if this is so, what else is Berger and Luckmann's book but a legitimation of the precarious social order! True, in other books Peter Berger has defined the task of sociology as "debunking" or the removal of mystification,[34] but by defining science so exclusively in terms of world-maintenance, he leaves little room for this critical dimension. The Functionalist trend, when uncorrected, tends to underestimate the creativity of sociology, making it a symbolic world legitimating the social system.

What is the reason that we find this extraordinary stress on legitimation and symbolic world-maintenance in the sociology of Peter Berger? The answer to this question is quite clear. For Peter Berger all social life is essentially precarious. Society is created by people acting together and for that reason remains at all times threatened by possible dissolution. What if people stopped acting together? Society would simply fall apart. Berger has no Durkheimian trust in the inner coherence of the societal forces. Berger follows, rather, the Weberian suspicion that people form a society because there is an authority that makes them do it. This authority is for Berger mainly symbolic. To keep social action going and make the social reality stable, we need symbols that make us believe that society has to be the way it is. We need world-maintaining symbols. We need a world-maintaining myth. We have to be made partially blind, or else live with the nagging fear that tomorrow the precarious construction of society may fall apart.

Society, in the perspective of Peter Berger, is in need of alienation to survive. For him, alienation is the illusion that the societal processes are fixed and unchangeable realities; alienation is the repression of the truth that society is simply people-doing-things-together and hence basically fragile and unstable. Whenever we repress from consciousness that the social order is simply man-made, we experience society as a compelling force making us act in this or that way, even if this does not correspond to our wishes. We experience alienation because society forces us to act against our will. If we all did what we really liked, Berger holds, we would find ourselves very quickly in social chaos. Some alienation is necessary for the protection of society. A few people may be lucky enough to be able "to do their thing," but unless there were vast numbers who feel compelled to conform, to work and bear the burden, the social reality would dissolve and with it the possibility for personal life. Alienation is anthropologically necessary.

We need many symbols of legitimation. Among all of these, the most efficient alienating force is religion. Religion casts a spell of sacredness on the structures of society and makes us forget that they are merely man-made conventions. Religion produces the sacred compulsion that is necessary to keep this mad world going. This sociological theory, we note, does not differ very much from Marx and Freud who also thought that religion was an alienating sacred canopy, except that Karl Marx believed—an accountable theological *a priori* —that humanity was destined to overcome alienation and be free. Peter Berger does not share this *a priori*. Contrary to Marx and Freud, however, Berger does recognize world-shaking religion. In particular he holds that the basic inspiration of Hebrew religion, expressed in its origins, its prophetic tradition and in the person of Jesus, is critical, de-alienating religion; but he thinks, if I understand him correctly, that this inspiration inevitably leads to secularization and the waning of religion, leaving the world without sacred norms. This, for Berger, is the present situation. In a secular society, the world-maintaining symbols must be supplied by non-religious legitimating systems, possibly even by scientific theories. But without religion society remains unstable. If I read Peter Berger correctly, religion is for him essentially a legitimating factor in society, and to the extent to which it becomes innovative and liberating, it prepares its own demise.

In this chapter we have come to a different conclusion. Religion, we have seen, is a complex, ambiguous reality with many trends, some of which may even be contradictory. Because of this complexity, religion is able to blind some people and make others see, it produces sickness in some and leads to health in others, it acts as legitimation for the *status quo* and as catalyst for social change. It appears that religion is capable of generating its own critique.

I have, moreover, great difficulties with Berger's view of alienation. I do not wish to look at life from a perspective that makes alienation appear as anthropologically necessary. It is of course quite true that life in society demands many services and sacrifices and, in this sense, prevents us from doing what we like and diminishes our freedom, but there is no reason to suppose that these limits will always be imposed on us against our will. Marx, we recall, clearly distinguished between imposed labor and creative work. In Marx's view man was essentially a builder, a cooperative builder. Prior to Marx, Hegel himself in his mature thought distinguished between two kinds of alienation:[35] there was the alienation (*Entfremdung*) which was inflicted on people and diminished their humanity, and there was the alienation (*Entäusserung*) which was freely chosen, grounded in love, and made people more truly human. Hegel held that people who discover themselves and assume self-possession are thereby rendered capable of forgetting themselves, identifying with society and freely assuming the burden of social responsibility. Hegel adopted this anthropology, I suppose, because he believed that operative in personal life is a transcending Spirit. The very word *Entäusserung* was taken from the biblical message that Jesus "emptied himself." But, then, there is no anthropological view that does not begin with an *a priori*. Since the concepts we devise and the social analyses we propose affect our imagination and eventually influence our very perception, I object to Peter Berger's theory of alienation. I do not wish to encourage an imagination that regards alienation as anthropologically necessary. I prefer to analyze the social process from the viewpoint that freedom is man's promised destiny.

Recommended Readings

RELIGION AND MAGIC

Bronislaw Malinowski, *Magic, Science and Religion*, Doubleday, New York, 1954.

Max Weber, *The Sociology of Religion*, Beacon Press, Boston, 1968.

J. Milton Yinger, *Religion, Society and the Individual*, Macmillan Company, New York, 1957.

RELIGION AND HEALTH

Gordon Allport, *The Individual and His Religion*, Macmillan Company, New York, 1950.

Erich Fromm, *Psychoanalysis and Religion*, Bantam Books, New York, 1967.

William Lynch, *Images of Hope*, New American Library, New York, 1967.

Rollo May, *Love and Will*, Norton & Comp., New York, 1969.

IDEOLOGY AND UTOPIA

Charles Glock and Rodney Stark, *Religion and Society in Tension*, Rand McNally, Chicago, 1965.

Charles Glock, *To Comfort and To Challenge*, University of California Press, Berkeley, 1967.

Karl Mannheim, *Ideology and Utopia*, Harcourt, Brace & World, New York, no date.

Rosemary Ruether, *The Radical Kingdom*, Harper & Row, New York, 1970.

Donald E. Smith, *Religion, Politics and Social Change in the Third World, A Documenation*, Free Press, New York, 1971.

Notes

1. Emile Durkheim, *The Elementary Forms of Religious Life*, trans. J. W. Swain, The Free Press, New York, 1965.
2. *Ibid.*, p. 470.
3. *Ibid.*, p. 474.
4. *Ibid.*, pp. 57-62.
5. *Ibid.*, p. 63.
6. Max Weber, *The Sociology of Religion*, trans. E. Fischoff, Beacon Press, Boston, 1964, pp. 20-31.
7. *Op. cit.*, Introduction, p. xxx.
8. Cf. *op. cit.*, Introduction, pp. xxxii-xxxiii, and Index, under "rationalization," p. 300. For Weber on rationalization, see also *From Max Weber*, edit. Gerth and Mills, Oxford University Press, New York, 1958, Index, under "rationalization," p. 484; Julien Freund, *The Sociology of Max Weber*, Vintage Books, New York, 1969, pp. 17-24; and Robert Nisbet, *The Sociological Tradition*, Basic Books, New York, 1966, pp. 141-150.
9. *The Sociology of Religion*, pp. 32-45.
10. *Op. cit.*, pp. 46-59.
11. See below, p. 134.

12. On Functionalism see Irving Zeitlin, *Rethinking Sociology*, Prentice-Hall, Englewood Cliffs, N.J., 1973, pp. 3-62, and Thomas O'Dea, *The Sociology of Religion*, Prentice-Hall, Englewood Cliffs, N.J., 1966, pp. 1-19.

13. See Milton Yinger, *The Scientific Study of Religion*, Macmillan, London, 1970, pp. 69-71, 74-77, where the author documents the trend in much of contemporary social anthropology to regard religion and magic as functional equivalents.

14. See Albert Pierce, "Durkheim and Functionalism," in Emile Durkheim *et al.*, *Essays on Sociology and Philosophy*, edit. Kurt Wolff, Harper & Row, New York, 1960, pp. 154-169, and Robert Bellah's "Durkheim and History," in Robert Nisbet's *Emile Durkheim*, Prentice-Hall, Englewood Cliffs, N.J., 1965, pp. 153-176.

15. Erich Fromm, *Psychoanalysis and Religion*, Bantam Books, New York, 1967.

16. *Op. cit.*, p. 18.

17. *Ibid.*, p. 19.

18. *Ibid.*, p. 22.

19. *Ibid.*, p. 37.

20. *Ibid.*, p. 48.

21. Cf. Edgar Bruns, *The Art and Thought of John*, Herder & Herder, 1969, pp. 78-86.

22. Max Weber, *The Sociology of Religion*, pp. 80-137.

23. Karl Mannheim, *Ideology and Utopia*, trans. L. Wirth and E. Shils, Harcourt, Brace & World, New York, no date, p. 78.

24. *Op. cit.*, pp. 192-196.

25. *Ibid.*, pp. 262-263.

26. *Ibid.*, pp. 43-47.

27. *Ibid.*, pp. 47-48, 98-108. Also see Karl Mannheim, "On the Interpretation of 'Weltanschauung' " and "Historicism," *Essays on the Sociology of Knowledge*, edit. Paul Kecskemeti, Routledge & Kegan Paul, London, 1952, pp. 33-133.

28. Charles Reich, *The Greening of America*, Random House, New York, 1970.

29. Karl Mannheim, *Ideology and Utopia*, pp. 211-218.

30. Rosemary Ruether, *The Radical Kingdom*, Harper & Row, New York, 1970. In the following section, I also rely on R. Ruether's as yet unpublished manuscript, "Messiah of Israel and Cosmic Christ." Cf also Harold H. Rowley, *The Relevance of the Apocalyptic*, Lutterworth, London, 1964; David S. Russell, *The Method and Message of Jewish Apocalyptic*, S.C.M., London, 1964.

31. See above, p. 91.

32. Peter Berger, *The Sacred Canopy*, Doubleday, New York, 1967, p. 100.

33. Peter Berger and Thomas Luckmann, *The Social Construction of Reality*, Doubleday, New York, 1967, pp. 95-97.

34. Peter Berger, *Invitation to Sociology*, Doubleday, New York, 1962, pp. 25-53.

35. Cf. Richard Schacht, *Alienation*, Doubleday, New York, 1971, pp. 45-62.

VI
The Discovery of the Symbolic:
Freud and Durkheim

The dominant intellectual trend in the wealthy societies of the 19th century was scientific Positivism. Even in Germany, in the second half of the century, scientific Positivism replaced the Romantic rejection of the rational Enlightenment. According to the sociologists we have studied, this scientific mind-set corresponded to the rational and atomistic nature of associative society (*Gesellschaft*), with its contractual and hence external bond between people. The extraordinary achievements of science and technology, moreover, persuaded scientists and philosophers that the scientific method was the only valid method of inquiry and scientific knowledge was the only reliable truth. These scholars looked upon reality, including human society, as a universe defined by quantity. All qualities, they thought, could eventually be translated into quantities. Scientific Positivism was based on a naive epistemology, according to which the observing subject gained knowledge of the observed object by gathering quantitative information about it and then constructing a verifiable theory explaining its behavior. This knowledge was regarded as objective and universal. Positivism engendered the hope that eventually, with the advance of science, the men of science would be able to solve all the problems of society.

At the end of the 19th century, sociologists and some other social thinkers, while adopting a moderate form of Positivism themselves, made the startling discovery that human culture and society, whether ancient or modern, could not be accounted for without paying attention to the symbolic

dimension.[1] The human world was not simply an aggregation
of quantities. It became clear to these thinkers that people did
not define themselves in purely rational terms, that their interrelationship was not purely contractual, that their behavior
was not simply analyzable in quantitative terms; operative in
the constitution of culture and society was people's symbolic
self-understanding. The symbolic structure of the mind affected
the creation of society, and this in turn determined man's own
self-creation.

In this chapter I wish to present the discovery of the symbolic by two great thinkers at the turn of the 20th century, Sigmund Freud and Emile Durkheim.

Sigmund Freud was brought up in an intellectual climate
determined by Positivism, and in his psychological books and
essays, especially in the early ones, he adopted a highly scientific and in fact mechanistic terminology for dealing with psychic phenomena. As a theorist, he never went beyond the Positivism he had inherited. Yet his great discovery that dreams
have meaning, and reveal in symbolic language aspects of personal life hidden from consciousness, was a turning point in the
Western intellectual tradition. Dreams could not be fully explained, Freud held, as remnants of the brain's waking function; they were not uncontrolled reflexes produced by external
stimuli or inner organic causes; they could not be accounted for
in purely quantitative terms. Dreams had meaning. It is hard
for us today to imagine how shocking Freud's theory appeared
to the community of scientists at the turn of the century. They
were looking for hard, quantitative data to come to a better understanding of the human mind. To attach so much importance
to the fleeting images that skipped through the mind during
sleep seemed to go against the scientific understanding of
human life. Even though Freud thought of himself as a scientist
and presented his theory of dreams as scientifically demonstrable, he was not followed by the scientific world of his day. Only
poets believed him at first.

Freud's famous book, *The Interpretation of Dreams*, written at the beginning of his psychoanalytical career, is dedicated
to the theory—demonstrable, he thought—that dreams reveal
the hidden and unconscious depths of the human mind.[2] In sig-

nificant night dreams, our unacknowledged wishes express themselves in symbolic language. Dreams are symbolic wish-fulfillment. Dreams manifest people's deep inclinations and their great frustrations. Yet the meaning of these dreams usually escapes the dreamer, even if the dreams themselves offer a certain amount of psychic release. Freud's controversial discovery was that dreams have meaning and that they are related to the core of a person's life. Freud held—and he is followed in this by all representatives of depth psychology—that there are psychic processes in us, of which we are not aware and yet which have great influence on our well-being and our action. They can even make us sick. We have no direct access to our own unconscious. Yet these psychic processes, Freud tried to show, express themselves in moments of spontaneity, such as laughter, mistakes in speech or action, and free fantasy, but more especially in the symbolic language of dreams. The dream is the royal road to the unconscious. It is a revelation of the hidden truth about oneself.

We note that the revelation of the deep takes place in symbolic language. The symbol is here not the second-best, an imprecise approximation of the truth, eventually to be displaced by the clear concept. The symbol is the proper mode of a person's self-manifestation, and it is the encounter with this symbol that may lead to self-knowledge and eventual psychic transformation. Healing is not due to the content of the dream analyzed by the psychotherapist and presented to the dreamer in conceptual form; healing may come to pass, rather, through a person's confrontation with his dream in the light of his discovery, made with the help of a therapist, how this dream speaks the hidden truth about himself. The persons in quest of healing and growth will not be helped by assimilating intellectually the interpretation presented to them by the therapist; what counts, rather, is that they stay with their dream, live with their dream, and use the interpretation worked out in collaboration with the therapist to make the symbolic language of the dream meaningful and powerful. The interpretation does not heal; what may heal is the message embodied in the dream. Symbols, for Freud, are not only the revelation of the unconscious; they also have power to transform the unconscious.

It is true that Freud tended to confine the meaning of the dream to the fulfillment of hidden wishes and even tried to interpret anxiety dreams in terms of repressed desires; but the psychotherapeutic practice, inspired by Freud, has widened the understanding of dreams as manifestations of a person's unconscious life, including of course his deep wishes. The various schools of depth psychology look upon dreams as the symbolic language revealing a person's hidden life, in a form that enables this person to encounter his (her) own depth, listen to its message, and by responding in a creative way initiate a significant transformation of his (her) personal life. The symbol is both revelation and power.

It is also true that Freud often tended to regard the content of the unconscious as made up of material repressed from consciousness, as if there existed no unconscious process in the mind that had not previously been conscious. Freud emphasized this aspect of the unconscious because it was the most important one in the psychotherapeutic process. In his more theoretical work, however, he recognized the existence of primary psychic processes that never reach the conscious mind, and he admitted something like a collective memory in the unconscious, handed on in largely hidden ways, which affects the creativity of individuals and directs their imagination.[3] Freud did not object in principle to the "collective unconscious," to which Carl Jung attached so much weight.[4] What Freud objected to in Jung's theory was the idea that the inherited symbolism was transhistorical, that it related people in every culture to the same metaphysical reality. For Freud this collective symbolism was strictly historical; it was produced by the significant experiences of a people in their evolutionary past. Freud objected to the use of the collective unconscious in psychotherapeutic practice, at least until the personal unconscious had been dealt with adequately. He feared that a hasty turning to a collective symbolism would only serve as defense against, or disguise for, the unresolved personal conflicts repressed in one's own past, especially in infancy. But with these restrictive remarks made, Freud's understanding of the unconscious, operative in men's lives, included not only the repressed material that had previously been conscious but also hidden memo-

ries that transcend personal history and link them to the
sources of creativity as well as to heavy burdens, the mortgages
of the past. Symbols have power in the constitution of human
life.

This position was new and startling. In a highly scientific
culture, the educated tended to regard symbols as unimportant
and useless as approximate formulations of a reality that could
be expressed with greater precision in conceptual terms, and as
signs that appeal to the emotions rather than to a person's
mind. Symbols were decorations in a room that was essentially
complete; they did not enter into the very making of the room.
Freud's theory of dreams and unconscious processes was repudiated by the scientific community of his time. Lay people lis-
tened to him, artists and poets. It was only gradually that psychoanalysis affected the self-understanding of Western culture.

Even theologians began to listen to Freud, despite his negative evaluation of religion as collective neurosis. For if the
symbol is the revelation of the depth and in fact the only way
in which the deep can manifest itself—without ever being replaced by a concept or a clear and distinct idea—and if the
symbol enables a person to confront the hidden dimension of
his life and by doing so to be significantly changed, then it
would be possible to use this notion of symbol for a better understanding of divine revelation. Since contemporary theology,
as we have repeatedly mentioned, tends to speak of God as a
presence in human life, as matrix and horizon of human history, it is possible to affirm the divine mystery as the deepest
dimension of human existence that reveals itself in symbols.
These symbols in turn enable the believers to encounter the
divine operative in their lives and by doing so to enter into a
significant transformation of their personal and social existence. The encounter with God's self-revelation in these symbols
is a saving event. We may even present Jesus Christ as the ultimate symbol in which the divine ground of the human and
cosmic reality reveals itself: by meeting him and believing in
him, people come to know their own depth, their own humanity as well as the divine mystery out of which they come to be.

Freud himself did not engage in philosophical reflection on
the role of symbols in man's making of man. But in his actual

therapeutic practice he did make use of symbols, of one symbol in particular, in a way that remind theologians of the role played by symbols in biblical religion. Sam Keen, in his public conversations, has often referred to psychotherapy as a process whereby people are taught to tell their story in a new way, and, by doing so, to experience deliverance from their psychic blocks and inhibitions. Telling one's story is never easy. When we actually do decide to tell the story of our private life as far back into infancy as possible, we inevitably do so under the guidance of some sort of symbol we have adopted for our own self-understanding. This symbol determines what we remember of the past and what we forget, and selects from the wealth of material the details we regard as worthy to be reported. If I think of myself as the one who always gets the short end of the stick, then I will tell of my past in the main those incidents, beginning in earliest childhood, which show how I have been disfavored. I find that I remember in detail the incidents when I have been cheated, when others have been preferred over me, when I did not get the love or the appreciation I thought I deserved. The rest of my childhood I have largely forgotten. It is in these painful disappointments that my true self appears. Or if I think of myself as the one who always wins, then I will tell my story by relating those events of my past that reveal my own superiority. I will be able to recall from my earliest childhood the moments of triumph and the incidents where people praised me, found me gifted or handsome, and regarded me as a special kind of person. The other incidents I have forgotten.

The telling of my own story, then, is always mediated by a particular self-symbolization. People who approach a therapist to be healed from symptoms of various kinds will tell their personal story through a symbolic self-understanding closely related to their illness. They may actually have no self-knowledge at all. They may have repressed from memory those incidents of their lives that had the most formative influence on them. Even if the events told by them in their story are true, they may still be ignorant of their past and in no way suspect the origin of their present turmoil. Now it is the claim of Sigmund Freud— and here, for many, he leaves the realm of science—that there is one single model story, one Story with a capital S, that applies to all individuals wherever they may live; and if people learn to tell their own story in dialogue with the normative story, then they will remember many significant events they have forgotten, they will come to understand their own dreams, they will acquire a realistic understanding of their own past and eventually experience a marvelous deliverance from the symptoms that made them suffer. What is this normative story? According to Freud, it is the story of King Oedipus who killed his father and married his mother.

The Oedipal story is the salvation myth in Freudian therapy. If people are taught how to tell their own story in the light of the normative story, they will eventually get in touch with their own deepest drama and be freed to leave it behind them. People in dialogue with the Oedipal story will begin to understand their own dreams, they will remember long forgotten experiences of childhood which reveal their desperate attachment to the mother and the hostility and fear of the father, and they will even recall many incidents in later life when the unresolved oedipal feelings of childhood manifested themselves in their relationship to men and women. Freud held that by learning to tell their story in a new way, through a new self-symbolization, they would be able to face the repressed material—and here dreams play an important role—come to greater self-knowledge, resolve the hidden conflicts of childhood and adolescence, and experience a new freedom in creating their own future.

How could Freud, the scientist, make the extraordinary claim that a legend belonging to Greek mythology is the one normative story revealing the central psychological complex of every single individual? This claim seems to move beyond the realm of science. In the past, only religions have spoken of normative stories. However Freud based the universality of the Oedipal complex not on metaphysics (as did Jung for his archetypes) but upon the biology of the family: he thought that being born of woman and being nourished and protected by this woman and the man to whom she belonged would inevitably introduce the male child into the oedipal constellation. What Freud overlooked was how much the structure of the family ×
and hence the experience of infancy and childhood depended on

✗ cultural factors and the social order.[5] Freud's theory, which proved so useful in the therapy of his own patients, reflects the middle class environment, characteristic of European society at the turn of the century. Freud did not realize that by making Oedipus Rex the normative myth of human life, he excluded women from his essential imagination; the typical human being was male. While I have no doubt that to this day, for vast numbers of people in Western culture, the Oedipal story is still a central model of self-knowledge and personal deliverance, nevertheless by investing this story with universal validity, orthodox Freudian psychoanalysis becomes an ideology that subjects people to a pre-conceived image and possibly imprisons them in a false imagination.

Again, the theologian reads Freud with amazement. Since Christianity contains normative stories, the Freudian application of the normative story as guide to personal transformation may well help the theologian to understand how his central stories of salvation enter into the re-creation of human life. The Exodus is a normative story, for it reveals not only God's mercy in redeeming Israel from slavery but also manifests the hidden divine will in regard to all peoples burdened by oppression. In contemporary liberation theology, this model story has acquired central significance. Oppressed societies and classes are trying to understand themselves and their histories through the revealed model of Exodus.

Even more central in Christianity is the story of Jesus Christ, crucified and risen, which offers the model of God's saving grace acting in human life, personal and social. How does this story affect the believing community? Let us adapt the Freudian use of the normative story. Christian believers, we hold, try to see their lives and tell their own stories in conversation with the life, death and resurrection of Jesus, and by doing so they are enabled to discover the sinful and destructive trends threatening their lives from within and from without, and discover—with surprise—the gracious power present in their lives, saving them from these trends and strengthening them to overcome the obstacles to love and surrender. Jesus here becomes the key to one's personal life. In him, the believers find their true selves. In other conversations, Jesus becomes the one who reveals the truth about life in society. Jesus reveals to us who we are as a people, as a community, or as a church. He initiates us into the self-symbolization through which we come to understand ourselves as sinful and redeemed people, as people with a destiny, called to hope in the future promises. This symbolization, we note, is not imposed upon us from without, for if God is the deepest transcendent dimension of human life as matrix and horizon, then Jesus as God's Word reveals to us not an extrinsic truth to which we must submit, but our own unexplored depth. In him we encounter our true selves.

Perhaps it is necessary to add that in making Jesus the normative story we do not propose him as the model for psychological transformation or social change. His story reveals the divine mystery that works itself out in and through human growth and the various transformations of personal and social life. Jesus is a theological model. In him salvation is offered to us. Making his story normative in their lives, Christians do not invalidate the model stories of psychological healing and social regeneration. Christians believe, rather, that through the various ways in which people are humanized and liberated, physically and socially, they are being carried forward by a mystery that transcends them and has revealed its features in Jesus Christ.

Let me add at this point that in the story of Oedipus Rex the maleness of the hero is of central importance, for it determines his relation to mother and father. In the story of Jesus, on the other hand, maleness in no way enters into his redemptive role. The story presents Jesus as open to the mystery of God; he heard the voice and followed it; he saw himself as the bearer of the divine; he believed in the coming kingdom and his own role in initiating it; he saw through the false consciousness of his society, and because he revealed to the people the falsifying structures of the religious community and the social order, he undermined the prestige of the authorities and was duly hated by them, persecuted and eventually nailed to the Roman cross. Yet his death was not the end. God triumphed over the powers of darkness and had the last word. Jesus fulfilled the promises. In all of this, there is nothing specifically male. The redemptive task could have been equally performed by a woman. This is worth noting since there are Christian theologians who oppose the ordination of women to the priesthood by referring to the maleness of Jesus.[6] No, the normative story in Christianity is not sexist.

Do Christians claim that this Jesus is the symbol of salvation for all mankind? Does it have universal application? For reasons we need not discuss at this point, contemporary theologians are trying to reconcile the Christian gospel with religious pluralism! There is room before God for other religions and other wisdom traditions. While Christians define their own existence in terms of Jesus Christ, the Christian churches of our day have tried to relativize this symbol in theologically responsible ways.[7] In particular, listening to the divine message contained in the crimes and the holocaust of this century, the churches have learned to acknowledge the place of Jewish religion before God.

After this theological digression, let us return for a moment to Sigmund Freud. Since he was so closely identified with the positivistic intellectual climate of his day, Freud was unable to reflect on the methodological implications of his own discovery. He was a brilliant psychotherapist and an original thinker who broke new ground in the understanding of human life; but even though his discovery of the symbolic had in principle overcome his Positivistic presuppositions, he was unable to re-examine his own starting point. Freud's discovery made such a re-examination necessary. Why? Because if our self-symbolization determines the telling of our story, then it also will determine the manner or the perspective in which we look upon the human world in general. It follows from this that scientists studying human behavior can no longer take for granted that they stand on wholly neutral ground observing the human world with objectivity. The human life which the observers study is not simply a given reality apart from them; it is inevitably mediated by the symbolic structure of their mind. The claim to objectivity made by Positivistic scholars disguises from them their own symbolic self-understanding and hence makes them blind to the ideological dimension of their research. We have in Freud, then, the seed for the overcoming of Positivism and the beginning of a new approach to the social sciences, one that takes into account the presuppositions of the observer.

* * *

The discovery of the symbolic took place in a dramatic way in the sociological work of the great French thinker, Emile Durkheim. As we shall see, Durkheim changed his mind in mid-career. Like Freud, he had been brought up in and was closely identified with a Positivistic intellectual climate. He took for granted the scientific method as the one valid approach to research and repudiated metaphysical inquiries of any kind. However, coming from the more rational Positivism of the French tradition, in contrast with the more empirical Positivism to which Freud belonged, Durkheim was convinced that the scientific method could discover the structure of the social reality, including the values on which it was based, and thus define the moral ideals which people must embrace to assure the well-being and development of their society. Here science included morality. Durkheim held that scientists, especially social scientists, engage in research and reflection out of moral commitment. Social science tries to discern the structure and the values of the social order to enable society to become more faithful to its destiny. It was in Durkheim's own quest to understand the society to which he belonged that he made the discovery of the symbolic.

In his early work, *The Division of Labor in Society*, published in 1893, Durkheim distinguished between two types of society, traditional and modern, in terms that have become familiar to us. We recall that Toennies' distinction between *Gemeinschaft* and *Gesellschaft* represented a certain consensus among social philosophers, even if they did not always agree in their evaluation. Durkheim was especially concerned with the social bond operative in the two types of society. Studying traditional society, Durkheim was greatly impressed by the observation that the wider society was made up of self-contained units adjacent to one another—families or clans or village communities. Traditional society was a collectivity of social units that were self-sufficient, able to produce their own means of subsistence, and hence essentially independent from one another. What then kept traditional society together? According to Durkheim, the social bond was the common symbol system. Social solidarity was created through sharing in the same rites, values, dreams and myths.

Modern society, according to Durkheim, was characterized by a complex division of labor. The units of modern society were interdependent, each in need of the others for the means of subsistence and the expansion of life. Durkheim tried to show that modern society—*Gesellschaft*—was not based simply on rational and contractual elements but—contrary to Toennies—also on the organic interdependence of all citizens in the creation of the social order. The social bond of modern, industrial and democratic society, then, was not weak, as was supposed by most social philosophers; it was in fact very strong, grounded in the complex division of labor. Despite the individualism of modern life, then, there does exist a profound social bond among people, a bond that serves as the foundation on which contracts are made and kept. Social contracts do not create the social bond; they actually presuppose it. What Durkheim tried to do in his *The Division of Labor in Society* was to clarify the moral foundations of modern society. While other sociologists had proposed that *Gesellschaft* inevitably undermined morality and promoted selfishness, Durkheim tried to show that the social laws operative in modern society were in fact creating a profound social bond and establishing values of a new kind, values that enabled people to transcend egotism and acquire a truly social commitment.

While traditional society was held together by common symbols and rites, modern society, held together by the complex division of labor, was no longer in need of a symbol system to remain firmly united and grounded in common values. In modern society, Durkheim then held, religion would disappear. While he disagreed with sociologists in the evaluation of *Gesellschaft*, he agreed with them in their theory of secularization. With the ongoing complexification of the division of labor, religion will eventually wither away: it will no longer have a social function in modern society. "That is not to say, however, that the common conscience is threatened with a total disappearance. Only, it more and more comes to consist of a very general and very indeterminate way of thinking and feeling, which leave an open place for growing multitude of individual differences. There is even a place where it is strengthened and made precise; that is the way in which it regards the individual. As all the other beliefs and all the other practices take on a character less and less religious, the individual becomes the object of a sort of religion. We erect a cult in behalf of personal dignity which, as a very strong cult, already has its superstitions."[8] Durkheim hoped that his own sociology, by laying bare the moral foundations of society, would actually help to make people more conscious of the social bond that unites them and thus overcome the isolation from the social matrix (*anomie*) that threaten individuals in times of change.

A few years later Durkheim made a study of suicide. To demonstrate the power of sociological analysis he tried to show to his contemporaries that even phenomena as irrational and unpredictable as suicide, on the surface the most private and least social of all actions, could be understood more clearly through a sociological analysis. In his book, *Suicide*, published in 1897, Durkheim distinguished between various forms of suicide. There were the selfless suicides, by which individuals in traditional societies executed the judgment of the community on a fault they had committed. Disgraced in the eyes of the community, they were willing to put an end to their lives. In modern society, however, most suicides took place because persons had been pushed to the margin of the social order or because the values on which they had built their lives were undermined by significant social change. Durkheim spoke of egoistic and anomic suicides. On the basis of empirical information provided by statistics available in various parts of Europe, Durkheim came to the conclusion that the rate of these suicides remained constant in a given area as long as the social order remained unchanged. Suicide was thus related to social conditions. With the advance of modernity, i.e., with the growth of industrialization and the spread of individualism, the rate of suicide increased. There were more suicides in cities than in the country, more among men than among women, more in Protestant than in Catholic areas, more among the individualistic middle class than among the more communally-minded lower strata of society. Since suicide is unplanned and unpredictable, how can there be social laws governing its frequency? Durkheim could explain the constant rate of suicide in traditional society; here he could invoke the symbol system that created the social bond and affected the minds of the people. The tensions in society were transmitted to people through this symbol system and could be thought of as pushing a constant number of individuals into suicide. But Durkheim was unable to explain the constant rate of suicide with unchanging social conditions in the more industrialized and individualistic parts. Since he had denied, in his *The Division of Labor*, that a symbolic system was operative in *Gesellschaft*, he did not know how the social order could communicate itself to the individual citizens and with growing tensions push some of them, at a constant rate, into suicidal action.

Here was Durkheim's dilemma. How could he account for the social law observed by him? Here are some of his reflections that led him to resolve his difficulty. "Victims of suicide are in an infinite minority, which is widely dispersed; each of them performs his act separately, without knowing that others are doing the same; and yet, so long as society remains unchanged, the number of suicides remains the same. . . . There must then be some force in their common environment inclining them all in the same direction, whose greater and lesser strength causes the greater or lesser number of suicides. . . . This force then must be collective. Each people has collectively an inclination of its own to suicide, on which the size of its contribution to voluntary death depends. . . . These tendencies are forces *sui generis* which dominate the consciousness of single individuals. . . . They have an existence of their own: they are as real as cosmic forces, though of another sort."[9] Durkheim, then, changed his mind. To account for the empirical evidence, he postulated a position previously denied by him, namely that modern society expresses itself in a symbol system that has an objective facticity and at the same time creates the consciousness of the individual citizens. At the end of his *Suicide*, he speaks of *la conscience collective*, the collective consciousness, which became the central topic of his later book

on religion.[10] Modern society, then, as much as the traditional one, is bound together by a common symbol system. The indi- ×
vidualistic and scientific mind-set, characteristic of modern life, is itself generated by a symbol system reflecting the social order which creates a common bond between people despite their greater personal freedom and their relative independence from traditional values. In modern society, symbols remain constitutive of personal consciousness—and of society.

With this discovery of the symbolic, Durkheim acknowledged that it was impossible to account for the social evolution of human life and consciousness purely and simply in terms of the material factors that enter into it. His discovery overcame both scientific Positivism that sought to reduce the human reality to measurable quantity and a rigid historical materialism that tried to account for the evolution of consciousness in terms of the evolving means of production. The creation of consciousness and society could not be understood apart from the symbolic dimension. We mentioned before that Durkheim did not clarify the dialectical relationship between society and symbol. No society is possible without symbols. Sometimes he says that society expresses itself in symbols and at other times he claims that symbols enter into the constitution of society; yet he fails to affirm these two contrary positions simultaneously and develop a dialectical understanding, according to which the social institutions create the symbolic structure of the mind and conversely, at certain critical periods, the symbols of self-understanding affect the life and structure of society.

While Durkheim's sociological approach had nothing in common with Freud's psychological analysis, both thinkers came to similar conclusions: people's self-symbolization enter ×
into the creation of their history, their culture and their society. Even if these two scholars were atheists by personal conviction and adopted a reductionist approach to the study of religion, they helped nonetheless to create a new openness to religion in modern culture. They made room in the social sciences for the symbolic dimension of human life.

Durkheim's discovery of the symbolic did not make him re-examine the Positivistic presuppositions of his scientific approach. He continued to think of himself as an objective observer of the social reality which he tried to understand by means of the scientific method. Durkheim, we recall, thought that this method enabled him to grasp the moral foundations of society, and in this he differed from the dominant empirical Positivism. In fact, measured by the value-neutrality characteristic of contemporary sociology, Durkheim's moral tone makes him a radical. But what he failed to consider was that if consciousness is created by symbols mediated through the social order, then this is also true of the mind-set of scientists. Scientists, then, are not objective observers. What scientists must do, in fidelity to truth, is to become aware of their own symbolic presupposition and its relationship to the social object studied by them. While Durkheim's discovery of the symbolic overcame Positivism in principle, he did not transcend it in a theoretical way. Durkheim continued to defend the purely objective character of social science.

At the end of *Suicide*, as we mentioned above, Durkheim moved from the affirmation of a collective consciousness to the concept of religion.[11] He anticipated a theme that he was to examine several years later in his famous *The Primitive Forms of Religious Life* (1912). Already in his earlier book, Durkheim felt that his discovery of the symbolic dimension enabled him to gain a better understanding of religion. He rejected the various theories of religion that ascribed its origin to purely personal experiences, feelings, needs, or frustrations, whether these theories were proposed by believing philosophers eager to defend religion or by atheistic thinkers bent on undermining it. Religion, Durkheim insists, is never found apart from a collectivity. Religion unifies people; it links them to their common history and strengthens them in their common task. Religion is the source of social identification. Why is religion able to do all this? Because it is the symbolic representation of the vision and the values immanent in society. In religion society gives expression to its highest ideals and deepest aspirations. Only a sociological definition of religion does justice to its total reality.

For Durkheim, we note, society does not remain purely external to the people who constitute it. He vehemently repudiated the individualism of his day and the utilitarian concept of society based on social contract. Since people's entry into personal consciousness takes place through participation in language, culture, institutions, and eventually the whole structure of society, this society becomes a constitutive element of their self-definition as persons. Because of this process of socialization—Durkheim did not yet use this expression—each person encounters society as a dimension of his or her own consciousness. All of us encounter within ourselves a reality which transcends us, to which we belong, and which exists beyond our death.[12] For Durkheim it is this encounter of people with the transcendent element in their own consciousness that creates morality: people experience within themselves that they must serve society. Biological and instinctual egotism is overcome by a more powerful, spontaneous dedication to the common good. People experience that they exist through society and their participation in it. Morality leads in the direction of self-sacrifice. The encounter with the transcendent in personal consciousness eventually gives rise to devotion, to worship, to religious experience. Our social matrix, present in consciousness, summons us to awe and surrender.

Religion, then, is people's encounter with the depth and the height of their society. The gods are simply "the hypostatic form of society,"[13] Durkheim writes. Through these gods, that is, through the symbolic representations, a society discovers its hidden potentialities, its richest resources, and its most daring dreams. Durkheim writes: "Religion is in a word the system of symbols by which society becomes conscious of itself; it is the characteristic way of thinking of collective existence."[14] Durkheim, the atheist, found himself pushed to the conclusion that every society will create its own religion. Every society in the process of living up to its highest ideals will generate the worship of its symbolic self-representation. In his *The Primitive Forms of Religious Life*, after having examined in detail Australian totemic religion, Durkheim concludes, "There is something eternal in religion which is destined to survive all the particular symbols in which religious thought has successively enveloped itself. There can be no society which does not feel the need of upholding and reaffirming at regular intervals the collective sentiments and the collective ideas which make its unity and personality."[15] The symbols generated by society ultimately lead to religion; they communicate the experience of the sacred and involve people in the worship of the principles out of which they become alive.

While Durkheim believed that the traditional religions of the West, Judaism and Christianity, were unable to survive the critical spirit of Enlightenment, his sociological theory made him expect new forms of religious life in modern society. These forms had not yet emerged since society was still in transition and turmoil. "The old gods are growing old and already dead, and others are not yet born."[16] Yet he repudiated Comte's conscious effort to produce a humanistic religion suited to the conditions of modern life. Religions, Durkheim clearly saw, cannot be rationally constructed. Religion happens; it is created through the experience of the sacred by which people are brought in touch with the deepest dimension of their social existence.

Sociologists have often regarded Durkheim's view of religion as purely ideological. Religion, they understand Durkheim to say, is the sacred power legitimating the existing social order. Religion creates social stability and provides a symbolic system that protects society from the forces that seek to undermine it or modify its structure. Some sociologists go so far as to suggest that for Durkheim religion was the worship of society. This, I think, is an inadequate reading of Durkheim's sociology of religion. For the great French sociologist again and again insisted that religion celebrates the deepest values operative in the social order, commemorates the moments in the history of society when its nature found the highest expression, and draws a symbolic image of what the society is meant to be in the future. "A society can neither create itself nor recreate itself without at the same time creating an ideal. This creation is not a sort of work of supererogation for it, by which it would complete itself, being already formed; it is the act by which it is periodically made and remade. . . . The ideal society is not outside the real society, it is part of it."[17] Religion, then, as the celebration of the highest aspirations of society, grounded in the significant moments of history, is able to generate a critique of the existing social order and create strong impulses to change it. "The society that reality bids us desire is not the society as it appears to itself, but the society as it is or is really becoming."[18] While at certain times religion may well serve as protector of the social order, at other times it judges the present social conditions by the ideal of society and produces movements of reform. The values in terms of which the existing society is found wanting are themselves generated by a deeper level of the same society.

Durkheim rejected Marx's view of religion as the inverted image of society. Religion was not simply the mirror of society that made sacred the existing power relations in the social order. While Durkheim believed that Christianity (as well as Judaism) had largely become an ideological symbol system protecting the *ancien régime* or other outdated social orders, he did not wish to define the essence of religion in terms of this particular historical development. Religion for Durkheim was not simply a dependent variable. His sociological research convinced him that culture and society were constituted by a process in which both the social infrastructure and the symbolic superstructure exercised a creative role. For Durkheim the passionate ideals that enabled a prophet such as Marx to condemn the existing social order were themselves generated by the best of the society and its tradition. He wrote, "Socrates expressed, more clearly than his judges, the morality suited to his time. It would be easy to show that, as the result of the transformation of the old society based on the *gens* and the consequent disturbance of religious beliefs, a new morality and religious faith had become necessary in Athens. . . . It is in this sense that Socrates was ahead of his time while at the same time expressing its spirit."[19] Religion for Durkheim, we conclude, cannot be equated with a sacred canopy protecting existing society: at its best, it produces a crisis period in history where society recreates and reconstitutes itself according to its own highest aspirations. Religion again and again turns out to be utopian.

* * *

Durkheim's theory that every society eventually generates a form of religion has led to an important contemporary controversy on civil religion in America. In a now famous essay,[20]

Robert Bellah finds evidence in the foundational documents of the American republic, the ceremonies of handing on public office, and the public holidays commemorating the important events of American history that there exists in America a civil religion with its worship, its rites and its divinity. The structure of this religion, Bellah tries to show, is the fusion of two symbolic legacies bequeathed on the republic, the Enlightenment heritage of trust in the laws of nature and nature's God and the biblical heritage of faith in the high destiny of the chosen people in their promised land. This civil religion, Bellah holds, can be distinguished from the historic religions of the churches and synagogues. The traditional biblical religions may be linked in some way to civil religion, but they retain their independence and autonomy, and in fact their relationship to civil religion varies greatly over the years from warm welcome to critical distance.

What is the role and function of civil religion? Readers have differed greatly in the understanding of Bellah's article.[21] Some regarded Bellah's civil religion as pure ideology legitimating the American way of life; others took an even more negative view of civil religion, seeing in it a dangerous idolatry whereby a nation worships its own success and motivates an aggressive foreign policy. In a subsequent article Bellah explained that neither of these interpretations corresponds to his own view.[22] While he admitted that civil religion could deteriorate and become ideological pretense or, worse, idolatrous worship, civil religion according to its own nature was the celebration of the greatest values of the nation and its highest ideals— Durkheimian religion—and provided transcendent norms for criticizing its actual collective life and its governmental practices. Civil religion was "the subordination of the nation to ethical principles that transcend it and in terms of which it should be judged."[23] For Bellah, civil religion was not devoid of utopian elements.

Another famous study on religion in America, written in the fifties, had presented a very different picture of the religious situation. In his *Protestant, Catholic, Jew*,[24] Will Herberg examined the faith of Americans in churches and synagogues and found little evidence for critical utopian trends. He came to the conclusion that while the churches among themselves and the churches together vis-à-vis the synagogues differed greatly in terms of doctrine and ritual, they preached and promoted the identical religious ethos. A superficial look at churches and synagogues suggests great diversity of religion in America, yet a more careful study reveals that Americans have a common religion. "A realistic appraisal of the values, ideas and behavior of the American people leads to the conclusion that Americans, by and large, do have their 'common religion' and that that religion is the system familiarly known as the American Way of Life."[25] Will Herberg presented a detailed study of this religion. He sums up the American religion in the single word "democracy"—which includes law and order, free enterprise, optimism and the middle class values that dominated American life in the fifties and made this period one of universal conformity. Civil religion, or what Herberg calls "the operative faith of the American people,"[26] is here a vast ideological system, subsuming the inherited biblical religion, that sacralizes the dreams and aspirations of the American middle class, persuades the lower classes to imitate as much as possible the middle class style, blinds people to the actual exclusion of whole sections of the population from the American consensus, breeds intolerance with public criticism, and fosters political aggression against nations that have repudiated the American values.

There is no reason to suppose that the studies of Herberg and Bellah are contradictory.[27] Herberg wrote his book in the fifties, an age of conformity characterized by an absence of public criticism. Even the churches and synagogues had become silent. In his study Herberg wanted to confront the religious institutions with what they had actually become. Bellah wrote his article in the sixties when criticism abounded. What he wanted to show to the young critics of American civic life and foreign policy was that they stood not against, but in the tradition of American civil religion. The inherited symbols of the American republic provided norms that condemned the injustices and the racism of American life and the aggressive posture of American foreign policy. The radical self-criticism of the sixties was not anti-American; it was rather an exercise of the American civil religion.

In a more recent article,[28] Bellah tries to show that the

original American ideals even generate a criticism of present-
day corporate capitalism. For the free enterprise policy of the
young republic recommended the family farm and the family
business as the defense of personal freedom and implied a criticism of the large corporations that were being formed in England at that time. American civil religion, then, can be the
bearer of utopia.

Civil religion, then, according to Darrol Bryant's analysis,[29] fulfills a threefold function: it serves as an intentional horizon projecting an image of the nation's destiny, as an integrating myth permitting all sections of the nation to be
equally members of society even if they perpetuate diverse cultural traditions, and as a public court protecting social values
and keeping people critical of the existing social conditions.
Looked upon from this point of view, civil religion becomes
ideological only if it collapses the ideal with the actual. In
Bellah's perspective, only a corrupt civil religion sanctifies the
present social order and fosters political trends toward national
self-aggrandizement. If this corruption proceeds, the civil religion may eventually lead the self-worship of the nation and an
idolatrous overevaluation of its role in history and become an
advocate of right-wing reactionary politics. Civil religion, we
conclude, is ambiguous. It is the bearer of utopia and ideology.

The discovery of the symbolic by the social sciences has
provided new conceptual tools for the study of religion and its
role in human life. We shall come back to this topic in a later
chapter. At the end of this chapter let me add that it is not
always easy and sometimes impossible to distinguish between
utopian and ideological trends in religion. Religion always promotes a certain behavior and legitimates certain values. But to
know whether a Durkheimian analysis of the religious phenomenon is called for, which sees in it society's élan toward its
highest ideal, or whether a Marxist analysis is in place, which
sees in it a legitimation of the *status quo*, is often very difficult
and sometimes cannot be decided apart from the scholar's personal political vision. In critical cases the final judgment of
such a question depends on the historical standpoint of the
sociologist and his vision of the future. If we suppose, for instance, that limit to growth has become the only intelligent and

humane politics of survival, then a religious movement that fosters diligence and makes laziness a sin would be an ideological defense of the inherited system, while a religious trend that stresses contemplation and does not invest time with a sense of urgency could in fact exercise a utopian function. If, on the other hand, the policy of minimal growth is seen as unrealistic, of benefit to the wealthy nations and of harm to the poor, then the evaluation of these religious trends would be the opposite one. Yet there is no neutral ground on which sociologists can take refuge. Sometimes only the actual course of history will enable us to discern the true nature of the ideas and ideals that have contributed to it. It is a principle of hermeneutical sociology that the analytical understanding of critical issues depends on the scholar's vision of the ideal society and represents, in some way or other, an active attempt to create this historical reality. We here touch upon a subject that will occupy us further on, the power exerted by the symbolic structure of the imagination on the making of culture and society.

Recommended Readings

Ernst Cassirer, *An Essay on Man*, Doubleday, New York, 1953.

Emile Durkheim, *The Elementary Forms of Religious Life*, Free Press, New York, 1965.

Sigmund Freud, *Moses and Monotheism*, Vintage Books, New York, no date.

———, *Totem and Taboo*, Vintage Books, New York, no date.

Erich Fromm, *The Forgotten Language*, Holt, Rinehart and Winston, New York, 1960.

Stewart Hughes, *Consciousness and Society: The Reorientation of European Social Thought, 1890-1930*, Vintage Books, New York, 1961.

Russel Richey and Donald Jones, edit., *American Civil Religion*, Harper & Row, New York, 1974.

Paul Ricoeur, *Freud and Philosophy*, Yale University Press, New Haven, 1970.

Joseph Royce, edit., *Psychology and the Symbol*, Random House, New York, 1965.

Notes

1. Cf. Stewart Hughes, *Consciousness and Society: The Reorientation of European Social Thought, 1890-1930*, Vintage Books, New York, 1961.

2. Sigmund Freud, *The Interpretation of Dreams*, Avon Books, New York, 1965, especially pp. 155-167, 385-439. For dreams as symbols, also see "Symbolism in Dreams," *A General Introduction to Psychoanalysis*, Pocket Books, New York, 1953, pp. 156-177, and "Archaic and Infantile Features in Dreams," *ibid.*, pp. 209-223.

3. For the primary processes and the archaic roots of the unconscious mind, see Sharon MacIsaac, *Freud and Original Sin*, Paulist Press, New York, 1974, pp. 26-28, 60-62.

4. "The era to which the dream-work takes us back is 'primitive' in a twofold sense: in the first place, it means the early days of the individual—his childhood—and, secondly, insofar as each individual repeats in some abbreviated fashion during childhood the whole course of the development of the human race, the reference is phylogenetic. . . . It seems to me that a symbolism, which the individual has not acquired by learning, may justly claim to be regarded as phylogenetic heritage": S. Freud, *A General Introduction to Psychoanalysis*, "Archaic and Infantile Features in Dreams" (translation adjusted), pp. 209-210. The phylogenetic unconscious is the underlying theme of Freud's study, *Moses and Monotheism* (Vintage Books, New York, no date), explicitly discussed on pp. 125-130.

5. For Wilhelm Reich's early criticism of Freud, see Paul A. Robinson, *The Freudian Left: Wilhelm Reich, Geza Roheim, Herbert Marcuse*, Harper & Row, New York, pp. 19-52.

6. Cf. Emily Hewitt, "Anatomy and Ministry: Shall Women Be Priests?" *The Ecumenist*, 11, July-Aug. 1973, pp. 70-75.

7. Gregory Baum, "Faith after Auschwitz—and Belfast," *Commonweal*, Nov. 15, 1974, pp. 153-159.

8. Emile Durkheim, *The Division of Labor in Society*, Free Press, New York, 1964, p. 172.

9. Emile Durkheim, *Suicide*, Free Press, New York, 1951, pp. 304, 305, 307, 309.

10. *Ibid.*, pp. 312-320.

11. *Ibid.*, p. 312.

12. Emile Durkheim, *The Elementary Forms of Religious Life*, Free Press, New York, 1965, p. 29. Cf. "The Dualism of Human Nature and Its Social Condition," in Emile Durkheim *et al.*, *Essays on Sociology and Philosophy*, edit. Kurt Wolff, Harper & Row, New York, 1960, pp. 325-340.

13. Emile Durkheim, *Suicide*, p. 312.

14. *Ibid.*

15. Emile Durkheim, *The Elementary Forms of Religious Life*, pp. 474-475.

16. *Op. cit.*, p. 475.

17. *Ibid.*, p. 470.

18. Emile Durkheim, "The Determination of Moral Facts," *Sociology and Philosophy*, Cohen & West, London, 1953, p. 38.

19. *Ibid.*

20. Robert Bellah, "Civil Religion in America," *Religion in America*, edit. W.G. McLoughlin, Beacon Press, Boston, 1966, pp. 3-23; reprinted with comments and a rejoinder in *The Religious Situation 1968*, edit. D. R. Cutler, Beacon Press, Boston, 1968, pp. 331-394; also available in Robert Bellah, *Beyond Belief*, Harper & Row, New York, 1970, pp. 168-189.

21. For a survey and analysis of the controversy and for evidence of its continued vitality, see *American Civil Religion*, edit. R. E. Richey and D. G. Jones, Harper & Row, New York, 1974.

22. *Op. cit.*, pp. 255-272.

23. Robert Bellah, *Beyond Belief*, p. 168.

24. Will Herberg, *Catholic, Protestant, Jew*, revised ed., Doubleday, New York, 1955.

25. *Op. cit.*, p. 88.

26. *Ibid.*

27. Cf. the discussion of Civil Religion in Andrew Greeley's *The Denominational Society*, Scott, Foresman and Company, Glenview, Ill., 1972, pp. 156-174.

28. Robert Bellah, "Coming Around to Socialism: Roots of the American Taboo," *The Nation*, Vol. 219, Dec. 28, 1974, pp. 677-685.

29. M. Darrol Bryant, "Beyond Messianism: Toward a New 'American' Civil Religion," *The Ecumenist*, 11, May-June 1973, pp. 44-51.

VII
The Secularization Debate

In the preceding chapter we have examined the discovery
of the symbolic by two great thinkers, Freud and Durkheim,
and suggested that this breakthrough led to a greater appreciation of religion on the part of the social sciences. Did this new
sensitivity simply prepare a greater openness of sociology to
the study of religion? Or did it also represent a new cultural
trend favorable to the practice of religion? On this question
sociologists are divided. A good number of sociologists, even
while appreciating the role of symbols in men's social existence, are convinced that modern, industrial society will inevitably lead to the disappearance of religion. This is the famous
theory of secularization. Other sociologists do not think that
this theory has ever been demonstrated. In this chapter we shall
examine the arguments proposed in favor of the theory of secularization as starting points for the study of contemporary religion.

We recall that already the 19th century witnessed several
theories of secularization, even if the term "secularization" has
been used in sociology only fairly recently.[1] In the preceding
chapters we have encountered three versions of this theory.
There was, first of all, the Comtean theory, endorsed in one
way or another by the great number of scientists and Enlightenment philosophers, according to which the advance of rationality and the scientific spirit would inevitably undermine
the religious heritage; religious myths would give way to scientific explanations. This theory of secularization was linked to a
philosophy of progress based on science, technology, and liberal democracy. A second theory of secularization we found in
the thinkers who regarded religion as a symptom of human

140

alienation and who anticipated the disappearance of religion as people were able to overcome the deprivations and frustrations inflicted on them in a previous age. The views of Marx and Freud belong to this category—even if, from another point of view, they also helped to overcome scientific Positivism and create a new sensitivity to symbols. Finally there was the theory of secularization proposed by the sociologists, many of whom were German, who regarded the transition from traditional society to modern, industrialized society as a decline of culture and spirit and who foresaw the waning of religion with regret. What all of these social thinkers observed, quite independently from their particular theories, was the passage of European society from an old order in which religion was a taken-for-granted dimension of social, cultural, political and personal life, to a new, as yet undefined order where religion was losing its social, cultural and political importance and where even its significance for personal life was being questioned by more and more people. But was it reasonable and scientific to make the description of this particular historical experience a sociological law of universal application and predict the disappearance of religion altogether?

To this day, sociologists are greatly divided in regard to the theory of secularization. Some still claim that the advance of industrialization and individualism inevitably leads to the disappearance of religion, while others claim that this theory is by no means demonstrated and that there is no fixed sociological law relating religion and modern society. The present state of the controversy is well brought out in two books published in England in the sixties, Bryan Wilson's *Religion in Secular Society*,[2] which makes a persuasive case for the theory of secularization, and David Martin's *The Religious and the Secular*,[3] which tries to show that the concept of secularization has introduced confusion in the study of religion and hence ought to be banished from the sociological vocabulary. In this chapter I wish to discuss the three arguments proposed by Bryan Wilson and make them the starting point for reflections on religion in North America today.

* * *

Bryan Wilson's first argument is taken from empirical studies. He presents an impressive amount of statistical evidence to show that the Church of England has lost power and influence over the last hundred years. A comparative study of the number of baptisms, confirmations, enrollments in parishes, children in Sunday school, Sunday school teachers, and Easter communicants show beyond a doubt that the power the Church of England holds over the imagination of the people is steadily declining. This conclusion is confirmed by studying the steady increase of secular over religious marriages. Similar evidence, one may add here, could be given for other European countries. At one time religion was fully established in European culture in the sense that religious symbols and religious institutions were part of the basic social structures that defined society; today religion has become a set of convictions that certain families cherish and hand on to their children, or something that people freely choose. This is the sociological process called secularization. On the basis of empirical research, then, Bryan Wilson tries to establish the law that the closer people are involved in industrial production, the less religious they become. Thus people in the city are less religious than those in the country, men are less religious than women, men and women of working age are less religious than children and the aged, the highly industrialized countries in Europe are less religious than the less industrialized ones, and so forth.

The great exception to the European pattern is the American experience. A study of church membership in the United States over eighty years reveals the opposite trend! In 1880 only 20% of Americans were church members; in 1960 they represented 63% of the population. Wilson accepts these high figures even though they have been challenged by some. Some sociologists think that because of the great mobility of the population, church members may have been counted more than once. Yet Wilson accepts the high figures as reliable; they are moreover confirmed by Gallup Poll data. At the same time, he is seriously puzzled by the contrasting pattern in America.

Andrew Greeley, in several important studies,[4] has examined the empirical data on religion in America and presented the contrasting pattern as an argument against the theory of secularization. The available information reveals a certain cycle of slightly higher and slightly lower church attendance and membership, for which it is difficult to find a sociological explanation, but there is no evidence whatever for the theory that increasing industrialization and individualism lead to a weakening of religion. The American experience, then, should offer enough evidence to show the inadequacy of the theory of secularization, at least in the Comtean and Weberian versions. One of the obvious reasons for this alternate pattern is the fact that in America religion had not been "established" and that consequently the starting point of its religious development was quite different from that of Europe. Still, this only shows that the impact of industrialization on religion in Europe cannot be made into a universal law.

How does Bryan Wilson deal with the counter-evidence of the American experience? He attributes little weight to it because religion in America seems to him rather superficial. He writes, "The travelers of the past who commented on the apparent extensiveness of the church membership, rarely omitted to say that they found religion in America to be very superficial."[5] In regard to the more recent period, he himself concludes, "Thus, though religious practice has increased, the vacuousness of popular religious ideas has also increased."[6] The evidence does not count because American religion is not of the right kind. The same curious inconsistency is found in the sociological studies of Peter Berger, another proponent of the theory of secularization. He writes, "The situation is different in America, where the churches still occupy a more central symbolic position, but it may be argued they have succeeded in keeping this position only by becoming highly secularized themselves, so that the European and American cases represent two variations on the same underlying theme of global secularization."[7] Again, American religion is not the right kind to constitute counter-evidence to the theory of secularization. It is apparent that both Wilson and Berger engage here in faulty reasoning. If the theory of secularization intends to express a law relating religion and secular society, then it is inadmissible to introduce qualifications that exclude some forms of religion from being admitted as evidence.

American religion is undoubtedly different from religion in Europe. In his important study on American religion, *Protestant, Catholic, Jew*,[8] published in the fifties and mentioned above, the American sociologist, Will Herberg, tried to account for the extraordinary success of organized religion in the United States. He observed that the many churches and synagogues, despite the enormous differences in religious beliefs and practice, stand for the same ethos, the same virtues, and the same social vision. They are all equally the embodiment of the American Way of Life. Commitment to religious belief and membership in a religious organization have become visible signs of being a true American, that is, of being identified with America's social and economic ethic. Despite its diversity, religion is an integrating factor in America. It enables the people of this vast land, coming from different ethnic, racial, religious and linguistic backgrounds, to be united in the same way of life, to live truly American lives, and at the same time to remain faithful to an aspect of their past. Herberg showed that the second generation of immigrants tended to reject their ethnic heritage in an effort to become complete Americans and that the third generation, now fully Americanized, in the search for social identity in a highly mobile population, tried to return to the ethnicity of their grandparents. Yet since they had forgotten the language and hence could not participate in their cultural heritage, they joined at least their grandparents' religion. Writing in the fifties, Herberg interprets organized religion in America as a legitimation of the American Way of Life, as conservative and ideological. According to Herberg, this religion did not generate a critique of the American ethos; it was almost completely identified with the dominant cultural trends. This, I suppose, was the kind of phenomenon Wilson and Berger had in mind when they spoke of American religion as superficial and secularized. Let me add, however, that it is by no means clear that other-worldly religion built around the worship of the sacred is for that reason any less ideological.

It would be a great mistake to make Herberg's study of religion in the fifties normative for the understanding of American religion. We recall our discussion, in the last chapter, of Robert Bellah's important article on civil religion which brought out the complexity of religion in America. First, civil religion is itself ambiguous. At certain times it upholds ideals for the collective life of the nation that judge the present political practice, and at others it may partially collapse into a religious legitimation of the actual political powers. Second, Bellah had indicated that the relation of civil religion to the historic religion of Judaism and Christianity may vary greatly; at certain times the churches and synagogues express their religious ethos interwoven with the ideals of civil religion, and at others these historic religions define themselves over against the civil religion of the day. Religion in America has been both conformist and critical. In its adaptation to North American life, religion has shown considerable creativity. Herberg has described but a single phase. It is my contention that sociologists who defend the theory of secularization do not make themselves sufficiently sensitive to the creative and critical aspects of religion.

Religion changes with culture and society. The question is: How does it change? Does it always adapt itself to the new social conditions in a conformist way, or does it, at certain times, respond to the challenges created by the new conditions in a creative way? When Alexis de Tocqueville visited the United States in the thirties of the last century, he observed that important changes had taken place in the Christian religion, changes that he interpreted, in part at least, as creative responses to new social needs.[9] Tocqueville, the great social thinker before the word "sociology" existed, analyzed egalitarian democracy in America and contrasted it with traditional aristocratic society, in terms that anticipated the later sociological distinction between *Gesellschaft* and *Gemeinschaft*. While Tocqueville appreciated the civil liberties of men and women in the new society, he was also aware that the political and economic institutions, guaranteeing these liberties, produced a new individualism, eagerness for personal advancement, a highly utilitarian ethics, and the domination of culture by business values. Here people were exposed to problems and anxieties hardly known in traditional society. Tocqueville was aware of the threats these developments posed to human well-being. In such a situation, religion could well acquire a new social role.

Tocqueville observed that in the individualistic, egalitarian society of America, the role of religion was to curb people's selfish desires and to create communities in which people could
find friendship and solidarity. Religion enabled people to overcome their social isolation. In a highly competitive society,
religion was a school educating people in selflessness and social
concern. The diversity of religion in America and the ongoing
multiplication of denominations, which a European observer,
judging from his own social experience, finds distasteful, actually had an important humanizing function in America and in
fact produced a greater sense of unity among the people.

According to Tocqueville, religion fulfilled another new
and unexpected role in America. According to the great French
social critic, the great danger of egalitarian society is the power
it bestows on public opinion. A society according equal honor
to all citizens tends to undermine people's respect for the great
men of wisdom and the authoritative traditions of the past; instead, people begin to invest with great authority the opinions
and attitudes upon which the majority of citizens are agreed.
People become victims of public opinion. In such a social situation, Tocqueville held, religion protects people's personal freedom and delivers them from the pressure of commonly held
ideas and prejudices. Religious faith links people to a great
wisdom tradition, grounds them in values that transcend the
immediate needs and purposes of society, and hence enables
them to hold out against the ever changing, superficial, and yet
often tyrannical public opinion. Tocqueville thought that in
America the Christian religion had responded in a new way to
the social needs of people.

Tocqueville tried to describe the changes that would take
place in religion in an egalitarian society and that had already
been partially realized in the United States. Religion will become less and less hierarchical, more direct, more democratic
in organization, less ascetic and world-denying. Religion will
want to temper, not deny, people's quest for well-being, comfort and success. Tocqueville foresaw that religious worship
would eventually resemble less and less an assembly at court; it
would become more like an assembly of equals. Since the main
function of religion is exercised in the local congregation, reli-

gion in an egalitarian society will not have a public and political presence, except through the religious sentiment of the citizens; but this, Tocqueville thought—anticipating here Talcott Parsons—is not a negligible quantity. All of this the French social critic saw happening not as a weak adaptation of religion to the existing social conditions but as an original response of religion revealing its power to save and protect human life in new social circumstances.

Tocqueville testified that even the Roman Catholic Church in the United States had been profoundly affected by the egalitarian society and acquired a simplicity unknown elsewhere. What he could not foresee, of course, was that through strong interference coming from Rome and the condemnation of Americanism and Modernism at the turn of the century, the democratic temper of Roman Catholicism in the United States would eventually be replaced by a highly authoritarian spirit and organizational style. In a very shrewd paragraph Tocqueville goes so far as to suggest that people whose consciousness is formed by egalitarian social institutions will have increasing difficulties with acknowledging God as Lord of the universe; their piety will tend to identify God with the community. Personally Tocqueville regarded such a development as pantheistic and harmful to the genius of Christianity. Still, he here anticipated the shift in the understanding of God as ground of being and matrix of community. Tocqueville recognized—as Hegel had done before him and many sociologists after him—that there is a close relationship between the social institutions in which people live, the consciousness which is theirs, and the form which religion assumes in their minds.

If religion is a creative factor in society, should one not expect it to help overcome some of the alienation inflicted by the conditions of modern life? Emile Durkheim eagerly looked for ways and means of overcoming the isolation and anguish produced by modern society in individual citizens. How can people be saved from the *anomie* that threatens them? The French sociologists did not think that traditional religion, Christianity or Judaism, had enough vitality to offer any help. He had, incidently, never studied the role of religion in America. What Durkheim advocated, therefore, was the creation of "intermediary societies"[10] which would provide social matrices for the personal well-being of the participants. Durkheim somewhat naively thought that professional associations would be able to fulfill this task. What Durkheim was actually doing, unintentionally to be sure, was describing the role religious communities could play in the humanization of modern, industrial society. The theologian studying Durkheim finds in his work the foundation of a new ecclesiology. This was in fact done by Andrew Greeley.[11] In traditional society, the churches either regarded themselves as the exclusive bearers of the symbolic life of society and hence identified themselves with culture and nation or they understood themselves as marginal communities rejecting the symbols of society and living in critical distance from the dominant culture. Sociologists have called these two types *churches* and *sects*. However if religious bodies assume the function ascribed by Durkheim to "intermediary societies," they transcend the distinction between church and sect and play a new and original role in the making of a humane society. This is the development that has actually taken place in America.

The originality of American religion is developed in Andrew Greeley's interesting book, *The Denominational Society*. The author shows that the sociological study of religion in America must operate with categories of its own. In particular, the distinction between church and sect which has been so helpful in studying European religion has confused sociologists when studying religion in a country which never knew, except very early, an established church. Religion in America is constituted in denominations. Denominational religion communicates a sense of belonging to its followers—the Durkheimian perspective—and inspires them with a sense of meaning or purpose in life—the Weberian perspective. Greeley writes, "In the disorganization, personal and social, that occurs as part of the pilgrimage from the peasant communalism to the industrial city, man attempted and still attempts to compensate for the deprivation he endured and for the absence of the social support and the intimacy of the village by evolving quasi-*Gemeinschaft* institutions—the nationality groups, the lower-class religious sects, the radical political party and, in the United States and Canada, the denomination."[12]

The religious denomination is different from church or sect. The denomination is pluralistic; it takes for granted that it is surrounded by others, and in this it differs from the church. At the same time, it is open to culture and society, and in this it differs from the sect. The denomination is an intermediary society that introduces people to social cohesion in a highly mobile and atomizing society. The great number of denominations in America are not obstacles to the unity of the population. For despite the conflicts and tensions which occasionally arise from the competing interests of the denominations, they do not provide alternate definitions of reality. They provide a sense of community to their members and a meaning of life besides the daily struggle for existence, and hence promote the unity of the people. The divergence of doctrine need not necessarily have divergent social effects. Andrew Greeley shows that sociologically speaking, even the self-understanding of the Catholic Church in the United States has become denominational. It is this original American development, and not the supposedly superficial or secularized character of American religion, that accounts for the differing pattern of church attendance and membership. Religion has flourished in America because it has played an important humanizing role in the lives of the people.

Is American religion as analyzed by Greeley necessarily ideological? Must it always be a defense of the American Way of Life? The answer is that American religion, like all religion, is ambiguous. It can be—just like American civil religion— both ideological and utopian. In particular, since denominational religion is pluralistic and hence need not be identified with the symbol system undergirding the national life, denominational religion often communicates a sense of personal freedom to its members. Already Tocqueville mentioned something like that.[13] Religion enables people to define themselves in terms of a transcendent identity. While the structure of society makes people define their identity in terms of the roles they play, as citizens, as workers, as mothers or fathers, etc., religion offers them a self-definition in terms that transcend these roles: in religion people share the vision and purpose of a wider community, movement, or church. Thanks to these wider identities, people are able to stand over against their roles in society. They are more than citizens, workers, or mother and father; they are capable of being critical of the roles they play, and this gives them a sense of personal freedom. American religion has often been ideological, but it has also been the bearer of utopia.

*   *   *

Bryan Wilson's first argument in favor of the theory of secularization, drawn from statistical evidence of the decline of the Church of England, had led us to a more careful analysis of religion in America. Wilson's second argument is taken from the close relationship between pluralism and secularization. Wilson thinks that pluralism in religion, and mutual tolerance and recognition, inevitably weaken the hold of religion on people's minds. Pluralism implies a certain relativism and hence tends to undermine the unconditional surrender to truth at the heart of every religion. Peter Berger has proposed the same argument. Religious pluralism inevitably leads to secularization.[14] If there are several religions, all of which are regarded as valid, it is possible to choose between them and adopt the one that seems best suited to one's life; in this way religion becomes a private affair, a spiritual hobby as it were, and loses its nature as the ultimate grounding of reality. Pluralism transmutes religion beyond recognition and ushers in its total demise.

After our analysis of denominational religion in America, this argument is no longer convincing. It may well be true that churches and sects, understood according to their sociological definition, cannot survive in a pluralistic society, for both of these types of religion understand themselves in exclusivist terms. Denominational religion, however, is pluralistic. It takes for granted the existence of diverse religious communities. There is no reason, moreover, to suppose that an absolute surrender to the divine mystery in one's own religion cannot go

hand in hand with a willingness to recognize the validity of
other religions or other versions of one's own. Especially under
the impact of the ecumenical movement, contemporary Christians in quest of unreserved fidelity to the absolute are usually
quite unwilling to regard their own religious organization as an
expression of this absolute. Religion is here indeed due to personal choice, but the important social function of denominational religion shows that it is by no means a purely private affair. Sociologists who hold that pluralism undermines religion
and ushers in its disappearance underestimate religion's own
proper creativity.

Bryan Wilson refines his second argument by proposing
and defending the idea that the movement toward an ever more
secular society is implicit in Protestantism itself. Wilson follows here the famous thesis of Max Weber, which in some
form or other has been adopted by a great number of sociologists. According to this thesis, the worldly asceticism of Cal-
vinist-Puritan Christianity has enabled the spirit of capitalism
and entrepreneurship to spread rapidly among the class of
manufacturers and merchants, supplied an inwardness to the
lower classes enabling them to break away from traditional
bonds and rise to greater social power, and eventually produced a work ethos that helped to create the modern, industrialized world and made it unique among all previous civiliza-
tions. Since Weber's opponents sometimes presented his thesis
in an exaggerated way, let me say that Weber did not claim
that Protestantism has produced the modern, rational world. It
did not occur to Weber to overlook the effects which the development of science and technology, the expansion of commercial enterprises, and the creation of new means of production
had on the creation of the modern world. His thesis was more
modest. He asked himself the question why the beginnings of
capitalism, which were found in several cultures and which
were present in sections of European society prior to the Reformation, underwent such an extraordinary development in
Western Europe and produced the modern, rational culture,
unique in human history. Weber showed that it was the new
Protestant asceticism, the new sense of divine calling, that removed the religious and traditional obstacles to the spread of

the secular orientation and provided a religious impetus for a new, worldly dedication. Obedience to God's call meant hard work, limited pleasure, appreciation of personal achievements, and a critique of government based on a new sense of individualism and free enterprise.

Wilson accepts the Weberian thesis not only for the period studied by Weber himself; he thinks that the various Protestant movements, including early Methodism and the Adventist and Millenarian movements of the later period, continued to create among their followers a spirit of worldly dedication that promoted the advance of secular society. He writes, "Christianity's genius was in the adaptability to new classes throughout the process of social change."[15] Each new wave of Protestant revival and renewal was able to supply a rising class with new self-confidence and religious discipline that enabled them to rise in the existing social and economic system. This thesis is verified in Richard Niebuhr's *The Social Sources of Denominationalism* for the United States and in S. D. Clark's *Church and Sect in Canada* for British North America. More recent research has shown that new Christian sects, such as the Pentecostals, still perform the same social function.[16] They supply people of the lower classes, devoid of formal education, with new, spiritual self-confidence, transform them into disciplined, hard-working and reliable persons, and thus enable them to do well as industrial workers, to become successful businessmen in a competitive world, and to rise on the social scale. These sects still teach people to be frugal, to save their money, and to invest it wisely. Research in Pentecostalism and other Christian sects in Latin America, the West Indies and Africa has shown that there, too, these religious movements enable people who have been torn from their village or their tribal existence and find themselves inwardly destroyed in the big city to lay hold of themselves, to become hard workers, and to enter the economic system and rise in it. Even the ecstasy of revivalist religion is not the symbol of world negation; for these ecstasies, circumscribed in the worshiping communities, enable people to express their frustrations, become quiet and reconciled, and return to their rational, confined existence in the social and economic order.

Protestantism, according to Wilson's analysis, leads people to a more worldly life, weakens the mystical and sacramental elements of the Christian tradition, directs people's attention to secular aims and purposes, and thus prepares its own disappearance. After the rise in the social and economic system, people lose interest in their religion and drift into a vague agnosticism. Protestantism initiates its own undoing. The worldly asceticism which Weber called "the Protestant ethic" is now being communicated in Western culture through the social and economic institutions; it has become quite independent of its religious source. The proof of this is that in the United States the Protestant ethic is found as much among Catholics and Jews as among Protestants. The Protestant work ethic expresses the spirit of the culture we have inherited.

There is much truth in Wilson's thesis. Ernst Troeltsch, contemporary and friend of Weber, was often afraid that Protestantism would create the conditions of its own demise. The glory of Protestantism was also its weakest point. And yet this persuasive thesis is not in itself a proof for the theory of secularization. Wilson again describes especially the English experience. In America, Protestantism has remained strong precisely because it is, in a certain sense, the "established" religion; it articulates the spirit that makes American democracy and the economic system work, and for this reason vast numbers of Americans continue to find themselves in the symbolism of their churches. It is in part the ideological nature of Protestantism in America that has made it a thriving religion. Yes, Wilson's thesis can be turned around as an argument against the theory of secularization. For it was Protestantism, in its various movements and denominations, that enabled the aspiring classes in the English-speaking world to acquire greater social power and thus prevented not only the violent social change of the French revolution but also the vehement anti-clericalism and aggressive atheism associated with radical social reformers in Catholic countries. Wilson himself writes, "Whereas in continental countries, and especially in Catholic countries, secularization was expressed in the development of secularist and anti-clerical movements, in the Anglo-Saxon countries it found less direct and more subtle expression."[17] If these observations are correct, then Protestantism is not only a secularizing influence but also, paradoxically, a factor that prevents the disappearance of religion.

One more remark on this topic. While it is true, from one point of view, that Protestant Christianity is the established religion of the Western capitalist and democratic society, it is equally true that Protestantism is much greater than that. Protestantism has generated new utopias. Religions, as I hope to show, move, change and produce their own self-criticism. Protestantism has brought forth many forms of Christian socialism with its negative judgment on the capitalist system and its critique of the work ethic.

Wilson's thesis of the secularization implicit in Protestantism has been placed into an even wider context by a number of social philosophers and theologians. It has been claimed that biblical religion itself, from the very outset, aimed at the secularization of life and that the process by which the various spheres of social life have made themselves independent of religion in modern times was in keeping with biblical religion and the spirit of Protestantism. Some theologians think that this development ought to be welcomed by the Christian Churches. We find this theory in the work of Friedrich Gogarten in Germany and Harvey Cox's *The Secular City* in the United States. It is claimed that Old Testament faith made a radical break with the cosmic religions of Egypt and Mesopotamia. God revealed himself as the totally other, the creator of heaven and earth, beyond the cosmos and in no way identified with it. Old Testament faith de-divinized or secularized the earth. Nature is not divine; it is not the locus of God's presence; the world is just world, and it is man's calling to live in this world, assume responsibility for it, and transform it into a garden. Peter Berger, following a few hints of Max Weber and the extensive studies of Eric Voegelin, expresses much sympathy for this theory.[18] According to this theory, then, the central inspiration of scriptural religion is a movement toward secularization. The New Testament records the struggle of Jesus against inherited taboos, sacred laws, and the domination of life by religious authorities. In Catholicism, according to this theory, the central inspiration of biblical religion was suppressed in favor of sacramental and divinizing religious trends. The Reformation recovered the original inspiration of the Bible and became a bridge, with Renaissance humanism, to the secular culture of our own day. The secularization implicit in Protestantism (Wilson's thesis) is here part of a wider historical movement.

Since Wilson's thesis did not appear to us as conclusive evidence for the theory of secularization, we need not concern ourselves with the wider historical perspective. Yet I do wish to raise the question whether this understanding of Old Testament religion is not based on peculiarly Protestant presuppositions and projects a problematic of the 19th and 20th centuries onto an ancient culture. It is not clear at all whether the radical separation between God and nature is actually found in books of the Old Testament. In the Bible God remains creator of the world; he is the ground and protector of nature, and he reveals himself in the dramas of the natural universe. The earth remains the locus of God's presence. While he is a redeemer God, he is not any less the God of the universe. In the New Testament in particular—as Rosemary Ruether has pointed out in her writings—we are far away from a secular understanding of the world. The world appears either as possessed by demons or inhabited by the Spirit; it is either demonic or sacramental; it is either an obstacle to God or a means of God's self-communication. The great secularization theory of Gogarten and Cox may turn out to be a highly Protestant reading of the evidence, supported by scholars identified with cultural Protestantism (as Weber himself was), at a time when secularization seemed the dominant cultural trend.

* * *

Wilson's third argument in support of the theory of secularization follows the social analysis of Toennies and Weber; the passage from *Gemeinschaft* to *Gesellschaft* undermines the traditional values, applies rational thinking to more and more social processes, and hence removes the religious elements from the various spheres of social life. Religion thus loses its social base; it has no longer a social function. Social life becomes dominated by more utilitarian and pragmatic purposes. Wilson does not describe this process in the tragic tones of the German sociologists; he does not speak of the decline of culture. What he affirms is that the spread of industrialization leads to the waning of religion. Who can deny that this is a powerful argument? It certainly describes a certain European experience.

Still, some sociologists have interpreted the process of modernization differently, and it perhaps is not surprising that this variant reading of the identical data has come from America. In a famous essay, "Christianity and Modern Industrial Society,"[19] Talcott Parsons tries to show that modernization is not so much a process of secularization as of differentiation. What does this mean? Differentiation is a central concept in Parsons' sociology. According to him, the application of reason to the various social processes and the growing complexification of society lead to increasing specialization of the various functions exercised in society and increasing coordination between them. The various tasks performed by society tend to be separated out and exercised by distinct institutions, interrelated among themselves. This sort of differentiation is observable in government, industry, business, education—in short, in all sections of society. This differentiation also leads to the detachment of the religious component from the non-religious spheres of social life. This theory enables Parsons to acknowledge the gradual disappearance of religion from public life and yet interpret the evidence in a new way. What takes place is not secularization but simply the differentiation of religion as a distinct sphere. Religion becomes more separated, independent, and personal, and yet remains related to society. The process of differentiation allows religion to reveal its true nature and power, which is to create personal commitment and, through this, to influence the choices and decisions people make. While the various spheres of social life are no longer linked to religious institutions and religious symbols, Parsons thinks that they remain dependent on a personal ethos of responsibility, a highly developed and critical ethics, which is grounded in the inherited religion, Christianity (and Judaism). Religion has by no means lost its social function, even if its

point of insertion in the social process is simply the human person. Parsons holds that the survival of the social order still depends on the spiritual link of people's willing and responsible
cooperation—on a certain inwardness, in other words—which
is mediated for the majority of people by traditional religion.
This highly personal religion is institutionalized in the concrete
churches and synagogues. This Parsonian perspective has been
partially incorporated in Andrew Greeley's analysis of American religion as the interface of two functions, the meaning and
the belonging functions of society. The process of differentiation, associated with the modernization of society, has made
religion a highly specialized sphere of life, embodied in specifically religious organizations that are independent of the
public institutions and yet make an essential contribution to the
well-being of modern, industrial society.

In the sixties, a number of theologians, following Gogarten and Cox, enthusiastically endorsed what they regarded as
the movement toward secularization in society. Basing themselves on a particular reading of the scriptures, they understood
this secularization as the promised destiny of humankind.
These theologians were at the same time deeply concerned
about Christian faith. The biblical faith they envisaged was the
believing response to God's summons, calling people to maturity and reconciliation and enabling them to transform the face
of the earth. This faith was to be nourished and kept alive in
religious communities that tell the same biblical story and celebrate the same events. Despite the movement toward secularization, then, these theologians assigned an important function
to the church. We notice, here, that what these Christian writers were enthusiastic about was not at all the theory of secularization but, on the contrary, the counter-theory of differentiation. The use of the word "secularization" in theology has
often been confusing!

The Parsonian theory of differentiation is perhaps a little
too ideological; it presupposes that the American system is the
perfect system toward which all previous societies have moved
and that it is the task of biblical religion to make this system
operate efficiently. Yet the opposite theories of secularization
are also too ideological; they too defend a particular world

view. This was in fact one of the arguments proposed in David Martin's *The Religious and the Secular*. In this book, Martin tries to show that all theories of secularization have been ideological; they have all been proposed to justify a particular philosophy of life. He mentions several examples. He refers to the optimistic, rational Positivism of Comte and the more modest form of empirical Positivism, both of which understand religion as a cluster of superstition. Martin also refers to the world views of Marx and Freud, both of which left no room for religion in a liberated society. Martin could also have mentioned the more pessimistic world views of Toennies, Weber, and the German intellectuals in the decades preceding and following the turn of the century, which associated industrialization with the decline of culture. This ideology of decline, analyzed by us in a previous chapter, persuaded these scholars of a radical conflict between modernity and religion. We find a strong expression of this same spirit in Spengler's *The Decline of the West*. In fact, Martin could have mentioned, as examples of ideology, various cyclical theories of culture, some of which, for instance Spengler's and Sorokin's, predicted the demise of religion inevitably associated with the breakdown of great ideals. Since there are, then, ideological elements operative in the various theories of secularization (as well as in the theory of differentiation) I prefer to conclude that there is no fixed law relating modernization and religion.

There are sociologists who look upon religion as an abiding dimension of social life. In the writings of Emile Durkheim and the social thinkers influenced by him, we find that religion may appear with greater or less intensity in society, and it may even disappear altogether for a certain period of time, but as society finds itself and assumes a more stable form, people will come to express their encounter with the ultimate in religious symbols and rites. This view is based neither on philosophical theories nor on psychological analysis; it is properly speaking a sociological theory. Society generates its own religion in the same process in which it constitutes itself as a strong and self-confident community. Sociologists who, from this perspective, study a society in which the inherited religion is breaking down will spontaneously look for new religious movements or various substitutes of religion. David Martin remarks that the sociologists who defend the theory of secularization tend to identify religion with organized religion and do not make themselves sensitive to other religious manifestations. Here again, the studies of Robert Bellah[20] and Andrew Greeley,[21] following Durkheim's lead, have brought out the variety of religious manifestations in contemporary, industrial society.

I do not wish to close this chapter on the theory of secularization without mentioning the great German social philosopher, Max Scheler, who has written an important sociological study to refute the Comtean theory of the three stages.[22] While Scheler followed Toennies and Weber in the evaluation of *Gesellschaft* and feared that the rise of the commercial and industrial bourgeoisie would lead to the decline of culture, he was passionately convinced that religion was a dimension of human life as inescapable as sexuality, love, wisdom and morality. Scheler adopted this viewpoint from personal and philosophical convictions. Yet to refute the theory of secularization which he hated and despised, he became a sociologist; he created a sociology of knowledge that was to specify the relationship of thought and ideas to the social situation of the thinkers. He tried to show that the theory of secularization formulated by Comte, endorsed by scientific Positivism and followed by the middle class, corresponded to the materialistic and pedestrian preoccupation of this class. The theory was a creation of bourgeois resentment! The bourgeoisie, imprisoned in its petty concerns, was jealous of the flights of spirit and the ecstasies characteristic of religion. Inverting Nietzsche's famous formula, Scheler made resentment the source of hostility to religion. The theory of secularization was nothing but the disguise of the human poverty and spiritual emptiness of the middle class. Scientific Positivism was the ideology of the class dedicated to making money. Scheler's brilliance and passion made him the original creator of the systematic sociology of knowledge, but his analysis of the role of religion in society was a curious combination of conservative sentiment, elitist prejudice and radical social thought. We recall that Marx also thought that Enlightenment atheism was the ideology of the bourgeoisie. Yet we find it difficult to take Max Scheler literally. His claim that modern secularizing trends are the products of resentment is based on an overly polemical view of the bourgeoisie and an inadequate analysis of the social role of traditional religion. As the great accuser of modernity, Scheler was not sufficiently sensitive to the ambiguity of religion.

Recommended Readings

Peter Berger, *The Sacred Canopy*, Doubleday, New York, 1967.

Harvey Cox, *The Secular City*, Macmillan Company, New York, 1966.

Daniel Callahan, edit., *The Secular City Debate*, Macmillan Company, New York, 1966.

Andrew Greeley, *Religion in the Year 2000*, Sheed and Ward, New York, 1969.

————, *Unsecular Man*, Schocken Books, New York, 1972.

Franklin Littell, *From State Church to Pluralism*, Doubleday, New York, 1962.

David Martin, *The Religious and the Secular*, Routledge & Kegan Paul, London, 1969.

Louis Schneider, edit., *Religion, Culture and Society*, John Wiley and Sons, New York, 1964.

Bryan Wilson, *Religion Is Secular Society*, Pelican Books, London, 1969.

Notes

1. Cf. Hermann Lübke, *Säkularisierung, Geschichte eines ideenpolitischen Begriffs*, Verlag Karl Albert, Freiburg, 1965.
2. Bryan Wilson, *Religion in Secular Society*, Pelican Books, London, 1969.
3. David Martin, *The Religious and the Secular*, Routledge & Kegan Paul, London, 1969.
4. Andrew Greeley, *Religion in the Year 2000*, Sheed & Ward,

New York, 1969, and "The Present Condition of American Religion," and "The Secularization Myth," *The Denominational Society*, Scott, Foresman and Company, Glenview, Ill., 1972, pp. 86-107, 127-155.

5. Bryan Wilson, *op. cit.*, p. 112.

6. *Ibid.*, p. 122.

7. Peter Berger, *The Sacred Canopy*, Doubleday, New York, 1967, p. 108.

8. Will Herberg, *Catholic, Protestant, Jew*, Doubleday, New York, 1955.

9. Alexis de Tocqueville, *Democracy in America*, edit. Phillips Bradley, Vintage Books, New York, no date, Vol. 2, pp. 21-33.

10. For Durkheim's description of these *Gemeinschaft*-type corporations, see his *Suicide*, Free Press, New York, 1968, pp. 378-384. For a summary of Durkheim's position, see Robert Nisbet, *The Sociological Tradition*, Basic Books, New York, 1966, pp. 155-158.

11. Cf. Andrew Greeley, *The Denominational Society:* "In our model of American religion, we view the denomination as the point of intersection of meaning and belonging functions in a society where an urban, industrial order emerged in a society that had no established church" (p. 2).

12. *Ibid.*, p. 2.

13. A. de Tocqueville, *op. cit.*, Vol. 2, p. 23.

14. Peter Berger, *The Sacred Canopy*, pp. 126-153.

15. Bryan Wilson, *Religion in Secular Society*, p. 42.

16. *Op. cit.*, pp. 43, 210-211, 219-220.

17. *Ibid.*, p. 53.

18. Peter Berger, *The Sacred Canopy*, pp. 113-121.

19. Talcott Parsons, "Christianity and Modern Industrial Society," *Religion, Culture and Society*, edit. Louis Schneider, John Wiley & Sons, New York, 1964, pp. 273-298.

20. Robert Bellah, *Beyond Belief*, Harper & Row, New York, 1970.

21. Andrew Greeley, *Unsecular Man*, Schocken Books, New York, 1972.

22. Max Scheler, "Uber die positivistische Geschichtsphilosophie des Wissens," *Schriften zur Soziologie und Weltanschauungslehre*, 2nd ed., Franke Verlag, Bern, 1963, and *Ressentiment*, Free Press, New York, 1961.

VIII
Creative Religion:
Max Weber's Perspective

Can religion be an independent, creative, original force in human life? In the preceding chapters we have met sociological thinkers who stressed the dependence of religion on society; religion here appeared as a faithful or distorted (inverted) reflection of the social and economic infrastructure. However, we also met authors who recognized in religion an independent variable. The young Hegel regarded "bad" religion as source of personal and social alienation, yet conceded that there was another kind of religion that actually promoted movements of de-alienation. We saw that Durkheim recognized religion as creative; for him, religion, though dependent on society, generated values for social reform. We mentioned Weber's view of religion as breakthrough overcoming magic; we spoke of Erich Fromm who recognized, in addition to the compulsive religion described by Freud, trends of humanistic religion that exercise a creative role; and we introduced Mannheim's concept of utopian religion as the source of a new, political imagination. Religion is ambiguous, but it seems to have its creative side.

Is there good sociological evidence for the power of innovative religion? Are we quite sure that, after the application of various ideological critiques, there will be anything left of the world religions? After all, it has happened that believing Christians who opened themselves to the negative critiques in the hope of purifying their own religious tradition found to their dismay that these critiques affected all aspects of their religion, left nothing intact, and ultimately dissolved their faith in the Christian message. Is there good sociological evidence, I ask, for creative religion?

As a Christian theologian, I trust that the mystery of God operative in human life again and again produces creative religion—and I suppose as a Christian believer, I understand my own personal inwardness not simply as a reflection of the human context in which I live, but also as an encounter with a ⅄ mystery that radically transcends this context. But I do not wish to raise this theological issue at the beginning of this chapter. What I want to ask instead is whether sociologists, relying on their sociological research, have presented strong evidence for creative, innovative religion.

The great sociological witness for creative religion is Max Weber. While Durkheim concentrated on the forces that held society together, Weber was more interested in the forces that carried society forward and modified the conditions of culture. One of the principal issues that preoccupied his mind was the origin of modern, rational culture, unique in the history of civilization. His early empirical studies had acquainted him with the problems of work and employment in Eastern Germany where German (Protestant) employers and Polish (Catholic) laborers were set over against one another. This study revealed to him that involved in these problems were not only material interests but also diverse symbolic world views. He pursued his intuition that religion had something to do with the creation of culture. In his famous book, *The Protestant Ethic and the Spirit of Capitalism*—already mentioned in the previous chapter—he studied the origin of the modern, hard-working, capitalistic world at the end of the Middle Ages and concluded that the Protestant worldly asceticism had something to do with its rapid spread and unequaled success. Weber's book determined the direction of his subsequent research, but it also produced one of the most important controversies in the intellectual community of the 20th century, a controversy that still continues.[1] What is the creative role of religion in the making of culture?

Let me repeat that Weber formulated his thesis in a modest way. He did not claim that Reformed Christianity was the cause of modern capitalism. He realized, of course, that the beginnings of capitalistic enterprises were present in pre-Reformation Europe as they had been in other cultures before that time, and he even specified the various social and economic factors that contributed to these developments. But why did these beginnings spread so rapidly in Europe and create new cultural conditions on an unprecedented scale? This was due, according to Weber's thesis, to the new spirituality. Weber did not deny that this new inwardness was, in part at least, an adjustment to the growing commercialism and entrepreneurship present in certain parts of Europe, but it was for him not simply an adjustment, not simply a giving in to social pressures. An original, creative, religious breakthrough took place in Calvinistic Christianity. God's call was experienced as a secular calling. Christians experienced the meaning and power of the gospel in their dedication to hard work and personal enterprise, and they regarded the success of their undertakings as God's approval and blessing. This new spirituality removed the religious obstacles to capitalistic expansion, for in the Middle Ages the Church had not only regarded as gravely sinful the taking of interest on money loaned, but had also held up contemplation, otherworldliness, patience in one's providential position, and even elected poverty as the ideals to be followed by the most dedicated Christians. The new worldly asceticism, moreover, supplied strong religious motivation for the secular effort to build a society that would reflect the new freedoms of the burgher and allow for his free enterprise in industry and commerce. Thanks to this new ethos, eventually embodied and handed forward to subsequent generations by secular social institutions (the school, the home, etc.), rational principles were applied not only to the expansion of trade and production, bookkeeping and investment policies, but to all institutions in society, including the government. This ethos, completely secularized in time, slowly undermined the traditional values. This was the ethos that had created and, at least in Weber's day, was still creating the modern world.

Weber's thesis offers a certain correction of the Marxist understanding of social evolution, and hence it has lent itself to many ideological uses. Needless to say, Weber himself was not an idealist who neglected the economic factor in the creation of culture. But he studied this factor along with others, social, political and even symbolic, that affect personal and social consciousness. Weber did not deny that under certain historical circumstances the economic factor may be the dominant one and provide the key for the understanding of cultural and social change, but there are other historical conditions, according to him, for which this is not true. For Weber, social class and class conflict were ideal-types. They were never, as they were for Marx, concepts representing the existing social realities; they were ideal-types applicable *more or less* to a given society. This becomes very clear, for instance, in Weber's study of the relation of religion to social class. He admits that there are times when the same religion serves the upper classes as ideology and the lower classes as otherworldly consolation, and for which the Marxist analysis holds true. But in studying the same history over a longer period of time, the relation of religion and class turns out to be very varied; it does not lend itself to easy generalizations. In history, religion has been both legitimating and innovative.

According to Weber's thesis, the new ethic, having become the inner logic of the system, continues to apply reason to the institutional processes of society. Weber calls this rationalization.[2] In his writings dealing with the modern world, rationalization means the application of technical, quantified reason to society; this leads inevitably to the ongoing specialization of institutions, accompanied by a corresponding complexification of their interaction. It creates, moreover, personal lives that are almost wholly dominated by the needs of this rational society. Occasionally Weber creates the impression that rationalization is a principle of evolution; yet when he reveals his feelings, it becomes clear that he regards the ongoing application of technical reason as a tragic principle of social change that will eventually reduce the true dimensions of human life and transform society into an iron cage. We referred to his famous sentences earlier in the book. Reason, in this context, means instrumental or functional reason, having to do with the means, not the end of the social process.

However in his book, *The Sociology of Religion*,[3] Weber seems to speak of the application of reason in a different way. Let us look at his theory of religious development. We recall Weber's distinction between magic, priestly religion and proph-

ecy. Magic refers to a turning to the gods for the sake of solving private problems; it is inspired by the intention to make the
gods do the will of the client. By contrast, priestly religion is a
turning to the gods for the sake of wider, communal concerns.
Religion transcends magic. It is inspired by the surrender to
the divine that orders and enlivens the community. Religion
appears here as breakthrough. It results from the application
of reason to magic, but in this case, reason is mainly substantial, concerned not so much with the means as with the end.
Reason here changes the orientation of personal life and reveals a person's place in the wider community. A similar
breakthrough takes place in the passage from priestly religion
to prophecy. Operative in the religious development is rationalization. For through the prophetic message the community is
brought to greater self-knowledge and gains a clearer understanding of its own ideals. Again the reason spoken of is substantial, for through prophecy people acquire a greater sense of
responsibility for their future. In the early chapters of his sociology of religion, then, Weber introduces a notion of reason
that differs from the instrumental reason at work in the institutional changes of capitalist society.

It is possible—though probably misleading—to read
Weber's sociology of religion as evolutionary theory. This is
the way in which Talcott Parsons presents it in his famous introduction to the English translation of Weber's book, published in 1963. Parsons shows that Weber creates categories for
the understanding of religion by abstracting from the total
social process sets of two principal alternatives of social structure (e.g., magic/religion, religion/prophecy, etc.) where one
reinforces the traditional order of society and the other creates
a breakthrough and becomes a source of evolutionary change.
Magic is conservative, and the breakthrough to priestly religion
leads to social change; at a later historical moment, priestly
religion legitimates the existing social order, and prophetic religion becomes a factor in the evolution of society. Weber tried
to detect in religion the moments of breakthrough. Parsons
writes, "Weber's primary interest is in religion as a source of
the dynamics of social change, not religion as reinforcement of
the stability of society."[4]

It is indeed possible to read the opening chapters of Weber's sociology of religion as presenting the categories of an evolutionary scheme as long as we do not remember that these are simply ideal-types. They do not propose a theory of inevitable evolutionary progress; they are simply useful tools for detecting the significant breakthroughs in the creation of consciousness and society. Weber did not believe in evolution; he did not think that scholars had enough evidence to speak scientifically of a necessary direction implicit in the historical process. And hence he did not regard religion as the breakthrough agent that kept on applying reason to the social processes, moved history in a progressive direction, and eventually produced the modern, Protestant, critical consciousness characteristic of the Great Society. There are tones in Parsons' introduction which suggest this. Weber was personally convinced that present in the human world were many diverse and irreconcilable values, all deserving of loyalty and admiration, which could never be brought together in a single synthesis. Every development in one direction, faithful to a certain ideal, would inevitably neglect other values, irreconcilable with it, and hence ultimately produce a reaction, a new movement, possibly mediated by religious breakthrough, that would seek to recover some of these neglected values. Polytheism, Weber felt, was the only realistic religion.[5]

Weber was fascinated by the idea of change and non-conformity. He made "charism," a word derived from the Pauline epistles, the starting point for his study of religion as well as the key concept for his theory of social change.[6] Charism is a mysterious power attached to a person which attracts people to him and makes them obedient to the will and the commands of that person. The charismatic person is experienced as a human with superior powers, out of the ordinary and not subject to the laws of daily reality. In some instances, the charismatic person is regarded as having divine powers. This, Weber thinks, is the origin of religion. The charismatic leader creates a community and begins a movement of people who accept his word and submit to his authority. To make this charism available to people living at a distance from the leader or to hand it on to subsequent generations, the original charism is institutionalized in rites, symbols or sacred writings and ritually communicated to a group of chosen disciples and their successors. This institutionalization of charism—which we find, for instance, in the great religions—always implies a certain weakening or cooling of the original charism. The fervor of the beginning is lost in the second generation. In Weber's terminology, the charismatic power of the founder is eventually transformed into traditional authority invested in the religious institutions. What happens again and again, according to Weber, is the outburst of new charisms: new leaders emerge who attract people and exercise power over them. Sometimes these new charismatic movements aim at restoring or reforming the religious tradition, and at other times they break away from the institutionalized religion or are forcibly excluded by it. In the history of religion, these charisms have never disappeared.

At the beginning of this chapter, we posed the question whether religion could ever be original and innovative. According to Weber, religion always begins in an innovative movement; it becomes tamed only through its routinization, but it continues to remain the locus of new charisms.

At the same time we must not overlook that Weber used "charism" as a value-free term. It does not necessarily refer to a religious phenomenon. It refers to the superior power some persons have over groups of people and hence applies to good and wicked leaders alike. Charism is present in the magician as well as in the prophet; charism is present in Hitler as well as in Pope John XXIII. Because of the value-free use of the term, Weber was able to make charism central in his theory of social change.

There are, according to Weber's ideal-typical analysis, three basic kinds of authority that constitute social life.[7] Authority is here defined as the power to make people obey. There is, first, *traditional* authority, associated with the rules and customs of ancient cultural systems, including their religious and political elements. Since these systems are venerated by their members and looked upon as almost sacred realities, people obey this authority without questioning it. This authority belongs to the order of things as they see it; it is part of their cosmos. However, because of new problems and changed circumstances, the tradition is eventually challenged. Some people desire to make the social order more rational. They ask questions regarding the social usefulness of the laws, and when they find them no longer serving the conscious purposes of the population or sections of the population, they advocate change. What takes place then is the transition from traditional to *legal* authority. In this reformed social order, people obey because the laws have been made on rational grounds by men who were legally appointed to legislate. The passage from traditional to legal authority is not usually smooth. It is often released by men with *charismatic* authority. They exercise personal power over people for a time, during which they succeed in modifying the traditional structures and introduce more rational social processes. No society is wholly constituted by legal authority; it always retains some traditional elements. But even if society should become almost completely dominated by legal authority, it is not for that reason assured of stability. Since even a rational society inevitably suppresses certain human values and neglects important aspects of human life, radical persons wielding charismatic authority are likely to emerge who break with the fundamental assumptions of the social order. What takes place here may be a much more radical questioning of society than the passage from traditional to legal authority. The critical, countervailing movement may, of course, peter out because it is unsound and based on wholly irrational impulses; or it may be crushed by those who exercise legal authority in society; or its special insights may be used by the leaders of society and integrated, in modified form, into the dominant social system. But what can also happen is that the countervailing movement, possibly joined by other such movements, eventually spreads among the people, affects the consciousness of the majority, and eventually produces a radical cultural transformation, or, by reaching a powerful group in society, produces radical political upheaval and reconstitutes the social order according to new principles. If the charismatic element is very strong in the countervailing movement, it may even give rise to a new sacred tradition, and the new society, after the revolution, will exercise power and demand obedience in the name of traditional authority. And so history goes on.

For Weber, the dynamic element in the history of institutions is charismatic authority. Curiously enough, he does not say very much about what this authority is. He speaks of extraordinary, inexplicable power attached as special talent to some persons. Charism is not a religious concept, even though Weber derived it from his study of religion. How is the charism related to the social order? As a sociologist, Weber could not suppose that it drops from the sky; even the extraordinary is socially grounded. Yet Weber did not follow this line of thought. He does suggest, however, especially in his writings on religion, that the charismatic person has power over people because he touches them where they suffer. The charismatic person is intuitively aware of what disturbs, wounds, and exasperates people in their society. This is true of the magician as of the prophet; this is true of the demagogue who seduces people to follow him on his futile political journey as of the radical reformer who inspires people to recreate the order in society. The person gifted with charism can put into words the hidden oppression from which people suffer, and hence, as he speaks, they verify his words through their own experiences. Charism cannot be acquired by intelligence and effort; it is a gift found in a person whereby he is able to intuit what goes on in people behind their social façade. The charismatic person gives voice to the common suffering; *he articulates the alienation* of the community; he speaks with an authority ultimately derived from the misery or unredemption of the many.

The charismatic person senses the hurts of people and *proposes a new imagination* by which this harm can be overcome. It is here that charismatics are distinguished from one another. The demagogue draws people with him along a road that leads to destruction; the mystagogue uses tricks to blind people and manipulate them for his own purposes; the prophet summons people to greater self-knowledge, releases new energy in them, and inspires them to recreate society according to higher ideals of justice and equality. Weber often speaks of charism as the breakthrough that applies reason to the social processes. This is operative, according to him, in the evolution leading from magic to priestly religion and prophecy. This sort of charism has also been at work in some of the significant social changes in Western history. In this sense, Weber saw the Protestant ethic as a charismatic breakthrough phenomenon. It produced a new imagination that enabled people to transcend the limitations of the past and enter upon a new way of life.

To understand charismatic authority as the dynamic element of history, we must look at the role of the imagination in the creation of the future. This theme has been greatly developed by social thinkers such as Karl Mannheim and Ernst Bloch. We mentioned in particular that Mannheim distinguished between ideological and utopian consciousness.[8] Utopian imagination makes people sensitive to the breaking points of the present system and nourishes in them a longing for a new kind of society, and as such exercises a significant role in social change. Mannheim thought that the disappearance of utopia would bring about a static state of affairs in which people become more and more like things and behave according to the fixed laws of the social system. In ordinary language, the word "utopia" is often used in a pejorative sense; it then refers to unrealistic dreams of the future that lead to passivity and despair. We already mentioned that Mannheim regarded such an imagination as ideological rather than utopian, for dreams that lead to inaction simply reinforce the present social order. Ernst Bloch called such unrealistic dreams of the future "abstract utopias" and distinguished them from "concrete utopias" that provide an imagination that actually influences people's thoughts and actions.[9] Concrete utopias are images of the future that are grounded in authentic intuitions of the ills and contradictions present in society. Concrete utopias negate the most oppressive elements of this society and present a vision of human life that, even if as such unrealizable, summon forth new ways of thinking and acting that could lead to actual social change. According to Mannheim and Bloch, the imagination of the future exercises great power in directing people's action. For if such an imagination is permitted to govern people's hearts and minds, then it will create a special sensitivity in them and make them look at reality from a certain, definite perspective; it will act as a symbol system that mediates people's perception of the world and guides their response to it—and thus enters into the creation of the human reality to which they belong. It is through the exercise of charism that the imagination of the future comes to play this governing role in people's lives. In religion, in particular, people submit to the imagination of the founder or the saint.

For Weber, curiously enough, the Puritan dream was the last valid utopia. He did not expect any more charisms in the modern, industrialized, bureaucratic world. Since the same kind of functional rationality would dominate the communist nations, they could hardly offer an alternative to the iron cage. Weber felt that every breakthrough would be leveled down by the application of empirical reason. He anticipated Marcuse's "one-dimensional man." Weber could not imagine a charismatic breakthrough of substantial reason that would question the end and purpose of human life. He thought, moreover, that the bureaucratization of life, taking place on all levels of society, would inevitably create monocratically governed, rigid and inhuman structures that the increasing rationalization would only make tighter until no room whatever will be left for freedom and flexibility. Was Max Weber right? Will we end in the iron cage? Can we expect no more charisms? Or was Weber fooled by the ideology of decline that characterized many German thinkers of that period? We shall come back to this question.

Let me add, at this point, a few more comments on Max Weber's remarkable theory of social change. When Weber looks upon society and culture, he sees both a dominant trend, a trend imposed by the major institutions, and countervailing trends, sparked by personalities with charismatic gifts of varying strength. Durkheim, we recall, and with him the majority of sociologists, look upon society principally as a unity; they concentrate on the equilibrium of the social system and understand the conflicting trends as so many factors that, in their own way, contribute to the ongoing balance of the social order. For Weber, on the other hand, the unity of the social system is imposed by authority (*Herrschaft*, as he liked to call it); it is the work of the dominant forces in society. Unity is the creation of the ruling classes. At the same time Weber also expected the existence of countervailing movements in society challenging the established order. The special insight of Weber is that these critical movements are themselves nourished by powers and by an imagination that are in some sense determined by the dominant forces and their contradictions. If the above analysis of charism is correct (and I repeat that Weber did not move far in this direction), then the countervailing forces are summoned forth by the dominant social order they seek to change. The charismatic person, we said, had power because he appealed to, and sometimes even articulated, the alienation that the dominant system imposed on people, and initiated his followers to a new imagination that was to overcome this alienation and, in some instances, actually anticipated and helped bring about the future development of society. The conflicting movements are social reactions generated by the dominant systems. In other words, the dominant system of society produces not only the dominant consciousness that keeps the system going, but it also produces, by way of critical response and passing through the creativity of certain personalities, the countervailing movements and the emergence of a new consciousness. The critical movements are generated in the womb of the old society.

Weber regarded history as undefined and open. Freedom was inserted in the historical process through the charismatic persons and the countervailing movements created by them. The bearer of the charism, in touch with the alienation of his community, produces a new imagination with varying effects; it may lead his followers into blind alleys or actually make them agents of significant social change. The spectrum is very wide here. Each social order creates its own opposing movements, but these may vary from irrational sectarian protest groups to revolutionary movements and reformist parties; the form of the countervailing trend depends on the utopian imagination that has produced it. Weber follows Hegel and Marx in recognizing the dialectical relationship between society and consciousness, or between infrastructure and suprastructure, but he did not accept that these dialectics carried history forward in a clearly defined direction. For Hegel, this direction was provided by immanent reason; for Marx, it was the logic of the class struggle that carried history forward toward the classless society. Weber had little sympathy for theories of total world interpretation. At the same time, he had no sympathy either for the rationalism or idealism that made political scientists think they could devise rational solutions for the problems of society and impose them on the social order. For Weber, who was a materialist (in the Marxian sense of the term), the suprastructure had critical power only to the extent that it had been mediated by the infrastructure, even if the point of mediation was the charism.

(Let me add that this last sentence also applies to psychotherapy after Freud. For the word addressed to us by the therapist, and thus present in consciousness, has therapeutic power only if it expresses, in a creative way, what has emerged from our own history and our own consciousness.)

Weber's theory of social change can be applied to social configurations of all kinds, to cultural systems, to political societies, to ecclesiastical organizations, etc. It is even possible to recognize the Marxist theory of revolution as a special case in Weber's analysis of social change. For if there is a society in which the economic system is the predominant cause of alienation and oppression, so dominant that all other factors, cultural, intellectual, religious and even political, have become instruments of the economic interests of the owning class, then the countervailing movements, sparked by charismatic personalities in touch with the alienation of the people, will oppose the economic system, divide the society into two conflicting classes, and, if strong enough, overthrow the political system that protects the owners of industry. But Weber, contrary to Marx, did not suppose that economics was the exclusive determining factor in every society. As we mentioned above, Weber regarded bureaucracy and technology as such powerful institutional factors in the creation of culture that he was convinced that they would cause oppressive conditions and dehumanization even in countries that rejected capitalism and opted for a "rational," centralizing and industrializing communism. Even here the "iron cage" is inevitable.

Let us return to the question of Weber's pessimism. Does the bureaucratization of life inevitably lead to the crushing of all charisms and countervailing and corrective trends in society? Have we become inevitably preoccupied with functionality and lost sight of questions concerning the end and purpose of life? Weber's theory of bureaucracy has been criticized by sociologists. Robert Merton,[10] in particular, has shown that the movement toward increasingly controlled and rigid bureaucracies, described by Weber, actually contains dysfunctional elements that will eventually undermine the working of the bureaucratic systems. These dysfunctional elements can be overcome only by introducing into these systems free discussions, uniting members of all administrative levels, regarding the aims of the institution and regarding the manner in which these aims are actually achieved. In other words, the drift of bureaucracy toward greater rationality will eventually include self-corrective processes which raise questions not only in regard to means but also concerning ends.

In a lecture given in 1919, Weber himself admitted that the drift toward growing rationalization eventually moves beyond purely functional or instrumental questions; it will eventually compel people to give an account of the ultimate meaning of their own conduct and raise the question whether the manifold values of life are hierarchically ordered and cohere under a highest value. Rationality, then, is not purely and simply confined to means.[11] Weber's pessimism is not scientifically established. Charisms are still possible; people can still, surprisingly and constructively, react against the alienation that the system inflicts on them.

The Weberian ideology of decline is not without consequences. For to adopt a language which supposes that the future is determined, that the unexpected will no longer happen and that freedom has been removed, is to engage in a discourse that could become self-fulfilling prophecy. This discourse extinguishes any new imagination. Christians hold that the future remains open, and the language they want to use about history is one that protects freedom and the possibility of the unexpected. The new remains ever a possibility. In my book, *Man Becoming*, I tried to show that to believe in God means precisely to trust that the new can happen, that tomorrow will be different from today, that the future is not wholly determined by causes operative in the present but remains ever open to the unexpected and marvelous.[12] I then applied this principle mainly in reference to personal life, but it is equally valid for the historical process. Translating this theological principle into the language of Max Weber, we would have to say that charisms remain possible and that countervailing movements making people transcend the alienation inflicted upon them by the system remain possible.

Weber's theory of social change, derived—as we have seen —from his sociology of religion, also renders an admirable account of the conflicts within the Christian church. The medieval sects, for instance, were countervailing movements opposing traditional authority, often inspired by charismatic figures who had put their finger on the ills of the established church. Most of these movements were crushed. A few were kept by leaders within the church—the Franciscans, for instance—as protected subcultures with rules of their own that did not apply to the church as a whole. Charismatic leaders, living under great pressure, produced a wide spectrum of utopias from the fulfillment of biblical promises to strange and fantastic dreams. At the Reformation, a religious countervailing movement, sparked by a charismatic personality of great power, achieved its purpose in part because it was joined by countervailing political movements resisting traditional authority. The new churches, especially those of Calvinist inspiration, repudiated the notion of traditional or sacred authority; they introduced democracy into church life and regarded themselves ruled by legal authority. Yet the charismatic movements that repudiated both ecclesiastical and secular society, the so-called radical wing of the Reformation, were brutally crushed by the joining of all forces against them. It seems that church reform can only be successful if it is carried forward by important sociopolitical trends in society.

Weber's theory of social change also sheds light on the changes that have recently taken place in the Catholic Church. Vatican Council II was prepared by countervailing trends of various kinds—liturgical, ecumenical, biblical, lay action, etc. —which had promoted, over a considerable period of time, aspects of the Christian life that had been neglected or suppressed by the official church. These movements had experienced the pressure of the hierarchical establishment, yet they proudly remembered the charismatic personalities, however modest, associated with their origin. It was only at Vatican Council II, through the unexpected action of Pope John, that these movements were fully recognized and allowed to influence the policy-making of the hierarchy. Through these new policies, the Catholic Church opened itself to critical scholarship, freedom of conscience, pluralism within unity, participation and team responsibility, and some elements of democracy. This liberal reform movement was then carried forward by the critical cultural trend of the sixties, impatient with the inherited society.

At this time, ten years after the Council, when a certain shift to the right has come to characterize political life, the Catholic Church on the whole seems to have lost interest in the renewal. A ready identification with the dominant groups in society, as well as the unwillingness critically to examine the church's collective life, prevents Catholic parishes, dioceses and higher organs from applying the conciliar principles to their own institutions. In the contemporary church the critical vitality expresses itself in new countervailing movements. A minority of Catholics are involved in centers, cells and groups of various kinds, including some schools, colleges, and religious congregations, all of which promote the aspects of the gospel disregarded by the official church, in particular those that have to do with the critical power of the gospel in the condition of the modern world. The various centers, interrelated and supportive of one another, constitute a web of renewal which may have no institutional power at this time, but which will again, under changed circumstances, affect the church's policy-making on a higher level. Weber's theory helps Catholics to appreciate that their involvement in a countervailing movement is a realistic policy of social change in their own church.

Weber recognized the creative and innovative elements in religion. He regarded them as so significant that he based his entire theory of social change on a model taken from his sociology of religion. Weber did not deny, of course, the extraordinary ambiguity of religion. He recognized the ideological trends in religion which had been brought out by the Marxist critique. He was very much aware that the Christian religion of his own age acted as a legitimating system for the traditional order of society. Yet he accepted the evidence from history that religion has also been an innovating force.

*   *   *

Utopian religion—we use the term in Mannheim's sense— can be both reformist and radical. That is to say, innovative religion can nourish social currents that seek to reform the existing institutions or it can produce an imagination that looks forward to the overthrow of the existing order. Weber was especially aware of the reformist trend. This is also true of the theological thinkers who applied Weber's principles, Ernst Troeltsch and Richard Niebuhr. It is doubtful whether they paid enough attention to the radical form of utopian consciousness.

In his famous book, *Christ and Culture*,[13] Richard Niebuhr introduced a fivefold typology to categorize the various responses of Christian believers to their socio-cultural environment. Since these types are probably known to the reader, let me describe them very briefly: type 1, *Christ against Culture*, refers to the sectarian rejection of the world; type 2, *Christ of Culture*, designates the identification of the gospel with the dominant cultural trends; type 3, *Christ above Culture*, refers to the medieval natural-supernatural hierarchical cosmos; type 4, *Christ in Paradox with Culture*, signifies the conflictual vision of the two realms, the inward realm where God is present to believers and the outward realm where they must do God's will but are unable to encounter him; type 5, *Christ, Transformer of Culture*, refers to the Christian faith that summons believers to the transformation of their social existence and to the encounter with God in the historical struggle between good and evil. For Richard Niebuhr, writing his book in 1951, types 1 and 2 were outside the authentic understanding of the gospel, type 3 represented the Catholic faith, type 4 characterized the conservative trend of contemporary Protestant religion, and type 5 was the vision of faith which he himself wanted to promote.

In this chapter dealing with innovative religion we are concerned especially with types 1 and 5. Let me say that Niebuhr was not sensitive enough to the faith of the radical Christians who looked upon Christ as a judge of culture. He classified them under type 1. He understood their faith as individualistic and world-denying and did not detect its hidden social meaning. In a previous chapter[14] we have mentioned the research of Rosemary Ruether in her book, *The Radical Kingdom*, and in a manuscript on christology not yet published, which clarifies the revolutionary elements in the Christian tradition. She has shown that the apocalyptical consciousness, produced among the Jews under conditions of prolonged oppression in the centuries preceding and including the early Christian period, was mediated to subsequent generations by elements of the Christian religion and became the source of the Western revolutionary tradition.

Richard Niebuhr was more interested in reformist religion. What examples does he propose for type 5, *Christ, Transformer of Culture*? He first mentions the Gospel of John and the writings of St. Augustine. Is this wholly justified? While these ancient writers acknowledged God's gracious presence in the transformation of human life, they tended to look upon this as personal transformations. Christ created a new love in the hearts of men, and this new love in turn would produce a new type of society. These ancient writers recognized God's gracious presence in the entire human family, but they did not and probably could not clarify the redemptive presence in terms of social change. The radical, apocalyptical writers, rather, foresaw the coming of a new age and the transformation of the structures of human existence. The writer of the Fourth Gospel and St. Augustine believed that Christ was present in the believing community now, initiating them into love and truth, in a manner that was basically independent of the social circumstances. While the seeds of type 5 are found in antiquity, the full-blown spirituality of *Christ, Transformer of Culture*, exists in the Christian church only after the Enlightenment. The typical figure chosen by Niebuhr is Frederick Maurice, the Anglican divine of the 19th century, who recognized God's gracious presence in all of humanity, discerned the movement of the Spirit toward mutuality and reconciliation in history, and advocated a social ethic which he called, in 1848, Christian socialism.

Niebuhr recognized elements leading to type 5, *Christ, Transformer of Culture*, in Calvin's writings. He fully appreciated the aspects of Calvinist teaching which made Christians see themselves as called to work in the world and establish God's justice on earth. Niebuhr acknowledges the revolutionary potential of this piety. At the same time, he felt that these trends were counterbalanced by a strong emphasis on the over-againstness of God. While Calvin created an action-oriented, innovative religion, he greatly stressed the dualistic character of the Christian message. "To the eternal over-againstness of God and man," Niebuhr writes, "Calvin adds the dualism of temporal and eternal existence and the other dualism of an eternal heaven and eternal hell."[15] Type 5, *Christ, Transformer of Culture*, as described by Niebuhr, implies a more immanent understanding of the transcendent God. God is present in the remaking of the world. And this view did not become important till after the Enlightenment.

It is my contention, repeatedly mentioned in this book, that over the last century and a half a significant change has taken place in Protestantism and Catholicism, well symbolized by Frederick Maurice, according to which God is worshiped as the mystery, present in human life and revealed in Christ, which calls and strengthens people to wrestle against the powers of darkness and restructure human life on this globe toward greater justice and reconciliation. We find this trend at first among certain Protestant and Anglican religious thinkers. In North America the social gospel discovered the immanent God. Let us listen to the conclusion of two Church historians. "The social gospel rested upon a few dominant ideas that characterized the intellectual climate in which it grew. Its primary assumption was the immanence of God, a conception derived from the influence of science—Darwinian evolution in particular—upon Protestant theology. Belief in an indwelling God, working out his purposes in the world of men, naturally involved a solidaristic view of society—which was conveniently supplied by sociology."[16] "The demand 'save this man, now' became 'save this society, now,' and the slogan 'the evangelization of the world in our generation' became 'the Christianization of the world in our generation.' The sense of an immanent God working in the movements of revival and awakening was easily transferred to social movements, and hence to the whole evolution of society. . . . To submit oneself to these immanent impulses of divinity was to adopt the social gospel and to embrace the social passion which lay at the heart of most of the movements of social reform in Canada in the period of 1890-1939."[17] With Maurice Blondel, out of a more personalistic human engagement, the new approach entered the Catholic tradition. Because of the collapse of much of German Christianity into cultural conformity, Karl Barth and neo-orthodoxy protested against divine immanence in any form. God was to be worshiped as the totally other. However in the second half of the 20th century, when Christians wish to identify themselves not with the dominant classes but with the exploited and oppressed, the major churches have moved to the theological position characterized by type 5, *Christ, Transformer of Culture*. This shift is found in the documents of the World Council of Churches, even though there is still a hesitancy about divine immanence which is unknown in the Catholic tradition. The same shift is clearly present in the documents of Vatican Council II.

The conciliar document, *The Church in the Modern World*, is perhaps the strongest public document ever made expressing faith in Christ, the transformer of culture. The preface explains the perspective adopted by Vatican II. "The Council gazes upon the world which is the theater of man's history, and carries the marks of his energies, his tragedies, and his triumphs—that world which the Christian sees as created and sustained by its Maker's love, fallen indeed into the bondage of sin, yet emancipated now by Christ. He was crucified and rose again to break the stranglehold of the evil one, so that this world might be fashioned anew according to God's design and reach its fulfillment."[18] This passage speaks of God's victory over evil, without distinguishing between person and society, between present history and future glory; in Christ is revealed a transformation that affects all aspects of human existence. Vatican II clearly acknowledges, in this document and in several others, the universality of divine grace. The divine call, fully revealed in Jesus, addresses people everywhere and summons them to a common task. Conscience is a sacred reality in all people. "Conscience is the most secret core and sanctuary of a man. There he is alone with God, whose voice echoes in his depth. In a wonderful manner, conscience reveals that law which is fulfilled by love of God and neighbor. In fidelity to conscience, Christians are joined to the rest of men in the search for truth and the genuine solution of man's social and personal problems."[19] Humankind is on the journey to the kingdom together, called and enabled by the same divine mystery. At Vatican II, the Catholic Church declared itself in solidarity with the whole human family, in which God is present as matrix, call and horizon.

How is such an extraordinary transformation of religion possible? In the Catholic Church this change is in continuity with very ancient doctrinal trends, acknowledging the immanence of God, the incarnation of the Logos in human life, and the divine destiny of the whole of mankind. In Protestantism, this change is in continuity with Hegel rather than with the original Reformers. We admit, of course, that this utopian religion, type 5 in Niebuhr's classification, is not universal in the Christian churches. It is expressed in the official teaching documents, it represents the viewpoint of the majority of Catholic theologians and a good number of their Protestant colleagues, and it inspires a significant minority of believers in the Christian churches. We also admit that this utopian religion exists in a variety of forms, some inspiring a reformist, left-liberal orientation and others a more radical, or even revolutionary, approach to society. We are even obliged to admit that in the mid-seventies the faith in Christ, the transformer of culture, is being challenged by conservative groups in the churches.[20] Still, it is hard to deny that a shift has taken place. The understanding of the gospel has been transformed. And this deserves an explanation.

Before we try to offer an explanation for this change, we want to raise the question whether faith in Christ, transformer of culture, simply expresses a wider endorsement of the Protestant ethic and the liberal dream. One might suggest that the growing strength of the middle class in the Catholic Church, especially in Western Europe and America, has led to a wider acceptance of liberal ideals and enabled Catholicism at Vatican II to catch up with the Protestant churches. There is no doubt a bit of truth in this theory. At the same time, there are significant differences between the Protestant ethic and the utopian gospel described above. The Protestant ethic was based on a dualistic understanding of the Christian message. God was the transcendent ruler of history who commanded his faithful servants to work in the world and transform it according to his will. The Protestant ethic corresponds to what Weber has called "ethical prophecy":[21] it presupposes the radical separation of God and human life. The transformist gospel, on the other hand, tries to overcome this dualism. Here God is affirmed and experienced as the transcendent mystery present in history and operative in the significant moments of human liberation, personal and social. Here we are closer to what Weber called "exemplary prophecy"[22] which presupposes God's immanence in human life and the mediation of the divine through participation in action. The transformist spirituality has a mystical dimension that is absent from the Protestant ethic—and from neo-orthodoxy. Life in the world is more than faithful obedience to the divine commandments; it is a redeeming encounter with the divine in the call to a reconciled life and the action in which people try to realize it. We have here the entry of contemplation in a Christian ethos of worldly orientation! The spirituality proper to the transformist faith is not a dualistic contemplation that withdraws people from the daily struggle, but a contemplation of the divine mystery as source, orientation and horizon of common action.

Secondly, the utopian gospel is critical of individualism. The Protestant ethic relates the believer individually to his God and makes him concentrate on his personal salvation, a religious attitude that tends to foster individuals in economics and society and promotes the liberal world view. The transformist faith, on the other hand, does not present a person's relationship to God as private and separated; salvation is mediated by people, by fellowship, by community, by the common effort to create humane conditions of human life and produce a new social order. Transformist faith fosters a movement away from individualism in personal life as well as in economics and society. It tends to be critical of free enterprise, the profit motive, and the principle of competition. The new spirituality recovers a greater sense of people's collective destiny and often formulates its opposition to individualism in terms of socialism and cooperative systems. For these reasons, then, *contemplation* and *socialism*, the transformist gospel cannot be regarded as a simple extension of the Protestant ethic. It corresponds, rather, to an important critical movement in the Protestant churches.

* * *

How did the transformist faith emerge in the Christian Church? Changes in religion depend on many factors, on the social and cultural conditions in which a religion exists, on the exigencies of its own institutional life, and finally on the charismatic element—charismatic used in the Weberian sense— which, though unpredictable, enables a religion to respond in an innovative way to new conditions. Changes in religion could of course either strengthen the dominant ideological trend or nourish the utopian current; the changes could strengthen the pathological tendencies or foster the liberating elements. The question I ask here is simply this: What happened in Christianity, in particular in the most rigid, conservative, and unrepentant church of the West, to generate a transformist understanding of the gospel?

To understand this shift in the understanding of the gospel, we must consider two distinct factors—first, the emergence of a new consciousness in Western culture, and, secondly, the peculiar creativity of the gospel in the face of evil. The discussion of the first factor belongs to sociological reflection; the discussion of the second factor takes us into theology.

1. We have already studied the creation of the *Gesellschaft*-type of society. The industrial and democratic revolutions at the end of the 18th century created an individualistic and atomistic consciousness that corresponded to the rational and scientific Enlightenment, often called the Early Enlightenment. At the same time, these new dominant institu-

tions also produced countervailing trends. (This, incidentally, again verifies Weber's theory of social change.) We mentioned the German thinkers at the turn of the 19th century who criticized Enlightenment culture, largely—if we follow Mannheim's sociology of knowledge—because of the prolonged feudalism and the absence of a large middle class in Germany. Still, their critical stance was taken over by the sociologists, including Marx, all of whom strongly reacted against the culture created by *Gesellschaft*. At the turn of the 20th century, despite the success and expansion of industrialization and technological development, the great critics of rational society emerge, including Durkheim, Weber, and Freud, who tried to overcome Positivism, discovered the symbolic dimension of human life, and often favored a wholistic rather than an atomistic understanding of society. These thinkers, including Marx, are often identified as the Late Enlightenment. It is here that we find the great critiques of rationalism, the effort to recover the emotions, a new outlook on action and involvement, the discovery of false consciousness, and the development of sociological theories. While the Early Enlightenment was hostile to religion, the Late Enlightenment, while often appearing unreligious, was basically open to religion. Christians could not carry on fruitful conversations with the Early Enlightenment, but there was no reason why conversation with the Late Enlightenment could not be promising. The first scholars who attempted such a dialogue in the Catholic Church were condemned as Modernists.

The Early Enlightenment found expression in the rational and individualistic structures of *Gesellschaft*. We have shown above how the democratic and industrial revolutions communicated an atomistic and scientific spirit among the people. At the same time, *Gesellschaft* had a more latent effect on consciousness, not perceived by its early critics. Its immediate effect was the spread of the scientific mind-set, but the more remote effect was the creation of historical consciousness. How did this happen?

The expanding technological-industrial institutions and the increasing flexibility of political structures created a new awareness—first, among the intellectuals who reflected on them, and eventually among the people whose lives were involved in them—that the social and cultural world was made by men, or at least was controlled by them, and hence could be remade to suit human needs. While at one time the human reality was *a given* for people, which they tried to understand and into which they wanted to fit their lives, in the new age society was experienced by people as unfinished, as something that still had to be built, as social process, the past of which was a given but the future of which still depended on people's choices. Thanks to the institutions in which people lived, they came to look upon reality as development, as an ongoing process which demanded their freedom, intelligence, and dedication. As the world was unfinished, so were they. People eventually ceased to regard themselves as finished subjects looking at a world pitted as object over against them (the scientific consciousness); they began to realize that subject and object are inseparably interrelated, that they have been produced by a common history of interaction, and that men and women, unfinished as they are, constitute themselves as subjects precisely by continuing to build the world as object. People thus began to feel responsible for their future. It was up to them as a community to build their world, and by building their world to engage in their own self-transformation. While the thinkers of the Early Enlightenment often saw this process as mechanically determined, the men of the Late Enlightenment discovered in varying ways how much people's freedom, their symbols and dreams, their feelings and intentions, enter into this action. People began to experience themselves as having been produced by an historical process and being responsible for creating their future by a similar process passing through their collective decisions. This is the historical consciousness. Some people who acquired this new consciousness felt themselves as part of an evolutionary process that moved forward toward progress and the great, liberal society, while others had a better understanding of the distortions and discrepancies operative in society and the human mind and hence saw this historical process more in terms of a struggle against opposing powers. Here again some of these felt that, despite these obstacles, history was destined to move forward toward the just, socialist society, while others who recognized the historical process and the struggle against obstacles remained unconvinced that history would inevitably lead toward the humanization of life. Yet all of these outlooks, while different in many ways, share in the same historical self-understanding.

Today, the historical consciousness is no longer confined to a few intellectuals who reflect on the conditions of modern life; it is in fact shared by a growing number of people as the unexpected, latent consequence of *Gesellschaft* on their consciousness. This new self-awareness may still represent a minority trend, for the scientific consciousness continues to predominate, but there are widely acknowledged signs that an increasing number of people understand themselves as responsible for their world and for their future. This development was not foreseen by Toennies and Weber, the great critics of *Gesellschaft*. Today it begins to be widely acknowledged. It was clearly recognized as the emerging consciousness in the documents of Vatican II. "In every group or nation, there is an ever-increasing number of men and women who are conscious that they themselves are the artisans and authors of the culture of their community. . . . Such a development is of paramount importance for the spiritual maturity of the human race. This truth grows clearer if we consider how the world is becoming unified and how we have the duty to build a better world based on truth and justice. Thus we are witnesses of the birth of a new humanism, one in which man is defined first of all by his responsibility toward his brothers and toward history."[23] This is the new cultural consciousness, I hold, in which Christians have experienced Jesus Christ as transformer of culture and interpreted the gospel as a transformist faith.

In this historical consciousness, the traditional imagination presenting reality as two worlds, the human world below and the divine world above, could no longer be entertained. What took place, as I briefly described in the first chapter, was the rejection of this sort of extrinsicism. Hegel was the first thinker to see this clearly, and some Protestant theologians followed him in this; in the Catholic Church this rejection took place by Blondel and some of the so-called Modernists, and since then by the majority of theologians. But even the spiritual experience of the faithful, at least of those involved in modern institutions and situated at the church's critical edge, no longer confirmed the traditional, radical separation of sacred and profane, the divine world and the human. Christians began to experience God, not as the voice from above that called them away from this world to a higher level, but as a transcendent mystery, present in life itself, which summoned people to greater self-knowledge, enabled them to assume responsibility for their world, and moved them forward into the future.

2. This takes us to the second factor responsible for the emergence of transformist religion in the Christian Church, namely the special creativity of the gospel in the face of evil. The gospel of Jesus, so Christians believe, is a power unto salvation. It promises to save us from the enemies of life. It proclaims the coming of God's kingdom that will crush the powers of darkness; it enables us to discern the sin in our midst and to be severed from it; and it permits us, in a limited way, to anticipate God's kingdom in the community of men and women touched by the Spirit. This is the way Christians talk about the gospel. Jesus offers redemption from evil.

But evil changes from age to age. The forces that threaten human life depend on many cultural, political, and personal factors. In every period of history, the de-humanization operative in society has a different face. It is possible, therefore—this is a theological affirmation, though in keeping with the Weberian analysis of religion—that the Christian Church will generate a new response to the form of evil present in its age. I only affirm the possibility of such an event, for it is by no means a necessary consequence or a reaction that can be taken for granted. Since religion, including the Christian religion, is ambiguous, since it is often dominated by ideological trends and troubled by institutional pathologies, it may not produce a creative response at all. The Church may just strengthen its defenses and protest its heritage without any living relationship to its age. This is possible. At the same time, the unexpected, the gratuitous, the marvelous may also happen. Even from a sociological point of view, we admit the possibility of charism. There may emerge in the church charismatic persons (in the Weberian sense) who are in touch with the alienation of the people and who will provide a new imagination that sparks a countervailing movement of innovative, utopian religion. From the theological point of view, we affirm that these special gifts may be the work of the Holy Spirit who enables some Christians to discern more clearly the features of evil and experience in a new way the saving power of the gospel. Breakthrough religion is always related to, and reacting against, the dehumanizing trends in the community. This is true from a Weberian perspective, and it has even more concrete meaning for the Christian theologian.

What I am proposing here is, in traditional theological terms, a theory of doctrinal development. It is of great theological importance to insist that such a development is never simply an adaptation to a new cultural consciousness or to new social conditions of life, but is or ought to be, at the same time, a creative response to the sinful world. Theologians dealing with the development of doctrine often neglect this second aspect. For this reason, they either restrict doctrinal development to logical or psychological deductions from previously held doctrinal formulations, or understand it simply as a translation of the Christian message into a new cultural consciousness. To my mind, the first tendency loses sight of the creativity of the gospel and cannot account for the transpositions of doctrine that have taken place in the church from time to time, and the second tendency is in danger of dissolving the cutting edge of the gospel and losing the sense of divine transcendence. To my mind, it is necessary to take into consideration the face of evil, characteristic of an age, to understand the creative process whereby the meaning of the gospel is renewed. In my writings, I have tried to show that if the face of evil changes in a dramatic way, then there may take place a shift of focus in the understanding of the gospel and this may lead to a radical reinterpretation of traditional teaching.[24] I have also insisted that the Jewish holocaust, which has made the church aware of its anti-Jewish ideology, makes demands on the formulation of its christology. Conservative theologians who oppose the reinterpretation of doctrine accuse the innovators of giving in to the spirit of the age and of assimilating the gospel to present cultural ideals and values. What these conservative thinkers overlook is that the transformist faith seeks to counter the evil of the day and understand the gospel as God's judgment on, and deliverance from, the destructive and sinful trends prevalent in contemporary society. By refusing to reinterpret the gospel, the conservative theologians actually show themselves willing to walk with their society, with its economic system and its dominant cultural forms. In my mind, then, as the grimace of evil changes in history, the Christian symbols of salvation take on a new meaning.

What is the face of evil in our times? This is a question that has preoccupied us in this book. We have learned from sociologists and psychologists to become aware of the alienation woven into our technological and industrial society, of the oppression and exploitation created by monopoly capitalism, of the subjugation of women, of the various falsifications of consciousness, of ideological and pathological religion. We are oppressed, and, simultaneously, oppressors, not only through the various institutions that de-humanize us, but also through false symbols that dominate our imagination. More than that, we are the generation after Auschwitz. We have seen the hidden power of certain myths. We have also come to realize that a certain church-centered understanding of Christianity has served as legitimation of the European invasion of other continents, including the Americas, and hence is related to the white man's hegemony in the modern world and his near-monopoly of many of the earth's resources. Thanks to the Enlightenment social sciences, we have been able to discern the structures of domination in our history and to articulate the alienation inflicted on people by society.

The transformist faith described above is the creative response of the gospel to this alienation.

Recommended Readings

Richard Allen, *The Social Passion: Religion and Social Reform in Canada, 1914-28*, University of Toronto Press, Toronto, 1971.

Salem Bland, *The New Christianity*, orig. ed. 1920, University of Toronto Press, Toronto, 1973.

S. A. Burrell, edit., *The Role of Religion in Modern Europe*, New York, 1964.

S. N. Eisenstadt, edit., *The Protestant Ethic and Modernization*, Basic Books, New York, 1968.

Goldwin French, *Parsons and Politics*, Ryerson Press, Toronto, 1962.

Robert Green, edit., *Protestantism and Capitalism: The Weber Thesis and Its Critics*, Heath, Boston, 1961.

Christopher Hill, *Puritanism and Revolution*, Secker & Warburg, London, 1958.

Peter D'Ailly Jones, *The Christian Socialist Revival, 1877-1914*, Princeton University Press, Princeton, N.J., 1968.

Gunter Levy, *Religion and Revolution*, Oxford University Press, New York, 1974.

Ernst Troeltsch, *Protestantism and Progress*, Boston, 1958.

Max Weber, *The Protestant Ethic and the Spirit of Capitalism*, Charles Scribner's Sons, New York, 1958.

Notes

1. For a history of the controversy and the application of Weber's method to other cultures, see S. N. Eisenstadt, editor, *Protestant Ethic and Modernization*, Basic Books, New York, 1968.
2. Cf. chapter V, note 8.
3. Max Weber, *The Sociology of Religion*, Beacon Press, Boston, 1964.
4. *Op. cit.*, Introduction, p. xxx.
5. *From Max Weber*, p. 152; cf. pp. 118-127.
6. Max Weber, *On Charisma and Institution Building*, edit. S. N. Eisenstadt, University of Chicago Press, Chicago, 1968; *From Max Weber*, pp. 245-252.
7. Max Weber, *Theory of Social and Economic Organization*, Free Press, New York, 1968, pp. 329-340. Cf. Robert Nisbet, *The Sociological Tradition*, pp. 141-150.

8. See above, p. 102.

9. See below, p. 282.

10. Robert Merton, "Bureaucratic Structure and Personality," *Reader in Bureaucracy*, edit. R. Merton *et al.*, Free Press, New York, 1952, pp. 361-371.

11. *From Max Weber*, pp. 151-152.

12. Gregory Baum, *Man Becoming*, Herder & Herder, 1970, pp. 235-241.

13. Richard Niebuhr, *Christ and Culture*, Harper & Row, New York, 1951.

14. See above, p. 105.

15. Richard Niebuhr, *Christ and Culture*, p. 218.

16. C. H. Hopkins, *The Rise of the Social Gospel in American Protestantism, 1865-1915*, Yale Univ. Press, New Haven, 1940, p. 320.

17. Richard Allen, *The Social Passion: Religion and Social Reform in Canada, 1914-28*, University of Toronto Press, Toronto, 1973, pp. 7-8.

18. *The Documents of Vatican II*, edit. Walter Abbott, Herder & Herder, New York, 1966, p. 200.

19. *Ibid.*, pp. 213-214.

20. See the "Hartford Appeal for Theological Affirmation," *Worldview*, 18, April 1975, pp. 39-41, and the responses to the Appeal in *Worldview*, 18, May 1975, pp. 22-27, and 18, June 1975, pp. 45-47.

21. Cf. Max Weber, *The Sociology of Religion*, pp. 55-59.

22. *Ibid.*

23. *The Documents of Vatican II*, pp. 260-261.

24. Gregory Baum, *Faith and Doctrine*, Paulist Press, New York, 1969, pp. 101-133.

IX
Critical Theology

This chapter deals with theology. The preceding chapters for the most part began with sociological reflections and only toward the end moved to theological considerations. By "theology" I here refer to its traditional definition as the reflection of believing Christians on their religion. Theology is the critical task of the believing community. Theology then presupposes faith—or, more precisely, theology is an expression of faith and thus enters into the very shape which faith takes in people's lives.

And what is "faith"? Again I here move within the traditional definition. To believe means to receive the message and be open to the gifts that accompany it. To believe means to share with others in the symbols of God and to define one's life orientation out of these. The symbols received in faith initiate the believers into a new self-understanding and relate them in a new way to the world. Faith, mediated by the biblical symbols, is the trusting acknowledgment of a divine mystery graciously operative in human history and creating a community of salvation. Coming to such an acknowledgment depends on the perspective in which we look at the world and open ourselves to the religious tradition, and over this basic approach or attitude we have no direct control. We cannot change, by will power, the angle from which we see our lives. Faith is a gift. People are amazed and marvel when, looking at the world and listening to the inherited religious language, they discover a hidden meaning in their lives and a direction in history and are able to redefine their existence as men and women with a destiny. Theology, then, presupposes and expresses faith. Theology is the reflection of Christians, in conversation with the entire believing community, on the world to which they belong and the religious tradition in which they participate.

It is my contention that Christian theology, after the Enlightenment, assumes a new and important role in the life of the church. Learning from the social sciences and the various critiques of religion, Christian theologians are able to discern the ideological and pathogenic trends in their own religious tradition and then, by opting for a wider meaning of the promised salvation, interpret the Christian gospel as a message of deliverance and reconciliation. The sustained dialogue with the critical thought of the Late Enlightenment I wish to call "critical theology." Critical theology is the critical application of the various theories of alienation to the self-understanding in faith of the Christian Church. This critical method may lead theologians to discover elements of false consciousness in their perception of reality and thus produce a significant change of mind and heart.

Traditional, pre-critical theology studied the Christian religion in the light of its divine gifts. The Christian religion was here understood as a spiritual reality mediated by doctrine and sacraments and expressing itself in the holiness of the faithful. Traditional theologians studied the development of Christian teaching and the meaning of the church's sacramental liturgy. According to the social thinkers, however, religious practice has a profound structural effect on people's lives far beyond the range of faith, hope and love. Religious practice, as we have seen, affects people's personal and social lives in ways that often remain quite hidden from them. The intended effects of the Christian religion may be quite different from the actual consequences. The early Puritans would have been surprised, I suppose, if they had been told that their perception of the gospel mediated an inner dynamics to society that would eventually lead to the rationalization of economic, social and cultural life. We are able to distinguish between what religion intends to be and what it actually produces in people's lives, i.e., between the intention and the consequences of religion. It is the task of critical theology to discern the structural consequences of religious practice, to evaluate them in the light of the church's normative teaching, and to enable the church to restructure its concrete social presence so that its social consequences approach more closely its profession of faith. For what must be in keeping with the Christian gospel is not only the church's teaching and practice but also and especially the actual, concrete effects of this teaching and practice on human history. Critical theology enables the church to assume theological responsibility for its social reality. In this preliminary sense, then, critical theology is "reflection on praxis."

We note that critical theology does not designate a particular area of theology; it does not refer to a theology of society or a theology of human life that accompanies a dogmatic theology concerned with the great moments of divine revelation. No, critical theology refers to a mode of theological reflection that is applicable to every area of theology—moral, dogmatic, ascetical, and so forth. We have observed in the preceding chapters that the doctrine of God, while dealing with a transcendent mystery, has in fact profound, unrecognized (and sometimes alienating) structural implications for social life and personal well-being. We have observed, moreover, that the traditional formulation of christology, while dealing with God's saving act in Jesus, actually had profound, unrecognized and totally unintended structural effects: it has inferiorized the Jews and prepared their social exclusion, and it has led to a church-centered understanding of history and legitimated the white man's colonial invasion of the world. It is the task of critical theology to bring to light the hidden human consequences of doctrine, to raise the consciousness of the believing community in this regard, and to find a manner of proclaiming the church's teaching that has structural consequences in keeping with the gospel. In the case of christology this means that a way of announcing God's Word in Jesus must be found which does not devour other religions but actually makes room for the multiple manifestation of God's grace. There is not a single doctrine of the church, nor a single aspect of spirituality, worship or church life that may be exempted from a critique that distinguishes between intention and structural consequences and evaluates the latter in terms of the gospel. The theological reflections in this book, I may add, have been in this critical mode.

Critical theology, I wish to insist, is not the submission of dogma to an anthropological norm as if the human were the measure of the divine; critical theology is rather the submission of the structural consequences of dogma to the revealed norm of the gospel. Critical theology, we note, is not an exhortative theology that complains of the unwillingness of church members to live up to their moral ideals. Critical theology is not concerned with personal virtue. What are examined by critical theology are the structural consequences of doctrine or institution, i.e., the effects on consciousness and society exerted by religious language and religious forms, quite independent of the subjective intention of the believers. The sociologists have convinced us that the symbolic structure of the imagination is able to legitimate an existing social order and, under certain conditions, even to overcome the present order and help to recreate culture and society. The structural consequences of doctrine and institution belong to the objective order. It is with these that critical theology is concerned.

In this chapter we shall discuss one application of critical theology. Since a major distortion of the Christian religion in the West has been the "privatization" of the gospel,[1] i.e., the excessively individualistic interpretation of the Christian message, and since this privatized religion has legitimated and promoted the atomization of the social order and an economic system of each man for himself, it is the task of critical theology to deprivatize the inherited religion. Such an exercise reveals the hidden political implications of religious language and practice; that is why German theologians, following John Baptist Metz, refer to the deprivatization of Christianity as "political theology."[2]

The theological starting point for the following critique is the thesis, commonly accepted by students of the Bible, that the preaching of Jesus Christ had to do with repentance and the coming of God's kingdom and that it had both *personal and social meaning*. Christ's message was addressed to people personally and collectively. Jesus proclaimed that the kingdom of God was near, that God was about to fulfill his promises made to the ancients and recorded in scripture, and that he himself was a special instrument and servant of God's ultimate victory over the powers of evil. Jesus did not present his work as the salvation of souls; rather he came to usher in a new age that would transform the very structures of human life. After the crucifixion and the Easter event, the disciples believed that in the resurrection the kingdom of God had manifested itself in an irrevocable manner, that God's victory over evil and all the enemies of life was assured, and that the final coming of Jesus as the fulfiller of the divine promises was not far away. In the "between-time," Christ was looked upon as the one in whom the kingdom had been anticipated. He communicated the Spirit to the community. He was the strength, the comfort, the guide, the divine revealer enabling the community to move forward in history, impatient with the enduring power of evil yet joyful that its days were numbered. The Christian message communicates both judgment and new life, and it is addressed to persons as well as society. The gospel has meaning for personal life and social history.

To reduce the Christian message to a truth about personal salvation is to suppress a basic dimension of this message and to transform it into an ideology sanctioning individualism. Critical theology counters the privatizing of the gospel with an effort to regain its double dimension of personal-and-social.

*   *   *

Let us begin with the notion of sin. There can be no doubt that the notion of sin in theological teaching and religious practice has become excessively individualistic. We have looked upon sin as a personal deed, a personal violation of a divine commandment, or an act of infidelity against God, freely committed with deliberation. What we have forgotten is the social dimension of sin, and by doing so we have lost the key for understanding the violence in our history and the collective evil in which we are involved.

In the scriptures, we find a twofold language about sin. There is personal sin knowingly and freely chosen, and there is social sin accompanied by collective blindness. There is sin as deed and sin as illness. An example of personal sin is King David's adultery with Bathsheba and the premeditated murder of her husband, Uriah, in which the king acted against his better judgment and for which he did penance after the prophet's reprimand. Yet even this story had a social message, for the prophets in Israel, accustomed to a confederate structure of authority, were suspicious of the new kingship and feared the possibility of despotism. They made the story of David's sin remind the people that the king was a sinner and that they should never abandon their critical attitude toward royal authority.

Social sin is more especially the topic of the prophetic preaching. There we hear of collective blindness, group-egotism, and the pursuit of a national life that betrays the covenant and violates the divine command. Peculiar to this collective sin is that it is accompanied by so much self-delusion and self-flattery that the people involved in it are not aware of their transgression. We remind the reader of what we have said of the biblical notion of "blindness" in a previous chapter. Here we have sin, understood as infidelity to God and destructive communal action, which is largely due to false consciousness. This sin is like an illness. It destroys us while we are unable to recognize its features and escape its power. While personal conversion to God's voice may make us discover the wayward direction of our collective life, we are quite unable to halt the involvement of society unless the new awareness is shared by the great number of people, and especially by the leaders.

The symbol of the purely private understanding of sin in the Catholic Church is the confessional. The confessional practice goes back to the early middle ages when the Church, in an attempt to civilize the Germanic tribes, imposed detailed rules of conduct on them, regarding as sin the violation of these rules, and transformed the ancient penitential ritual into the regime of private confession. This regime created a highly private, legal, and act-oriented understanding of sin. When the Reformation insisted on a more attitudinal understanding of sin, the Catholic Church defended the medieval confessional practice. This practice has created the imagination among Catholic peoples that sin is always a conscious and free decision to violate a divine commandment. To overcome this privatized understanding of sin and the dangerous political consequences, many contemporary Catholic theologians have recommended that the practice of private confession be replaced by a communal celebration of the sacrament of repentance[3] in which the people, gathered in community, listen to God's word, reflect on their sins, including their objective involvement in the injustices of their institutions, repent of their past, and then receive sacramental absolution—the divine pardon and the divine help to continue their struggle against evil. If Christians are in need of special counseling, and this happens occasionally in every person's life, they should seek out a religious counselor. Self-discovery, important and salvational though it be, need not be linked to the church's public sacramental celebration of conversion and forgiveness.

In the scriptures, sin is both personal and social, and the two aspects are closely interrelated. In our theological tradition, we have presented sin mainly as private. The biblical passages dealing with sin as illness have been too exclusively understood as referring to the inherited sin, the so-called original sin, which expresses the wounded state of human nature into which infants are born and thanks to which they share in the common inclination toward evil. At one time theologians linked this inherited distortion to Adam's transgression in a literal sense and saw in it a quasi-ontological legacy which had no direct connection with the sins of people and the evil of their collective life. Catholics often wondered why the inherited sin, for which we are not responsible, should be called sin at all. In fact, original sin was an embarrassing doctrine for many Christians. Contemporary theologians, on the other hand, have tended to identify the inherited sin with what the Bible calls "the sin of the world"—that is, the structure of evil, built into society, which wounds people, distorts their inclinations, and prompts them to do evil things.[4] The inherited sin, then, is mediated through the unresolved conflicts of parents and families as well as through the discrepancies of the institutional life into which infants are born and in which they grow up. Psychotherapists such as Freud and Laing have shown how the conflicts of parents are handed on as distortions to their children; and Marx and the sociological tradition have demonstrated that institutions create consciousness and that the injustices built into these institutions falsify the awareness of the children socialized into them. The contemporary understanding of original sin brings to light the connection between personal and social sin. Seen in this light, the ancient teaching on original sin contains an important message for our age; it corrects the liberal misunderstanding that we are born into a neutral environment, in which the good is available to us if we so choose. According to the church's teaching this is not so; we are born into a distorted environment, grow up with a partially falsified consciousness, and the good becomes available to us only through many conversions—only as we resist the easy inclination of our wounded nature and follow the challenging, transcendent summons addressed to us in life. In modern *Gesellschaft* in particular, infantile narcissism is reinforced by the individualism of the consumer society. Only as we enter a counter-culture, such as the *ecclesia*, are we able to move toward a less alienating and more reconciled experience of life.

What is social sin? This is an open theological question.[5] I wish to reply to it by relying on the sociological considerations proposed in the preceding chapters. Some theologians define social sin in terms of its object; social sin, then, is an evil act of a person or persons that adversely affects the life of society. Social sin is a deliberate act by one or several people damaging the common good. This certainly is an aspect of social sin, but as a definition it does not situate the sinfulness of the world at a deep enough level. We are still in the realm of conscious and deliberate action and hence remain very close to personal sin. I propose to define social sin with reference to its subject. What is proper to social sin is that its subject is a collectivity. Social sin resides in a group, a community, a people. I am not attempting to revive here the issue of collective guilt which occupied theologians after the war. Can a nation as a whole be guilty of the crimes committed by its government? This is not the question I pose here. What is proper to social sin is that it is not produced by deliberation and free choice. It produces evil consequences but no guilt in the ordinary sense. According to the biblical description, social sin is committed out of blindness. People are involved in destructive action without being aware of it. I wish to recognize several levels in social sin.

The *first* level of social sin is made up of the injustices and dehumanizing trends built into the various institutions—social, political, economic, religious, and others—which embody people's collective life. As people go about doing their daily work and fulfilling their duties, the destructive trends built into their institutions will damage a growing number of persons and eventually destroy their humanity. This evil may go on without anyone being fully aware of it. For the contradictions implicit in institutions remain hidden at first; only after a long time do the negative effects appear, and when they do, they are not immediately recognized as effects of the system. It takes a long time before the discrepancies implicit in institutional life translate themselves into dehumanizing trends and are acknowledged as such.

A *second* level of social sin is made up of the cultural and religious symbols, operative in the imagination and fostered by society, that legitimate and reinforce the unjust institutions and thus intensify the harm done to a growing number of people. Here again we have total ignorance. We have called such symbolic systems "ideologies." Such an ideology would be the privatized notion of sin we are discussing in this chapter, for by persuading people that the source of evil is only in the human heart we make them blind to the destructive trends built into their institutional life.

On a *third* level, social sin refers to the false consciousness created by these institutions and ideologies through which people involve themselves collectively in destructive action as if they were doing the right thing. This false consciousness persuades us that the evil we do is in fact a good thing in keeping with the aim and purpose of our collective well-being. Examples drawn from our own society would be the achievement-orientation of the dominant culture, its individualistic and competitive spirit, and our arrogant collective self-understanding with its implicit racism. This false consciousness exists, of course, in varying degrees of intensity, from a total identification with the dominant trends of society, including all of its social effects, to a greater and greater distancing from these trends accompanied by growing awareness of the injustices implicit in them. It is on this level that the wrestling against social sin begins! For here people, open to the Spirit, are able to become aware of, and turn away from, the taken-for-granted injustices built into their society. This is the level where conversion takes place.

Finally, if my analysis is correct, we have a *fourth* level of social sin which is made up of the collective decisions, generated by the distorted consciousness, which increase the injustices in society and intensify the power of the dehumanizing trends. These collective decisions, made by councils or boards of various kinds, appear as if they are based on free choice and deliberation while in fact they may simply be the rational consequences of the distortions built into the institution and duplicated in consciousness. At the same time, this is the level where personal sin clearly enters into the creation and expansion of social sin. For here, out of conscious evil intention and greed, a person or a group of persons can magnify the evil done by institutional life and give a twist for the worse to human organization.

Examples of this four-leveled sin could be drawn from the preceding chapters. I wish to give a simple illustration from a pastoral letter on world hunger entitled *Sharing Daily Bread*, written by the Canadian bishops in 1974. The main cause of the present impasse, according to this letter, is the free market system. No amount of generosity extended to the underdeveloped nations will significantly alleviate world hunger until the market system itself is changed. "The present market," the bishops write, "is designed primarily to make profits, not to feed people. The supply and distribution of food is determined mainly by effective demand, not by human need. Effective demand is usually defined in terms of ability to pay. Food supplies are often controlled in such a way as to drive up prices on the market." According to this pastoral letter, then, a contradiction is built into the system producing and distributing food. Human society does not plan to grow adequate food supplies for its population and then distribute them to people according to their objective requirements. Instead the institution which regulates the production and delivery of food is defined by a principle, the profit principle, which has no direct relation to people's needs.

What do we conclude from this pastoral letter? Implicit in

the free market for food is an injustice which no amount of personal generosity and good will shall be able to overcome (first level of social sin). What will have to change is the system. In the present society, however, the free market is legitimated by cultural and religious symbols (second level). The very raising of the question is regarded as disloyal and subversive. To indict the market system is to question a sacred element of our society. This system, which is the most pervasive in our society, has created a consciousness in us which makes us cooperate with it, look upon it as an irreplaceable element of society, and apply its principle to ever wider aspects of the social life (third level). What the pastoral letter tried to do was to raise the consciousness of Catholics in regard to the injustice built into the system. At present, the corporate decisions by which the market distributes food can become the locus of free collective sins—that is, of deliberate acts, committed by people for the sake of greater profit, that increase the injustices in the distribution of food (fourth level). As an example the pastoral letter mentions the artificial raising of food prices. Here personal sins give the system a twist for the worse.

It follows from the preceding that a dialectical relationship exists between personal and social sin. The alienating institutions have been created by people with inevitably limited perspective and some sinful inclinations. And the personal sins of the few can make the institutional discrepancies even worse. Personal sin may harm the neighbor or many neighbors, but it may also affect corporate life, distort the institution, and magnify its destructive effects. The sin of a person in authority who uses his power and his organization for selfish ends still belongs to the category of personal sin. Even a joint decision involving several conscious agents in unjust actions is still personal sin, at least to the extent that this decision is truly deliberate. But the structures which such a corporate decision produces, and which in turn, by a logic of their own, inflict alienation on people, are bearers of social sin. These structures will eventually modify the consciousness of the people involved in them and produce an alienating self-understanding. Personal sins, then, by a dialectics that can be analyzed in each case, are translated into social sin.

Human limitations and personal sins compounded have created social sins, and conversely social sins create an environment that promotes personal sins. The damaging of human life through social structures fosters attitudes that lead to personal infidelities and betrayals. The powerful in society are tempted to use their power for self-serving purposes. Economic injustices encourage greed and superficiality among the successful, which easily leads to the sins of the rich; the same injustices produce anger and despair among the disadvantaged, which easily leads to the sins of the poor. Criminals and social outcasts are the shadowy underside of an achievement-oriented society which destroys those who cannot or will not succeed and turns them into human caricatures. It is hard to think of a single personal crime that is not grounded in particular social conditions. To say this is not to belittle personal freedom or to find excuses for wicked deeds. What is asked for here is simply the need for a twofold analysis: an analysis that takes into account both the personal and the social factors.

We touch here upon the weakest side of traditional moral theology. This branch of theology has become so excessively individualistic that it concerns itself almost exclusively with the personal pole of the personal-social dialectics. Here we blame the sinner and condemn the criminal. We leave a certain room for social pressures by taking into account the gradual loss of freedom that reduces culpability. But we do not submit the social environment to the detailed criticism that we apply to the actor. It is true that moral theology today often includes the study of social justice, but it does not relate this social concern to the understanding of personal sin. Yet we have learned from the sociologists that institutions create consciousness and that it is necessary to examine the institutions to which people belong if we want to understand and evaluate their personal thoughts and actions.

In traditional moral theology we only look at the actor. Most people in society, in the climate created by the churches and the dominant culture, evaluate the faults of people in this excessively privatized manner. We complain that newspaper reporters love sensation and distort the news, without analyzing that in a capitalist economy the newspaper business is competitive, that each newspaper must struggle for survival, and that in such a situation questionable means are easily used to attract attention and make people buy more copies. Such a reflection does not intend to reduce individual action to automatic responses to social conditions; what is asked for is simply the double analysis. Our present moral impulse, encouraged by the dominant current in culture and religion, is to find fault exclusively with the actor. We blame the thief and the robber, but we do not at the same time examine the social order. Since our present system calls for the maximization of production and hence demands that we constantly expand our markets, companies spend much money on advertising to influence people's imagination and increase their desire for new goods. Television advertising in particular makes us feel that unless we have this or that commodity, we do not live up to the expectations of society. Some people who have been successfully persuaded by society that to have things is the purpose of human life, and yet are cut off from financial resources, may become cheaters and thieves indeed by free choice, and then the society which has manipulated their imagination sits in judgment over them. Christian theologians at least ought to make the double analysis. If they omit the social analysis, they let society off the hook, encourage the privatizing trend, and draw upon a false understanding of human life. Conversely, if they fail to make the personal analysis, they underestimate personal freedom and in this way also distort the image of human life.

Let me illustrate the two different approaches, the privatizing moral theology and the insistence on double analysis, by recalling the political events of the Canadian October Crisis of 1970, during which two public servants were kidnapped by a small circle of radical separatists, the so-called Quebec Liberation Front. When one of these men, Mr. Laporte, a minister of the Quebec government, was killed, the entire country was profoundly shocked. This had been the first political murder in Canada for over a century. A Catholic bishop of an English-speaking Canadian city made a public statement: we are horrified by the violence in our midst, he said, and may God grant Canada unity and peace. Quite unconsciously, following the privatizing trend, the bishop restricted his analysis to the vio-

lence of the extremists, and when he expressed his hope for
Canada, he took for granted that God was on the side of
national unity. The bishops of Quebec also made a public
statement on that occasion—a joint statement in fact. They too
began by expressing their horror at the violence in the country.
But then, in the second sentence, they asked all Canadians to
reflect on the injustices in their country that made such an
awful crime a possibility. The Quebec bishops chose the double
analysis. They tried to derive a lesson from the cruel event that
would not simply legitimate the *status quo* but raise the awareness of people in regard to the real problems of their country—
in this case the subordinate status of French-Canadians in an
unequal national union. This contrasting response symbolizes
to me a turning point in the Church's moral theology.

This brief reflection on sin as personal-and-social corresponds to the dialectical relationship between consciousness
and society we have mentioned several times in the preceding
chapters. The privatizing trend, overlooking the reciprocal relation between personal transgression and social contradiction,
has therefore a hidden political meaning. It makes people think
that the dreadful things that happen in the world are due to the
evil deeds of single individuals and that there is no need to examine the social institutions to which they belong. The privatizing trend in the Christian religion, supported by the dominant
culture, lets society off the hook—I have used this expression
before—and hence protects institutional power and privilege.
In other words, the privatizing of the gospel is ideological.

When we listen attentively to sermons or carefully read
spiritual literature, we easily detect the notion of sin held by
Christian teachers and discern implicit in it a view of society
and a political message. For if Christian teachers present sin as
those acts and attitudes that undermine the values and the authority of the dominant groups, they make the support of the
present social order a duty of religion. If they prefer obedience
to disobedience, conformity to criticism, modesty to public
controversy, patience to impatient longing for justice, then they
make the gospel a symbolic language for the defense of the
dominant forces in society. Another kind of Christian preaching indicts as sin conformity and compliance with the world.

Sin is here the uncritical surrender to the norms of society and the authority of the inherited institutions. This trend is strongly represented in the New Testament. Jesus initiated his followers to conflict with the existing institutions, including the family. "I have come to cause divisions: for henceforth in one house there will be divided father against son and son against father, mother against daughter and daughter against mother, mother-in-law against daughter-in-law and daughter-in-law against mother-in-law" (Lk. 12:52-53). The preaching of Jesus, in a trend amplified by his followers, accused "the world"—that is, the dominant structures and the received norms—as the principle of evil. We read, "Do not love the world or the things in the world. For if anyone loves the world, the love of the Father is not in him" (1 Jn. 1:15). The world as locus of sin is under the power of darkness (cf. Jn. 12:31; 14:30; 16:11). This is not the only trend in the New Testament. But on the whole we find in biblical preaching a view of sin that includes the personal-and-social and raises questions in regard to the existing institutions. All Christian preaching on sin, we conclude, has a built-in image of society and hence a political message. We have been largely blinded to this by the privatizing trend of our own tradition.

In the Catholic Church the privatization of sin eventually led to the denial that the church as church could be sinful. Since all sin was private it was unnecessary to engage in critical reflection on the church's corporate life. Bishops and popes admitted, of course, that they were personally sinners and in need of divine mercy, but they did not acknowledge that their collective life, embodied in ecclesiastical organizations, was marked by sin and hence in need of an ongoing critique. Systematic criticism of the institution was regarded as disloyal. When people, individually or in groups, left the church, fault was found with them: they were unfaithful, they had betrayed their heritage. What remained unexamined was to what extent the contradictions in the ecclesiastical institution had contributed to this exodus. Similarly, when priests leave in great numbers, churchmen tend to blame them and accuse them of infidelity, without asking the corresponding question regarding the discrepancies in the ecclesiastical institutions that have contributed to the great number of resignations. Once we discover the inseparability of the personal-and-social in human action, and thus the need to deprivatize our religious tradition, we come to realize that a church's unwillingness to subject its corporate life to a systematic and principled critique is the great barrier that prevents it from proclaiming the gospel with power. Some theologians defend the uncritical attitude toward the social reality of the church by appealing to the divine gifts and the divine guidance bestowed upon the community, and hence to the trusting faith that is necessary to make these gifts exert powerful influence among the people. But why should we think that the gifts to the church and our trust in the gospel would be weakened by the community's engagement in self-criticism? One could turn the argument around and pose the question whether the Christians afraid of collective self-criticism are not the ones who lack faith in the divine gifts. Unless we move in the direction of deprivatizing the notion of sin, we are in danger of making the Christian faith a protection against injustices in church and world and thus transforming the religion of Jesus into an ideology.

*　*　*

Once we deprivatize the notion of sin, we must also regain the full, personal-and-social meaning of conversion. For the sake of brevity, I shall only indicate the direction of this theology. According to the biblical message, the divine reply to human sin is judgment and the promise of new life. God's gracious and critical word makes people recognize their sins, calls forth their conversion, enables them to wrestle against the structures of evil, initiates them into a new life of love and dedication, and makes them yearn for the ultimate pacification of humankind. Conversion, therefore, can no longer be understood as the repentant recognition of one's personal sins; included in conversion are the critical recognition of, and the turning away from, the social dimension of sin, present in the various collectivities to which a person belongs. The *metanoia* to which the gospel summons us demands that we examine our own personal lives as well as the injustices and contradictions in the various institutions to which we belong, be they political, economic, educational, ecclesiastical, or whatever. The raising of consciousness in regard to institutional life is part and parcel of the conversion away from sin.

The preaching of personal conversion to Jesus, understood in an individualistic way, as it has been done in many Christian churches, represses one side of the gospel and hence has strongly defensive or even reactionary political implications. For the stress on private conversion makes people blind to the structures of evil in society. People are made to think that the inequities of their society are due to personal sins and can be removed only through the personal conversion of the sinners. What people who stress the conversion to Jesus as their personal savior fail to see is that the evil in society has a twofold root, in the sinful hearts of men and in institutionalized injustices, and that this evil can only be overcome by a movement that includes social change. The stress of Jesus as personal savior is always linked, therefore, to the defense of the political *status quo*. The individualistic religion of traditional evangelical and fundamentalist Christians legitimates the individualism of our economic system, and while they present their message as non-political, it has significant political consequences. The privatization of sin and conversion, fostered in Catholicism by the confessional practice, is promoted in the Protestant churches by the traditional evangelical stress on personal conversion to Jesus. Jesus saves! Today, it is worth noting, we find critical movements not only in the major Christian churches; we also witness the emergence of a left-wing evangelicalism which seeks to recover the social meaning of sin and conversion.[6]

In critical theology it becomes imperative to deprivatize and despiritualize the notion of salvation. Again we can only point in this direction. According to biblical teaching, Jesus is not the savior of souls. Jesus is announced as savior of the world, as bringer of a new age and servant of God's kingdom. When his message convicts people of sin and demands their conversion, this must be understood in terms of the inseparable dialectics of personal-and-social. And when his message promises salvation and mediates it to the believing community then this must be understood in the widest sense as the deliverance of people from all the enemies of life, including the oppression and alienation inflicted on them by the social structures of domination.

The effort to deprivatize the notions of sin, conversion and salvation leads to the recovery of a wider understanding of grace and holiness. For here, too, we do not want to confine the power of God in recreating human life to purely personal transformation; what the gospel promises is that God's presence to men in grace and their response to God in trust and obedience introduce them to a new life of conversion and holiness whose structures anticipate in some way, despite the ongoing need of redemption, the kingdom of love and peace promised for the last days. The new life of holiness then refers to the transforming power of God in history that changes people's hearts and leads them to structural changes. The prayer of Jesus, "Thy kingdom come, thy will be done on earth as it is in heaven," does not simply refer to personal holiness nor simply to the total deliverance of people at the horizon of history, but to the ongoing personal and social conversions by which God's victorious power is anticipated in a sinful world.

Critical theology demands that the language about Jesus and his salvation reflect the two interrelated dimensions of personal-and-social. Such a language is found in the biblical tradition. Such a language is also present in the liturgy. The eucharistic worship mediates the bi-polar understanding of salvation in the Christian Church. For in the eucharist Jesus identifies himself with the believing community: Jesus enters the congregation through his word and sacrament, offers salvation to people in the community, and transforms them into a single body representing redeemed life on this earth. The middle ages saw the emergence of a more individualistic understanding of holy communion as a purely private divine gift to the individual, an approach to the sacrament that profoundly affected Catholic and Protestant forms of worship after the 16th century. The liturgical reforms of the 20th century, in the Catholic Church and some Reformation Churches, have tried to overcome this privatizing trend and recover the social dimension of eucharistic worship. Liturgy is the occasion, or should be the occasion, when Christians grasp more firmly the personal-and-social meaning of salvation.

In some Protestant churches an unfortunate controversy has begun which creates the impression that a basic conflict exists between evangelical concern and social action.[7] Some conservative voices have opposed the social involvement on the part of the churches with the more spiritual stress on Jesus and his salvation. Other conservative voices have expressed the feeling that the churches' social concern dangerously neglects the mystery of divine transcendence. These Christians complain that their church leaders have become too interested in social justice, and that this represents a loss of evangelical substance. This accusation seems unfounded to me. For what the conservative critics call social action is in fact evangelical obedience to Christ and commitment to his personal-and-social salvation. When these critics contrast secular social involvement with their more personal, more spiritual, or more dogmatic religion, they suppose that their own approach is non-political and transcends the historical order. Yet this is illusory, for the privatistic understanding of conversion and grace, implicit in their approach to religion, legitimates the individualism of the dominant political and economic institutions. The stress on evangelism is not above politics: it usually expresses an option in favor of the political *status quo*. In terms of Richard Niebuhr's typology, mentioned in a previous chapter,[8] the conservative critics in the Christian churches object to the transformist understanding of the gospel (Christ, the Transformer of Culture) and try to influence the churches to return to the more conformist understanding of the gospel (Christ and Culture in Paradox) which does not apply the promises of Christ to the future of society. Critical theology insists that the salvation of Jesus Christ has a bi-polar, personal-and-social meaning, and any attempt to leave out one pole distorts the original message.

Christian advocates of social criticism and social action, reacting against the individualistic religion in which they were brought up, occasionally formulate their Christian involvement in a purely secular and moral way and fail to show that their social commitment is related to God's act in Jesus Christ. This is an understandable but unfortunate reaction. The deprivatizing of the gospel does not intend to destroy religious meaning; on the contrary, it seeks to recover religious roots that have been lost and to reawaken hope in divine promises that have been forgotten. The choice that presents itself to Christians is not between a political and a non-political gospel; every religious commitment implies a vision of human life and hence has social meaning and consequences. Today it has become the church's task to assume conscious and critical responsibility for the political implications of its religious teaching and institutional presence.

It is not surprising, therefore, that in the present the division among Christians no longer follows the inherited, confessional boundaries but passes right through the various churches. The cultural crisis has its theological equivalent. Christians are divided, it seems to me, on whether they should regard it as their religious duty to shore up the inherited social consensus and the cultural values that are being questioned, or whether they should join the critical forces in society and work for the re-creation of social life in greater accord with the future promises. The doctrinal discussions of official ecumenism today only too often have a conservative impact. For here Christian churches concentrate on doctrinal controversies of the past instead of listening jointly to the signs of the times in the present cultural crisis. The new questions that confront the churches together will enable them to formulate the meaning of the gospel in the sinful world of our time. The Christians of the 19th century who concentrated on the cultural mission of the church have rightly been criticized for losing a sense of divine transcendence. In many countries of the West, Christians often reflected and acted out of an identification with a successful culture and the interests of the ruling classes. In the second half of the 20th century, on the other hand, the Christians who profess a transformist gospel and have a strong sense of their secular mission have identified rather with the underprivileged sections of society and the hungry nations of the world. This is not an historical setting where the transcendence from the gospel is forgotten. For the extraordinary Christians who courageously walk the way of identification with the poor often find themselves exposed to the contempt of the authorities and marginalized even in their own churches. In this setting, the cross assumes a new meaning in many parts of the world. The lives of courageous Christians, marked by the cross, reveal that society punishes those who utter the truth and hunger and thirst after justice. The critical voices in any society are endangered. The Roman cross on which Jesus died becomes the eloquent symbol of the breakdown and breakthrough, repeatedly necessary in religious, cultural and political traditions for the sake of the wholeness to which mankind is destined. The cross is not the sign standing at the end of history, proclaiming its inevitable failure; the cross is situated at the center of history revealing the cruel suffering inflicted on the prophets and the painful remaking of consciousness and society by all who want to enter into the newness of life. Struggling against the structures of domination, the Christian churches must transcend the controversies that seemed important to them in a previous age and move forward to a new consensus, in keeping with scripture and their history, that responds to the face of evil in our times.

The preceding remarks on the deprivatization of sin and conversion lead us to a better understanding of the nature and task of critical theology. At the beginning of this chapter we defined critical theology as the critical application of the various theories of alienation to the Christian self-understanding. Critical theology is reflection on the church's praxis and enables the church to assume theological responsibility for its social reality. Theologians engaged in this pursuit, we said, may discover elements of distorted consciousness in themselves and be led to a change of mind and heart. Theology is based on conversion. After deprivatizing the notion of sin and conversion, it becomes even clearer that critical theology is based on, and leads to, a critical analysis of the church's institutional context and a turning away from its destructive and sinful trends. The raising of consciousness is at the heart of critical theology. We want to examine the kind of commitment that this implies for the critical theologian and the Christian community in general.

In Latin America the critical reflection on praxis has led to the creation of liberation theology,[9] in which the raising of consciousness, or "conscientization," holds a central place. This approach has even been adopted by the General Conference of Latin American bishops held at Medellín in 1968. To discover the social dimension of sin in their societies, the Latin American Christians focus almost exclusively on economic injustices. Why is this so? The various countries in Latin America are divided into the vast under class of dispossesed people, without access to education and the goods of life, and the small, visible class of wealthy families, the owners of the land and the means of production, who are linked, often as intermediaries, to the international capitalist system, and derive their power, in part at least, from the nations in which the center of capitalism resides. In Latin American countries, there is no broad middle class as we find it in the industrialized countries of Western Europe and North America. The Latin American countries are basically divided into two classes, the rich and the dispossessed, and the radical inequality between these two constitutes the overriding fact of their national existence. The blatant economic injustice determines every form of human association and distorts every expression of social and cultural life. The state becomes purely and simply the protector of the small ruling class. In these countries, then, the economic factor dominates all others—the political order, the cultural trends, the ecclesiastical system, etc. All expressions of society are reflections of the economic order. In this situation, the class domination becomes the key for understanding the misery in which people live and the form which social sin has taken. The Catholic Left in Latin America holds that the class struggle defines the reality of their countries and that conversion, in such a social context, implies an identification with the oppressed class and its struggle for economic justice. The critical Catholics in these countries engage in the education of ordinary people to raise their consciousness in regard to their own exploitation. They want the people to understand the oppression inflicted on them by a small upper class, protected by military and police power, which acts as an instrument of a vast economic system, the center of which lies outside their own continent. But they also want to become more aware how this oppression has falsified their own perception of reality, how they have assimilated the ideological elements of culture and religion, and how they have unknowingly contributed to the stability of the exploitative system.

Liberation theology in Latin America is, in a wider sense, critical reflection on praxis. The praxis which is the object of reflection here includes the dominant social process in which the church as an element of culture participates and the new action flowing from faith and solidarity. Liberation theology is then not a new theological system alongside other such systems; it is not a new, updated body of social teachings; it is, rather, a new mode of reflection that arises from action, modifies people's perception of their world, and thus leads to greater engagement in action. Liberation theology wants to be the theoretic component of the church's identification with the dispossessed class and its active involvement in the movement of liberation.

It is consistent for this Latin American theology to be critical of academic theology and the university system of the successful nations. Theology must not be allowed to become a wisdom restricted to a privileged group nor to reflect the structure of domination that unites teachers and the theology taught in traditional schools. Theology of liberation often presents itself as the work of Christian communities rather than the achievement of professional theologians, even if such theologians occasionally become the spokesmen for these communities. These groups meet at regular intervals over a period of time, discuss what Jesus and his church mean to them in the struggle for liberation, and record, with the help of a secretary, the conversations and critical reflections of the participants. After a certain period of time, the person acting as secretary rereads the remarks that have been made, gives them a certain systematic form, proposes them to the group as the summary of their reflections, and, after their approval, publishes them as liberation theology.

Let me mention another characteristic of the Catholic liberation theology of Latin America. It presupposes throughout that Catholicism is a dominant cultural force on the entire continent, linking the many countries to a common tradition, and possessing a network of communication and influence without parallel.[10] It presupposes, moreover, that the dispossessed people, struggling for justice, in some way belong to the Catholic Church and that the Catholic symbols have retained a place and a power in their imagination. While the Christians of the Catholic Left work in small fellowships, they remain strongly identified with the Catholic tradition, despite their critical stance toward its institutions, and they do not even wish to separate themselves from the alienated and alienating religion of the illiterate people, for it is this historical Catholicism that they perceive as the instrument of liberation on their continent.

Latin American liberation theology cannot be applied as such to the Christians in North America and Western Europe. To restrict the analysis of present social ills to class conflict and the economic factor is, in my view, quite inadequate. This does not mean that it could not be the correct analysis in Latin America! We have said before that the Marxist analysis of social change through the class struggle is a special case, under certain historical circumstances, of Weber's more general theory of social change.[11] The structures of domination in North America undoubtedly include the injustices implicit in the economic system, but they also include other significant factors as independent variables: institutionalized racism, the growing immobility of bureaucratic centralization, the devastation of natural resources through industrial expansion, the exclusion of women from public life, etc. These factors are interrelated. But while these factors in Latin America, according to the Catholic Left, are completely subordinated to the economic system and hence cannot be examined at all apart from the class struggle, in North America they have their own independent destructive influence. In North America, it is not at all clear whether there is a single dominant form of oppression, to which all others are subordinated.

The American radicals of the sixties tried to find a single source from which all forms of exploitation were derived or a single model according to which all forms of oppression could be understood. They turned to the dehumanization created by technocracy or to the oppression inflicted on the black people in the United States.

Many young people in the United States followed Max Weber's famous prophecy of the "iron cage." They were convinced, following Weber rather than Marx, that the institutional reform of society only increases the bureaucratic apparatus and makes the system more unbending and impersonal than before, and that the industrialization and growth of technology increases the power of instrumental reason over the human imagination and makes people into conformist followers of short-range pragmatic and pedestrian goals. They had no hope in a possible reconstruction of modern, industrialized society. For them, technocracy represented the most oppressive trend in modern society, the trend to which the whole of culture was subordinated. Nor could this trend be modified or weakened by a revolutionary shift from the capitalist economy to a centralizing socialism. The young people wanted to opt out of the present society, discover a new and simplified form of life, find access to a more liberated consciousness, and in this way prepare a new mode of human association which could point the way to the future. What these young people did not realize was how much their movement depended on the affluence of American society at that time.

There was, however, another radical analysis of American life based not on the experience of the young idealists but of the suffering of a marginalized people. Since in the United States the exclusion of the black from the political structures and cultural ideals at the very beginning produced a form of oppression that pervaded the entire country and had a visibility painted in black and white on every institution and every community, the black movement for emancipation in the sixties produced a powerful model, according to which other liberation movements in the United States understood themselves. Racial oppression came to be regarded as the symbolic key to all the ills of the country. Since the American consensus excluded the blacks from the definition of American institutions, the black radicals created a language of liberation by inverting the inherited American symbols: America the good became

Amerika the bad, the land of the free became the place of oppression, the home of the brave, the racist land, and God's own country, the Babylon of sin. The black thinkers developed a radical analysis of oppression in terms of negation and conflict that was not derived from Hegel and Marx, but from their own American experience and the biblical symbols of inversion they had learned in childhood, according to which the first shall be last and the last first.[12] Black radicals gave new political meaning to the ancient Exodus language, which remained alive on the American continent through the Protestant dissenters who had left European persecution to find religious and civil liberty on this continent. It was the Negro struggle for effective social and political equality that taught the other liberation movements the terms in which to analyze their own oppression, including the students' protest and the women's movement. Even French-Canadians[13] occasionally turned to the black people in the United States to interpret their inferior position in Canada, even if they usually prefer, living in a British Dominion, to draw their images from colonialism. The racial oppression of Negroes in American history has been made to typify every form of oppression in the United States.

While the model of oppressor and oppressed may be useful to analyze particular forms of injustices, it does not help to analyze the complex interrelation between various forms of oppression, even of racial oppression, in the United States. This complexity is typified in some parts of the country where blacks and Mexican Americans struggle for new recognition and access to resources, not always helping one another but sometimes standing in each other's way. The economic factor has obviously had an enormous influence on the shape of racism and entered into the institutionalized exclusion of blacks and Mexican Americans from the mainstream of society, but economics does not totally account for racism. The American experience has shown, rather, that however important the economic analysis may be, it alone does not suffice to understand the structures of domination of this continent.

It is unrealistic, in my view, to look for a single form of oppression in North America, to which all others are subordinated. What we have is a complex intermeshing of technocratic depersonalization and immobility, economic domination and exploitation, racial exclusion and inferiorization, and other forms including the subjugation of women. Americans will want to listen to their neighbors in the South to learn the effects that their own economic system has on the dependent countries and estimate the devastating influence of "the international imperialism of money."[14] Still, the analysis of social sin in North American will inevitably be complex.

Correspondingly, the commitment to justice and human emancipation, to which Christians are summoned, cannot be expressed by identification with a single movement. To shed light on the North American situation let me turn to Max Weber's theory of social change which, as we saw, tries to account for the conflicts in any society. For Weber, we recall, the dominant social, political and cultural institutions produce reacting, countervailing movements, sparked by charismatic personalities which reflect the alienation inflicted on people by the oppressive institutional trends of the dominant system and, in one way or another, promote significant social, political or cultural changes that promise to deliver people from their suffering. The strength of these countervailing trends depends on the degree of alienation from which people suffer, on the new consciousness which the quest for liberation creates in them and on the adequacy of the new imagination out of which the critical movements are generated. The success of these movements, however, is not guaranteed by historical necessity or, I would add, by divine promises. Still, it is possible that these movements affect the awareness of an ever greater number of people, reach some powerful leaders in society, create provisional institutions that express the new ethos, and ultimately, inducing crisis and polarization, produce significant social change. At the same time, it is also possible that these movements are crushed, or that they become unrealistic and bizarre, or that the pervasive mind-set created by technocratic society does not permit them to get very far. Yet if these countervailing movements express the quest for justice and authentic humanity, then Christians will identify themselves with them— even if the outcome is uncertain.

The raising of consciousness in the complex situation of

North America means the acknowledgment of the multiple forms of exploitation, and the turning away from the social dimension of sin implies an identification with the aims of the emancipatory movements. This commitment inevitably leads Christians to the difficult question how to relate these various movements to one another in a just and justifiable manner. This question, I wish to insist, cannot be solved prior to the commitment to be solidary with them. To remain aloof, to seek a neutral place (which does not exist), to examine these movements simply from the outside without identification with their aims, will not provide the historical standpoint from which these movements and their interrelatic.iship can be understood. To withhold this commitment until the question of their interrelationship has been resolved means never to be able to transcend the dominant system. Conversion away from sin, personal-and-social, implies an identification with the poor, the dispossessed, the disfavored and with the movements toward their emancipation, an identification that precedes the critical reflection on policy and strategy. This is the radical element of the gospel. Faith precedes calculation, conversion to Christ precedes the mapping out of the converted life, solidarity with the least of Christ's brothers and sisters precedes the search for an adequate plan of joining them in their struggle.

Critical theology in North America is, therefore, different from the liberation theologies of Latin America. What is different is the combination of factors in the analysis of social evil, what is different is the form which the political commitment takes, and what is different is, as we shall see, the new imagination drawn from diverse historical experiences. At the same time, structurally these critical theologies are identical. They are reflections on faith-conversion, they are grounded in social commitment in favor of the oppressed, they raise consciousness, lead to social involvement, and regard themselves as the reflective or contemplative component of the liberating human action, in which God is redemptively present to the sinful world.

We find this approach to North American liberation theology in the work of Rosemary Ruether.[15] Since Christ identified himself with the poor, since the gospel has been a critical trend from the beginning, since the church existed partially underground during the first centuries, since the biblical revelation of sin spells out God's judgment on the injustices of the dominant system, and since the gospel has stirred up critical movements within the historical church and created critical styles of the common life, Christians should feel an affinity with the emancipatory movements in society and identify themselves with the quest for liberation and authentic human existence. This identification with the multiple aims of human liberation, beginning in the United States and reaching out to join the struggle for freedom in Latin America and the world in general, has been the foundation of her theological achievement. In Western Europe a similar approach has been adopted by Edward Schillebeeckx. He too demands the church's identification with the emancipatory movements in history.[16] He, too, thinks that the Christians' solidarity with these movements provides the hermeneutical principles for understanding the gospel message and interpreting authentically the meaning of Christian dogma. The whole of theology is here grounded in the church's solidarity with the oppressed. Critical theology, then, cannot be exercised from any historical standpoint whatever; it cannot be produced if theologians seek a neutral place, apart from the conflictual trends in their society. Critical theology can only be created by reflecting Christians who identify with the historical movements from servitude to liberation taking place in their society.

It is at this point that the question arises what the commitment to liberation means in practical, social, and political terms. We saw that the Catholic Left in Latin America felt that in their societies, polarized between a tiny upper class holding all the trump cards and the great mass of dispossessed people, the Christian commitment has revolutionary consequences. In North America with its wider distribution of classes, the oppression of people is due to several intersecting institutional trends, of which the corporate economic system, with free enterprise exercised only on the highest level, is one, though possibly the most important. We have insisted that there are other dehumanizing trends. Committed Christians differ here on the strategy to be chosen for the reconstruction of society and culture. Some Christians have confidence that the existing critical movements will eventually succeed in modifying the political and economic order—*the reformist option*—while others have abandoned this hope, opt for a more radical stance, and long for the breakdown of the present system and the rebirth of a new society—*the radical option*. Both, it seems to me, are genuine forms of Christian commitment. The first option urges Christians to join people in the existing institutions struggling for the introduction of some public ownership into the economic system and social change on various levels of society, while the second option makes Christians seek a more radical life, at the margin of existing social and political institutions, which expresses itself in new forms of fellowship, in simplicity and poverty, anticipating in its non-dominative style and cooperative ventures the structures that ought to define the social order of the future. It is my view that the full Christian witness in North America needs these two options. Neither one by itself embodies the full meaning of the gospel for our times. While these two political decisions may lead Christians along different paths, the two groups need one another to spell out in a living conversation the anguish and the hope that is given in Jesus Christ.

In making their political decisions, whether reformist or radical, Christians have to reflect on the history of their society not only to detect the hidden, destructive ideologies contained in it, but also and especially to regain the positive symbols of their tradition that produced life and vision in the past and that could, in a new key, generate the ideals for a new social order. We saw that the Catholic Left, despite their criticism of the institutional church, united around the Catholic tradition deeply woven into their history in the hope that the ancient symbols of love and unity could create, in a contemporary context, a new imagination of fellowship and promise, and supply the inwardness and the yearning for the reconstruction of the social order. To discuss what this search for inherited symbols means for North America we have to distinguish clearly between Canada and the United States. What this means for Canada has rarely been formulated; the unequal union between the English and the French was so problematic from the beginning that it is not certain whether Canadians actually share in any common symbols derived from their history. I hope to develop theological thoughts on Canadian society in a future essay. Critical theology in the United States will have to foster a new imagination linked to the symbols of American history—the revolution, the declaration of independence, the dream of justice and freedom for all, the ideal of democracy including the democratization of economic life, the new land free of the oppressive character of feudal society. We return here to the question raised in an earlier chapter, in regard to American civil religion. Must the symbols of the American past, linked to the biblical story of exodus and promise, produce a civil religion that legitimates corporate capitalism, racism, imperialism and the American way of life? Or is it possible that these same set of symbols, read out of new and shattering political experiences, produce transcendent values that judge the oppressive elements of American society and generate a new vision of justice, freedom and parity. From the viewpoint of sociology, it seems clear that a new political imagination can only be successful in a people if it ties into the great moments of their history and in some way corresponds to their ancient dreams. It may indeed be derived from the scriptures or some other distant source, but unless it is understood as revealing the significant moments and conflicts of a country's past and presents itself as having been endorsed by previous experience, it will appear an alien insertion, appealing at best to an elite, and remain powerless in people's minds. What counts in any reform movement—or any revolution, for that matter—is to reinterpret the significant images and symbols that people have inherited and thus to regain them and reclaim them as sources for a new social imagination and guides for a new kind of social commitment.

Recommended Readings

Rubem Alves, *A Theology of Human Hope*, Corpus Books, Washington, 1969.

Gustavo Gutierrez, *A Theology of Liberation*, Orbis Books, Mary-knoll, N.Y., 1973.

Frederick Herzog, *Liberation Theology: Liberation in the Light of the Fourth Gospel*, Seabury Press, New York, 1972.

Patrick Kerans, *Sinful Social Structures*, Paulist Press, New York, 1974.

Johannes B. Metz, *Theology of the World*, Herder & Herder, New York, 1969.

Jürgen Moltmann *et al.*, *Religion and Political Theology*, Harper & Row, New York, 1974.

Rosemary Ruether, *Liberation Theology*, Paulist Press, New York, 1972.

Juan Segundo, *A Theology for Artisans of a New Humanity*, 5 vols., Orbis Books, Maryknoll, N.Y., 1973-75.

Notes

1. The language of "privatizing" and "deprivatizing" the gospel was introduced in Catholic theology by John Baptist Metz; see, for instance, "The Church's Social Function in the Light of a 'Political Theology,' " *Concilium*, Vol. 36, Paulist Press, New York, 1968, pp. 3-18. Metz defined "political theology" as "a critical corrective of contemporary theology's tendency to concentrate on the private individual, and at the same time to formulate the eschatological message in the circumstances of our present society" (p. 2). "The reversal of this privatizing tendency," Metz writes, "is the task of political theology" (p. 5).

2. See above, p. 71.

3. For a critical examination of the confessional practice, see the articles in *Sacramental Reconciliation*, edit. E. Schillebeeckx, *Concilium*, Vol. 61, Herder & Herder, New York, 1971.

4. Cf. Peter de Rosa, *Christ and Original Sin*, Bruce, Milwaukee, 1967; A. M. Dubarle, *The Biblical Doctrine of Original Sin*, Herder & Herder, New York, 1965; Karl Rahner, *Hominization: The Evolutionary Origin of Man as a Theological Problem*, Herder, Freiburg, 1965; Piet Schoonenberg, *Man and Sin, A Theological View*, Univ. of Notre Dame Press, Notre Dame, Ind., 1965.

5. The notion of social sin is found in recent ecclesiastical documents. "The riches of Canada are unequally shared. This inequality, which keeps so many people poor, is a social sin" (Statement by the Canadian Catholic bishops, "Sharing National Income," issued on April 12, 1972, *Catholic Mind*, October 1972, p. 59). In the Statement "Justice in the World," issued by the Third Synod of Bishops, 1971, we read, "We have been able to perceive the serious injustices which are building around the world a network of domination, oppression and abuses which stifle freedom." The bishops speak of those "who suffer violence and are oppressed by unjust systems and structures," and include in the church's mission "the liberation from every oppressive situation." They conclude, "Action on behalf of justice and participation in the transformation of the world fully appears to us as a constitutive dimension of the preaching of the gospel" (*The Pope Speaks*, Vol. 16, 1972, p. 377). See Patrick Kerans, *Sinful Social Structures*, Paulist Press, New York, 1974.

6. Cf. R. Pierard, *The Unequal Yoke: Evangelism, Christianity and Political Conservatism*, J.B. Lippincott, Philadelphia, 1970; D. O. Moberg, *The Great Reversal: Evangelism Versus Social Concern*, J. B. Lippincott, Philadelphia, 1972.

7. For an example taken from the Canadian church, see "The Fifteen Affirmations," in "Restating the Inherited Faith," *The United Church Observer*, Vol. 37, June 1974, pp. 8-9. Also cf. chapter VIII, note 20.

8. See above, p. 178.

9. Gustavo Gutierrez, *A Theology of Liberation*, Orbis Books, Maryknoll, N.Y., 1973, pp. 25-32, and Juan Segundo, "Capitalism—Socialism: A Theological Crux," *Concilium*, Vol. 96, Herder & Herder, New York, 1974, pp. 105-123. On Latin American liberation theology, also consult Juan Segundo, *A Theology for Artisans of a New Humanity*, Orbis Books, Maryknoll, N.Y., 1973; Gérard Bessière, "Do Revolutionaries Pray? Testimonies from South America," *Concilium*, Vol. 79, 1972, pp. 109-116; Segundo Galilea, "Spiritual Awakening and Movements of Liberation in Latin America," *Concilium*, Vol. 89, 1973, pp. 129-138; Joseph Barnadas, "Christian Faith and the Colonial Situation in Latin America," *Concilium*, Vol. 90, 1973, pp. 129-136; Gustavo Gutierrez, "Liberation Movements and Theology," *Concilium*, Vol. 93, 1974, pp. 135-146; Juan C. Scannone, "The Theology of Liberation—Evangelical or Ideological?" *ibid.*, pp. 147-156; and the articles in *The Mystical and Political Dimension of the Christian Faith*, edit. Claude Geffré and G. Gutierrez, *Concilium*, Vol. 96, 1974.

10. "La conjoncture internationale, les églises et les chrétiens: une entrevue avec Gonzalo Arroyo," *Relations* (Montréal), Vol. 34, juillet-aout 1974, p. 216.

11. Cf. above, p. 174.

12. Cf. Rosemary Ruether, "A New Political Consciousness," *The Ecumenist*, 8, May-June 1970, pp. 61-64, and "Sad Songs of Zion by the Waters of Babylon," *Event*, September 1971, pp. 18-23.

13. Pierre Vallières, *White Niggers of America* (translation), McClelland and Steward, Toronto, 1969.

14. The expression, "the international imperialism of money," drawn from Pope Pius XI's encyclical *Quadragesimo Anno*, has been used several times in the documents of Pope Paul VI, e.g., *Populorum Progressio*, NCWC News Service, #26.

15. Rosemary Ruether, *Liberation Theology*, Paulist Press, New York, 1972; "Paradoxes of Human Hope: The Messianic Horizon of Church and Society," *Theological Studies*, 13, June 1972, pp. 235-252; "Better Red Than Dead," *The Ecumenist*, 12, Nov.-Dec. 1973, pp. 10-14; "Sexism and Theology of Liberation," *Christian Century*, Dec. 12, 1973, pp. 1224-1229; "Male Clericalism and the Dread of Women," *The Ecumenist*, 13, July-Aug. 1973, pp. 65-69; "Anti-Semitism in Christian Theology," *Theology Today*, 30, Jan. 1974, pp. 365-382; "Crisis in Sex and Race: Black Theology vs. Feminist Theology," *Christianity & Crisis*, 34, April 15, 1974, pp. 67-73; "Rich Nations/Poor Nations and the Exploitation of the Earth," *Dialog*, 13, Summer 1974, pp. 201-207; "The Persecution of Witches: A Case of Agism and Sexism? *Christianity & Crisis*, 34, Dec. 23, 1974, pp. 291-295.

16. "In contemporary society, it is impossible to believe in a Christianity that is not at one with the movement to emancipate mankind": Edward Schillebeeckx, "Critical Theories and Christian Political Commitment," *Concilium*, Vol. 84, 1974, p. 55. Cf. the entire article, *ibid.*, pp. 48-61, and *The Understanding of Faith*, The Seabury Press, New York, 1974, pp. 124-150.

X
Deprivatizing Psychoanalysis: A Digression

In the last chapter the deprivatization of the notion of sin enabled us to come to a clearer understanding of the Christian gospel as revealed, critical social message. Before leaving the topic of deprivatization, I wish to ask whether it is possible to apply similar critical thoughts to psychoanalysis. For the psychotherapeutic tradition beginning with Sigmund Freud is a theory and practice that tends to presuppose a highly private understanding of evil. What causes suffering and turmoil in social relations is personal sickness. Psychotherapy assumes that the reason why people are troubled and engage in destructive action lies in their own unresolved psychic conflicts. Once these conflicts have been resolved in psychotherapeutic practice, people will become peaceful, recover their energies and expand their lives in significant ways. We have here a remarkable parallel to the privatized understanding of religion: the source of evil is situated in the human heart. Only as people through personal conversion are able to leave behind their destructive inclinations will the world become a better place. The critical reflections that try to deprivatize the notion of sin are, therefore, highly relevant for the psychoanalytic tradition.

While Freud himself was not sensitive to the privatizing implications of psychoanalysis, many of his followers were keenly aware of them. They tried to deprivatize the Freudian discoveries and show that illness is not only located in individual persons but also and especially in people's collective existence. Wilhelm Reich was the first who tried to transform psychoanalysis into a politically responsible movement.[1] He tried to show that the oedipal constellation of the family, which according to Freudian psychoanalysis is the matrix of personal psychic evolution, is itself largely the product of the social order to which people belong. The relation of mother and father is determined by social and economic factors, and together, through their interaction, parents act as agents of the social order introducing their children to the roles they have to play as adults in society. It was in the sociological determination of the family that Reich sought a bridge between psychoanalysis and social criticism. Since Reich's early work, the mainstream of psychoanalytic practice has always been accompanied by a Freudian Left that dealt with the political implications of the psychotherapeutic process.

Many psychiatrists are not aware of the political meaning of their practice—as little, we may add, as Christian teachers are aware of the political implications of religious doctrines and personal spirituality. It is perhaps not surprising, therefore, that political thinkers who locate the sources of evil in the contradictions of institutional life often repudiate both psychoanalysis and religion. It is my contention that by doing so these political thinkers fall into a reductionist understanding of human life that in the long run will have damaging social consequences. Critical theology, as we have shown, wants to institute an immanent critique of religion that deprivatizes the spiritual life and brings out the social meaning of divine revelation. And since at this time the psychotherapeutic movement in its various forms has considerable influence on Christian communities and the formulation of their ideals, it is the task of critical theology to ask whether the quest for personal healing can be made socially aware and politically responsible. It is often disturbing to see how easily Christians who have become impatient with the legal forms of religion turn to highly privatizing spiritual trends for inner renewal; such privatizing trends are found in some charismatic prayer meetings as well as in some forms of the psychotherapeutic movement. Since I myself have defended the position that Christian spirituality after Freud must be in dialogue with psychotherapy and take into account the psychoanalytic critique of religion, and since I have advocated that Christian preachers learn to proclaim the gospel in a way that does not stir up psychic guilt and protect infantile passivity but rather promotes psychic healing,[2] I wish to spell out more clearly the hidden political implications of Freudian psychiatry and at least refer to the attempts of the Freudian Left to deprivatize psychotherapy.

Let me look at six tendencies in classical Freudian psychoanalysis that foster political passivity in the patients and hence reinforce the existing social order. The first such tendency, already mentioned above, is to look for the cause of the patient's predicament in his own disturbed psychic life. You are in trouble because you are sick. A man who bears hostile feelings toward his superior and suffers from depressions whenever he comes to the office may consult a psychiatrist. He is unable to function at work, he says, and he is greatly disturbed in his private life by the obsessive preoccupation with his superior. It is likely that the psychiatrist will pay little attention to the dehumanizing circumstances prevailing at the office and to the rational foundation of the patient's anger. Sensing the intense hostility the psychiatrist will ask the patient about his relationship to his father and help him to recover the repressed infantile hatred which he has transferred on his superior. The patient gets the impression that his present predicament has nothing to do with what happens at the office; the source of his misery is in himself. He has projected his own inner turmoil on the social situation. Such an approach to therapy leads to privatization. It lets the institution off the hook; it stops people from engaging in social criticism.

The psychotherapists of the Left want people to analyze their situation in psychic as well as social terms. They attach great importance to the psychological analysis, for if indeed the angers of a person are largely determined by repressed infantile hostility, then such a person will not be in touch with the real situation of her life and choose ineffective ways of wrestling against her real oppressor. Unless a person deals with her unresolved conflicts, she will engage in pseudo-aggression, that is, she will wrestle against the oppressive forces with means that ultimately make her lose. People can adopt a realistic strategy only if they clearly see what they are wrestling against and are free of purely personal projections.

The second ideological tendency of mainstream psycho-analysis, related to the first, is that it all too easily turns people's eyes away from the present to the past. You are in trouble because you are still a baby. What really troubles you, the patient may be told, is not the situation in which you live at this time, but the unresolved conflicts of your own childhood. Psychoanalysis could make people concentrate on their past and use their encounters with present events only to recall the significant childhood experiences. The continual attention to the past could keep people from struggling to change the conditions of life in the present. Psychoanalysis, then, tends to legitimate withdrawal from political involvement.

Again the Freudian Left would reply that this turn to the past, if correctly understood and practiced, need not withdraw people from their involvement in the present. On the contrary, it is precisely the therapeutic attention to the past that eventually enables people to be fully present to their social situation. For as long as we are caught in psychic traps set in the past, our imagination and our energy remain absorbed by them and we have very little freedom to wrestle with present problems. Only as we encounter our childhood, come to greater self-knowledge, and relive some of the unresolved infantile conflicts are we able to leave the past behind and dedicate ourselves with all our power to deal with present issues.

The third legitimating tendency of psychoanalysis is the readiness of the therapist to regard the social world to which the patient belongs as the reality to which he must learn to adjust. Freud himself chose an unfortunate vocabulary: he distinguished between "the pleasure principle" operative in people's instinctual orientation and "the reality principle" confronting people externally in the social order. It was the task of therapy to enable a person to find enough satisfaction in his quest for pleasure so that he could live reasonably happy within the given reality. It has been pointed out by many social critics that by applying the metaphysical word of reality to the social world full of contradictions, Freud gave it a dignity it did not deserve and legitimated the existing institutions of society in the eyes of his cultured followers. Let me add that Freud also used the word "reality" in a more comprehensive and less ideological sense. For he calls "education toward reality" the commitment of humanist and scientist to serve humanity and means by this an education that delivers people from their illusions and opens them to the total human reality. And if there is hope in this world—and Freud was not always sure of this—then it is found in the truthful contact with the human reality—a reality which in this context includes the instinctual basis of human life.

The Freudian Left does not think that the reactionary tendency to invest the given social order with the aura of reality demands the total repudiation of psychoanalysis. Left-wing therapists and theoreticians think that it is possible to formulate the purpose of depth psychology and a person's healing encounter with his own unconscious, without making the social order the reality principle and without speaking of health as an adaptation to this reality. In left-wing therapy one speaks not of adaptation but of creativity produced by the therapeutic process, a creativity which enables people to live their lives with greater power and engage in social action to change the structures of their world. While society provides the framework necessary for personal life and offers symbols and values that enter into the very making of the person, this social framework itself has been created by people and hence is capable of being modified in turn. We recall here the dialectical relationship between persons and society we have defended throughout this book. It is possible to understand psychotherapy as a practice by which people are freed for personal creativity as a source of social change.

This leads us to a fourth legitimating trend in Freudian psychoanalysis, at least as it is understood by many theoreticians and practitioners, according to which the instincts are the biological drives in human life that must be tamed by the strictures of civilization. This trend is taken from the writings of Freud in which he looks upon culture, art and religion as compulsive neuroses, that is, as products of repressed, and hence inevitably distorted, instinctual energies. While it is the task of therapy to bring people in touch with the demands of their instinctual life and thus help them overcome the repression responsible for their neurotic behavior, Freud feared that such a liberation would impose heavy burdens on society. According to his theory of collective neurosis, a fully therapeutic community would fall apart. People would satisfy their instinctual desires, and no energy would be left for cultural achievements, for art and religion, for the building of a humanistic civilization. Culture may indeed be a compulsive neurosis, but without such a repressive force, Freud feared, people would return to tribal existence and social life would become less human and less humane. For the sake of art and morality, then, one must defend the repressions imposed by society. The instincts may be the source of personal satisfaction and well-being, but they are the enemy of social life. This tendency in psychoanalysis lends itself to the legitimation of the inherited institutions, even if they impose severe injustices on personal life. Law and order are the only guarantee for humanistic culture.

While it is possible to defend the above viewpoint from Freud's own writings, there are also insights in Freud that permit a more hopeful interpretation of human culture. Psychoanalysis need not become a legitimation of law and order. In particular, I wish to refer to Freud's distinction between repression and sublimation. Repression is the exclusion from consciousness of instinctual drives. Because of the severe restrictions and sanctions imposed by the social order, some instinctual energies are kept by force in the unconscious and from there seek expression and release in personal life without being detected. The repressed energies will return in disguise so that the acting person will not recognize them. The return of the repressed implies a certain amount of deceit and distortion. The cultural activity produced by repression will embody the broken connection to the instincts and thus promote illness rather than health in the community. On the other hand, Freud speaks of sublimation in different terms. Sublimation is also an unconscious process, but unlike repression it is not produced by social pressure and threats of punishment. Sublimation produces cultural activity based on a person's contact with his instinctual drives. Sublimation mediates libidinal energy to the creation of culture and the humanization of life. How does this take place? In his book on Leonardo da Vinci,[3] Freud explains that sublimation takes place whenever cultural activity, science and art are grounded in and prolong childhood inclinations which, in infancy, served the libidinal or sexual drive. Leonardo's inexhaustible scientific curiosity, which made him anticipate the technological developments of centuries, was grounded, energetically speaking, in the restless and anguished curiosity of the infant, born out of wedlock, unsure about who his mother and father were. Freud, needless to say, does not derive Leonardo's genius from his infantile experience; Freud clearly recognizes in creative freedom a phenomenon that cannot be explained psychoanalytically.[4] But he claims that in his cultural activity Leonardo was nourished by his instinctual energies. His creativity was not based on repression and neurosis. In this book, Freud is quite willing to universalize his observations. There is a cultural activity, he claims, that is not based on a break with the libido (repression) but on the continuity with libidinal energies (sublimation), a continuity which cannot be consciously chosen nor imposed by social restrictions. How then can this continuity be consciously sought? Freud hints that sublimation is possible when people trust their deepest wishes. For if we break the false wishes created in us by society and get in touch with, and follow, the deeper wishes that reveal the orientation of the infancy libidinal energies, we may be led to a cultural creativity, art or religion that prolongs the libidinal bent in us and enables us to sublimate our instinctual energies in the creation of a humane society. Such cultural activity is not based on distortion nor does it promote sickness in the community. In order to discover this sort of sublimation what is needed is not a more restrictive society, but personal freedom and a supportive community.

The fifth ideological tendency in Freudian psychoanalysis is the defense of authoritarianism. Opposition to authority is easily seen as an unresolved oedipal conflict. This authoritarian structure is symbolized by the very encounter between therapist and patient. The therapist enables the patient through transference to regress to childhood and relive the unresolved infantile conflicts in the therapeutic encounter. In this situation the therapist has great power. This is symbolized in orthodox psychoanalysis by the aloofness of the therapist, by his physical position in the room, and by his refusal to reveal himself as a human being with problems of his own. In this situation the patient is altogether dependent on the therapist, for it is the therapist who knows better than the patient what is good for the patient's own growth and development. If the patient sees things differently, the therapist is able to interpret this as resistance, as neurotic resentment against authority, as a sign of an unresolved oedipal complex. It is true, of course, that infants depend on the parent in this unprotected way, but when such a dependency structure is recommended and utilized later in life, after the maturing of the person, it tends to legitimate the structures of authority and suggest that the way to personal and social well-being is found in submission to the right and benevolent authority. There is in fact a certain similarity between priest and therapist. For both are parent figures, both create relations of dependency, both are mediators of powers that transcend them, and both set themselves apart and hide their personal lives. Critical theology which detects the authoritarian trend in classical psychoanalysis is also sensitive to the political implication of ecclesiastical ministry. For here, too, authoritarian leadership of the priesthood easily becomes a symbolic legitimation of authoritarianism in society. This is perhaps one of the most serious problems of Roman Catholicism.

Left-wing psychotherapists have become very sensitive to the problem of authoritarianism and look for various ways to overcome this ideological trend in their practice. While they recognize the importance of transference and regression and realize that therapists who revealed their own lives to a patient in the early stages would place an enormous burden on him, they do their best to move the patient to a stage where he can resolve the transference and enter into a new, more adult relationship to his therapist. Left-wing therapists eventually want to present themselves as brothers or sisters rather than as parent. This is true especially of group therapy where all participants are patients and therapists at the same time and where, after a certain period, even the directing therapist feels free to speak of her own personal problems and receive the help of the group members. Left-wing therapists—I suppose like left-wing priests—try to find a style of exercising authority which clearly reveals that they are as much in need of the truth they communicate as are others, and that together with others they constitute a community of mediation where all give and all receive.

Finally we come to the sixth and possibly the gravest ideological trend in classical psychoanalysis, namely, the anti-feminist element. Freud had stereotyped the roles of men and women in society according to the middle class ideals of his own age, and labeled all attempts of women to emancipate themselves from the exclusion from education and leadership as penis envy or repressed hatred of their own sex. In addition to this, Freud acknowledged a profound resentment in people, transcending their oedipal fears and angers, derived from the baby's helpless dependence on the pre-oedipal mother, which tries to explain and thus legitimate the unrelenting subjugation of women in society. Psychoanalysis can be understood as saying that there is ultimately no remedy for this subjugation. Some contemporary thinkers hold that this anti-feminism is so deeply rooted in the fibers of psychoanalysis that no immanent critique can ever deliver it from this vice. The essential psychoanalytic language is anti-feminist.

At the same time when Freud discovered the unconscious, the basic processes of repression, defense, projection and sublimation, the central role of sexuality and the power of dreams and symbols, he raised the self-understanding of Western men and women in a significant and irreversible way so that even those who refute the great discoveries use arguments drawn from his psychoanalytic theory. While Freud brutally legitimates the subjugation of women, he also enables us to analyze the false consciousness that has produced such a subjugation. According to writers such as Herbert Marcuse[5] and Rosemary Ruether,[6] Freud's account of the repressive nature of society and the dependent status of women is quite truthful if understood as a description of the social situation contemporary to him. The culture that is compulsive neurosis is the one produced by bourgeois industrial society. If Freud's study of the psychology of women is read not as a normative but simply an historical account, then it reveals what Western bourgeois society has made of women. Freud's description of society and the place of women can be understood as an indictment of the inherited social order. The Freudian Left, therefore, does not reject the psychoanalytic tradition altogether, for it may be possible, by an immanent critique, to free psychoanalysis from its anti-feminist ideology. Psychotherapy could help people to break the hold which the society-defined notions of men and women have over them and reach out for the greater freedom where each person can express herself in fidelity to her inner powers.

The preceding remarks on the ideological trends in psychoanalysis and the attempts of the Freudian Left to overcome them bring out the relevance of critical theology to the psychotherapeutic movement. These remarks wanted to show, however briefly, that it is possible to be involved in this movement with a profound sense of political responsibility.

It is possible to deprivatize Freud's great discoveries. It is possible to read psychoanalysis as shedding light on personal as well as collective life. Some Freudians deny that psychoanalysis can be applied to society. Yet when Freud himself early in his career began to interpret dreams, he discovered a principle that is equally applicable to all spontaneous, imaginative, expressive creations. It is possible to search for repression and sickness—and their resolution—in art and poetry, in all forms of cultural self-expression. And to the extent that social institutions are an expression of people's spontaneous inclinations, they too can be interpreted in psychoanalytic terms and seen as the locus of repressive and liberating forces. This book is not the place for attempting such a critical reading of society. What is important in this context is the recognition that the deprivatization of psychoanalysis, like the deprivatization of the Christian gospel, leads to social theory.

Recommended Readings

Jerome Agel, edit., *The Radical Therapist*, Ballantine Books, New York, 1971.

Philip Lichtenberger, *Psychoanalysis: Radical or Conservative?* Springer Publ., New York, 1969.

Sharon MacIsaac, *Freud and Original Sin*, Paulist Press, New York, 1974.

Herbert Marcuse, *Eros and Civilization*, Vintage Books, New York, 1962.

Paul Robinson, *The Freudian Left*, Harper & Row, New York, 1969.

Hendrik Ruitenbeek, edit., *Going Crazy*, Bantam Books, New York, 1972.

Notes

1. Cf. Paul Robinson, "Wilhelm Reich," *The Freudian Left*, Harper & Row, New York, 1969, pp. 9-73.
2. Cf. Gregory Baum, *Man Becoming*, pp. 127-161. Also "Pastoral Psychology: The Future," *Journal of Pastoral Counseling*, Vol. 7, Spring-Summer 1972, pp. 60-68.
3. Sigmund Freud, *Leonardo da Vinci*, Vintage Books, New York, 1961, pp. 25-30.
4. *Ibid.*, pp. 118-119.
5. Herbert Marcuse, *Eros and Civilization*, Vintage Books, New York, 1962, pp. 71-95.
6. Rosemary Ruether, "Freud and Jung: Friends or Enemies of Women?" *The New Woman and the New Earth*, Seabury Press, New York, 1975, chapter 6.

XI
Symbol and Theology

In the preceding chapters we have repeatedly spoken of symbols. We have seen that Durkheim and Freud, though Positivists, discovered the symbolic dimension of human life and history. We have seen that symbols which dominate people's imagination have great power in the creation of their future. The young Hegel showed us the alienating power of certain religious symbols. This theme has been greatly developed in Marxian sociology. Yet even the sociologists who followed this trend often returned to the Hegelian question whether there are not some religious symbols that have reconciling effects. In particular we spoke of Karl Mannheim's distinction between ideological and utopian forms of imagination. Since symbols are so central for the theological understanding of religion and its ambiguity, we shall examine various concepts of symbols, show how they are interrelated, and apply them to the presentation of the Christian message.

1. Symbols are signs or images addressed to people's memories. This is the first and most obvious meaning of symbol (s 1). Symbols make us remember important events of our personal and social histories and hence evoke the emotions associated with these events. Sometimes we only feel the mood connected with these symbols without being able to name the occurrences or experiences to which they refer. Symbols summon forth hidden memories and past dreams and tie them into our present aspirations. Symbols are able to frighten us if they make us concentrate on the awful in the world, and they can console and delight us when they sum up the moments of freedom and joy we have experienced and link them to the future promises contained in the stories out of which we define our

lives. Symbols then have power over the emotions. At the same time the meaning of the symbol (s 1) is largely dependent on a person's subjective response. The same symbol may invoke a variety of moods. And because symbols (s 1) are imprecise in meaning and unpredictable in their effects, some people feel that they easily confuse clear thinking. By appealing to memory and emotions, symbols might disguise the true proportions of an issue and prevent cool and critical intelligence from laying hold of the problem and solving it.

In Catholic life, symbols of this kind (s 1) have played a considerable part. Catholics decorate their churches and even their homes to recall to one another the great events of salvation and create a mood conducive to faith and openness. Protestant Christians who have put more stress on critical intellect have tended to be suspicious of symbols as mediators of religious emotions. Despite the sobriety of modern scientific and technological culture, Catholicism has struggled to retain its appreciation of symbols. Symbols continue to be important in Catholic liturgy and life. They appear, at this first level of analysis, as artifacts designed for a purpose. Symbols (s 1) remain external to the believers; they simply appeal to their memories and emotions. Symbols (s 1) are not free of a certain ambiguity; their meaning and power remain highly subjective. They may disguise reality as much as they may bring out its fuller significance.

The Modernists at the turn of the century tried to overcome the excessively conceptual understanding of religious truth that characterized Catholic theology in the age of Enlightenment. Dogma for these religious thinkers was largely symbolic. But they found it difficult to elaborate an adequate notion of symbol and hence often understood symbol in the most obvious sense as sign or image addressed to the memory (s 1). Religious truth, then, was not an idea to be assimilated by the intelligence but a symbol (s 1) evoking strong feelings that would lead people to religious commitment and holy living. The power of religion was not through the mind but through the heart. This, at least, is how the Modernists were read. If these scholars had been left at peace to examine the nature of symbols, they would have profited from the discovery of the symbolic on the part of the social thinkers of their day and eventually found a more adequate understanding of symbol for their theology.

2. This takes us to the second meaning of symbol, one we have previously drawn from the thought of Sigmund Freud. Symbol (s 2) here signifies a story or an event of any kind that reveals the hidden depth, in the encounter with which we undergo significant transformation. For Freud, we recall, such symbols emerge in dreams. Here the story reveals a person's unconscious conflicts and wishes and by deciphering the dream and working through its message, the person may be significantly changed and may experience healing. The symbol in this context is not external to the people whose lives it transforms. And while it may have several meanings and messages, it is not imprecise in any of them. The symbol (s 2) reveals and clarifies the hidden structure of reality. It mediates an encounter between a person and his or her unconscious life; in this the symbol could never be replaced by a concept or idea. The symbol is not an approximation of the truth to be replaced by a more precise objectification produced by the intelligence; it is the proper and unique mode in which the hidden structure of reality can be disclosed to the human mind.

We have suggested above that this concept of symbol (s 2) has been used by contemporary Catholic theologians to gain a better understanding of divine revelation.[1] For the majority of Catholic theologians, following Maurice Blondel, have rejected the extrinsicist understanding of revelation as a truth uttered into human life from a divine world apart from it; they have rather come to regard revelation as the manifestation of God's hidden self-communication in human life and history. The divine presence operative in human life from the beginning in a hidden way has become manifest in Israel and finally in Jesus Christ who came and is to come. In this perspective Jesus Christ is a symbol (s 2). What is revealed in the man Jesus is the hidden divine structure of human history. In him, the believers encounter the hidden truth about themselves and their destiny. In Jesus, the believers discover the nature and power of sin as opposition to truth, in him they recognize the hidden face of God made visible, in him they grasp the communal and

universal nature of redemption, in him they are able to communicate with the divine ground out of which they move forward into the future, and in him they meet the divine horizon
toward which they are summoned. To say that Jesus is God is
to say that in Jesus who came and is yet to come, the ultimate
meaning and destiny of human life is being made manifest.

In this second sense of the word symbol (s 2), then, it is
possible to say that Christian truth is symbolic. Christian truth
reveals the hidden structure of human life and by doing so significantly transforms the self-understanding of those who receive it. This understanding of symbol differs from the previous, external notion of symbol (s 1) which remained
imprecise and subjective. Christian truth has definite meaning
because it illuminates the hidden aspects of human life and
redirects man's history and self-definition.

How apt the notion of symbol (s 2) is for the understanding of Christian truth appears when we consider that the
main thrust of Christ's preaching had to do with the kingdom
of God, the reign which had been promised, which was about to
be realized, of which Christ was the servant and which in
some sense was anticipated in his own life. The message of the
kingdom is symbolic (s 2). This message does not deal with a
reality apart from human life; it reveals rather the truth about
a reality partially present in human history and urging it forward as principle of transformation. The kingdom makes
known the divine judgment on the sinful world and discloses
the divine presence to this same world, freeing people from
their sins and moving them forward to a more abundant life.
The reign of God is a symbol (s 2) revealing the ambiguity of
the present existence and the graciousness situated at its core
as a pull forward toward a more human future. Symbol (s 2)
here discloses the hidden structure of reality.

3. In the writings of the young Hegel we found a third understanding of symbol. Symbols (s 3) are the structures of the
imagination that affect the way in which people perceive the
given and respond to it. According to Hegel, we recall, certain
religious symbols induced alienation in the lives of people and
created an oppressive, exploitative society. Hegel's position has
sometimes been interpreted as an idealism that attributes inor-

dinate powers to the human mind. Yet a reading of Hegel more in line with the sociological tradition recognizes him as a social thinker who clearly saw that the human world is not fixed, that it has been produced by people, and that the symbols dominating their imagination had a profound effect on the world they created. The patterns governing the imagination make people select what they regard as significant aspects of life, combine them into meaningful wholes of one sort or another, connect them with values, and relate them to a vision of the future. In this perspective, human experience itself is not a datum presented to the mind but a phenomenon partially created by the mind. According to the classical view, experience takes place in the senses, and only after the impressions have been received are they presented to the mind as objects of reflection. According to the sociological view, however, experience involves the creativity of the mind. Experience has a structure in which the symbols governing the imagination have a creative part. The selecting, uniting and orienting produced by the imagination enter into the very content of experience. The world of experience to which we belong is in part produced by the symbolic structure of the mind.

According to the same sociological perspective, men's response to the world is also determined by the symbols operative in their imagination. For not only do these symbols order the perception of the world, they also link this perception to the values and purposes that determine human action. These symbols define the vision of life out of which people operate and thus orient their actions in a certain direction. Symbols guide people in their encounter with the world as well as their response to it. Experience in this perspective is always a mediation of the past into the future; it is always directed, it is always creative. And the organ responsible for this direction and creativity is the symbolic structure of the imagination. Hegel was not a philosopher who exaggerated the power of ideas; he was a social thinker who understood the power of the imagination in the mediation of experience and the creation of the world.

We realize that this understanding of the human mind is a departure from classical philosophy which looked upon human reason as radically distinct from the senses and, secondly, which supposed that the structure of the human mind was identical in all people. It was then commonly held that we all have the same concepts, that we all enjoy the identical logic, that we all think the same way. While there may indeed be common logical elements and a common basis of understanding among peoples of different ages and cultures, the sociological perspective clearly recognizes that the human mind itself is historically constituted, that it is created through the mediation of symbolic structures which are derived from a particular social history. Different historical peoples may have distinct mind-sets. While classical philosophy placed the objective basis of truth in the outer world of things and Kantian idealism rooted objectivity in the categories of the mind shared by all men, the sociological perspective recognizes objectivity in neither of these. For the world-which-confronts-us and the-world-which-we-are enter into a dialectical relationship and keep on affecting one another. The symbols in the imagination (s 3) represent one side of this dialectic, namely the part the mind plays in creating the world.

It is admittedly very hard to visualize what is meant by symbols (s 3). We are so used to symbols as something we can look at (s 1) that we find it difficult to conceive of symbols that can never become objects of the mind because they belong to the mind's structure. Symbols, as Paul Ricoeur has often said, are not *that which* but *that through which*. Symbols (s 3) are not signs or images apart from the mind; they are dominant patterns in the imagination that mediate experience and create the world to which we belong.

Can the symbols (s 3) be related to the notion of symbol previously discussed (s 2)? It is certainly possible that the symbols that rule the imagination are in fact symbols that reveal the hidden structure of reality. This makes sense on the sociological level, as we shall see, in connection with the fourth meaning of symbol. And it also makes sense on a deeper ontological or even theological level. For it is conceivable that the symbols that rule the mind (s 3) are in fact those that disclose the hidden structure of reality (s 2) and thus lead people into a reconciled life and make them build a world in keeping with the deepest inclination of their being. If symbols (s 2) reveal the divine presence in the universe, then their assimilation in the imagination (s 3) would make people follow the divine will and lead them on the way of salvation. Theologians may therefore usefully combine symbol (s 2) and symbol (s 3) and inquire what this complex view of symbol means for the understanding of faith.

If symbol (s 2) is divine revelation intending to initiate people into the hidden truth, how does it gain power over their lives? How does it become symbol (s 3) recreating the world in which people live? While in classical Catholic theology it was supposed that faith resides in the intelligence, it may be more realistic and ultimately more profound to say that faith resides in the imagination. People have abiding faith if the symbol revealing the divine presence to them begins to dominate their imagination, order their experience and create a new world for them. If divine revelation takes place in symbols, then the imagination is its proper locus in the human mind. This supposition does not deny that the revealed symbols give rise to reflection and are therefore connected with rational content, but this noetic aspect of the symbol is subordinate. Since symbols are not *that which* but *that through which*, what counts in the first place is that the imagination be structured by them.

Even classical theology was well aware that despite its highly conceptual understanding of revelation and faith, what really counted was the vital assimilation of religious truth. In Scholasticism this was expressed by insisting that faith must be alive with hope and love before it mediates divine justification. John Henry Newman created the famous distinction between notional assent and real assent to religious truth.[2] Notional assent was the purely conceptual assimilation of Christian doctrine while real assent included the total commitment of a person and charged the religious ideas with genuine feeling and vitality. This distinction has the weakness that it still puts the substance of faith in the intelligence and makes its power a derivative of the will. The sociological approach to symbols adopted in this chapter makes it clear that the revealed symbols have meaning and power only as they begin to structure the imagination; faith then mediates our experience and guides our responses to reality. This offers a realistic explanation of how Christian revelation transforms human life and history.

Faith is the conversion of the imagination to the revealed symbols, but faith does not stop in the imagination. Since people are intelligent, it is inevitable that they reflect on the revealed symbols and formulate for themselves some sort of conceptual image of reality, including the divine dimension. Symbols lead to doctrine. Yet such doctrine is always derived and approximate. Such doctrine, moreover, is ambivalent, for it may sustain the mind and lead the believer back to the symbol or it may tempt the believer to objectify divine revelation and make God into an object of the human mind. If doctrine is understood as the primary element of faith, it seriously distorts the Christian religion and undermines its saving power.

Let me illustrate these reflections with a concrete example. We believe in Jesus and the kingdom announced by him when we recognize in him and his preaching the revelation of the hidden, divine structure of the universe and permit our imagination to be governed by these symbols. What does this mean? It means that we learn to experience life as problematic, that we become sensitive to the destructive trends in the world and at the same time expect to discern in life itself a gracious presence, a call to rebirth, a movement toward reconciled community. Then the message of the kingdom becomes *that through which* we experience the world and move from past to future in precious moments of freedom. To have faith means that Jesus, in whom the kingdom has become visible, rules the imagination. Jesus then is *that through which* we experience ourselves and other people. All people including ourselves then become infinitely valuable to us since they are seen as the locus of the divine. We discern in our community the sin that opposes true humanity and the gracious dynamic that carries us forward to freedom and reconciliation. But if Jesus and the kingdom were simply *that which* and became objects of the mind assimilated conceptually, they have no power to transform human life. Unless doctrines are derived from symbols alive in the imagination and lead back to them as the primary structure of faith, they disguise the meaning of religion and become obstacles to the truth.

Since we have inherited such a highly conceptual understanding of faith and revelation, it is necessary to insist today
that the entire creed is composed of symbols that are revealed
in historical events (s 2) and become patterns of the imagination (s 3) that recreate human life and reconcile people to
their divine origin and destiny. We will have to learn to present
the creed in this way. Further on, we shall raise the question of
what the message of eternal life means and how it becomes effective in men's lives.

We must now ask how the symbols revealed to us in the
great events of salvation become part of the imagination in
faith. How do we assimilate the symbols as part of our lives?
The churches have answered this question by calling Christians
to participate in the believing community. There they share life
with people enjoying the same vision. There they are surrounded by the signs of faith. There they listen to the scriptures, celebrate the liturgy and study Christian teaching. I suppose that in
this context we may relate the symbol as sign or image (s 1) to
the wider meaning of symbol. For in the process of assuming
the revealed symbols in the imagination, people are greatly
helped by the visible signs and images that are part of Catholic
life and worship. These symbols enliven the imagination. They
make revelation concrete and help to overcome the mind's rational bent to transform religion into a conceptual system.
More than that, these symbols (s 1) have been created by artists who were immersed in the symbolic world (s 3) and for this
reason may disclose much more than we anticipated when we
began these considerations. Symbols (s 1) may themselves be
manifestations of Christian faith and hence appeal to men's
imagination to assimilate the symbols of this faith (s 2 and s 3).
Symbols (s 1) then are not wholly external to the believer. Even
symbols (s 1) may be *that through which* and not simply *that
which*. The manifold meaning of the symbol is, then, no disad-
vantage. For the various notions of symbols presented here are
interrelated and in some sense inseparable. One passes into the
other. And yet, for the sake of clarity, it is worthwhile to make
these distinctions.

In our reading of sociological literature, we found a fourth
meaning of symbol. Symbol (s 4) is the reflection of society in

the mind. If institutions create consciousness, if society creates the mind-set out of which people understand their lives and act, then the coordinates of the imagination are produced by society itself. For Marx, we recall, these symbols were inevitably an inverted image of society; they provided a mental framework in which the existing social order, despite its contradictions, appeared as necessary and rational. For Durkheim, on the other hand, the symbolic structure of the mind was an authentic reflection of life's social matrix. The shared values and aspirations of society expressed themselves in symbolic form and generated a shared mental life and eventually a common religion. But whether sociologists regard society mainly as oppressive system or mainly as the social matrix of life, they all appreciate the effect of institutions on consciousness. The social structures of society, the political institutions in which we live, the processes of production and the economic system—all have a profound influence on the mental make-up of people and create the basic imagination through which people perceive and respond to the world.

Is this understanding of symbol (s 4) in contradiction with the previous types (s 2 and s 3)? From many observations made in this study the answer to this question is clear. Since there is a dialectical relationship between mind and society, it is possible to regard the genesis of symbols from two different viewpoints, one as derived from sharing personal imagination and the other as produced by the social institutions into which people are socialized. Both aspects deserve to be studied.

It is possible to adopt a Weberian perspective and study the creation of new symbolic gestures revealing a hidden message and the gradual assimilation of these symbols in the imagination of more and more people until they succeed in recreating society according to the new vision. Or it is possible to pursue a Marxian-Durkheimian perspective and study the society and the symbolic mind-set it creates, and only then turn to the possible modifications of these symbols through the particular place people occupy in this society, through the action in which they engage, and eventually through the religious experiences they enjoy. Here the line of analysis moved from the common mind-set created by society to the particular symbols people in fact adopt as their own. Karl Mannheim has shown that while society provides the common symbolic coordinates for perceiving the world, it is possible within this context to follow ideological symbols that protect the inherited order or to identify with utopian symbols that summon people to social change. Both the ideological and the countervailing symbols are in some sense generated by the dominant social order and reflect its structure either by confirming or questioning it. It follows from this that even though consciousness is created by the society to which we belong, there is room within that setting for creative religious symbols which are related to the inherited mind-set as sacred legitimation or as sacred critique, or as a mixture of both.

These two perspectives, the Weberian and the Marxian-Durkheimian, are not contradictory; they are dialectically related. For if we begin with individual persons, then we must realize that their minds have been historically constituted by participation in their social history; and if we begin with society we must realize that this society is not a given but has been produced by people acting in common. There is no way of escaping the dialectics.

What does this fourth type of symbol signify for theology? In the first place it is important for theologians to realize that the symbolic mind-set is never wholly created by the religious tradition but that it depends substantially upon the material conditions of life and its cultural expressions. We found it impossible to agree with Marx that religion is purely and simply the ideological inversion of the social order, or with Durkheim that it is purely and simply the celebration of the depth dimension of society. Society is not all of one piece, nor is religion. Consciousness is created by material factors as well as cultural and symbolic ones in some dialectical relation. Since the mind's basic symbolic structure is created by society and the place people occupy in it, religion must be understood within this context as confirming or modifying this basic structure. Religion, in other words, is always a secondary socialization process. Religious symbols must be understood in the context of the society in which they are proclaimed and celebrated and hence vary in meaning and power in accordance with this historical context. This is an important hermeneutical principle for the study of religious symbols.

Can this fourth type of symbol also be a religious symbol? It is conceivable that religious symbols (s 2 and s 3) eventually create a perfect community which embodies them in its social structure. To the extent that this is achieved, I suppose, children born into this community will be initiated into the religious symbols by their very participation in the social life. Yet since the Christian gospel sets itself off from the society and transcends it, it is impossible for Christian symbols to be wholly identified with the symbols of the social order.

The consideration of symbols (s 4) leads to an important ecclesiological principle. We become aware that the structure of the church has an effect on the consciousness of its members. The organization, the power relations, and the social architecture of a religious community profoundly affect the religious symbols in which the believers understand themselves and their common calling. For instance, the organizational fact that in the Catholic Church power, on every level, is exercised by a single man over the community and that team responsibility remains almost unknown has a profound effect on the religious perception of Catholics. The church's institutional life at worship and at every organizational level generates a religious imagination that modifies in a significant way the perception of the divinely revealed symbols. These institutional effects on the religious consciousness could even introduce conflicts or contradictions between the organized church and its message. In a critical ecclesiology it would be important to examine whether the church's organization in some way reflects the symbols proclaimed in the Christian message. Talcott Parsons has called this "the symbolic adequacy"[3] of church organizations. Churches engaged in testing and critically reviewing their collective life must ask themselves whether their institutional life in some way embodies the self-understanding proclaimed by them and hence whether the mind-set created by these institutions (s 4) is in keeping with the symbols (s 2 and s 3) derived from divine revelation. For instance, if a church presents itself as a worldwide brotherhood and sisterhood of the Spirit, created by faith and baptism, it is difficult to reconcile this with purely regional boundaries of the ecclesiastical organization (as we find it in the national churches) or with the existence of a separated priestly class (as we find in some highly sacramental churches) or with an authority structure that sets one man, one male in fact, over a whole community and separates him from the fellowship (as we find in the Catholic Church). The question can be raised whether the religious consciousness of Christians is more strongly determined by the symbols proclaimed or by the symbols embodied in the ecclesiastical institutions. There can be no doubt that the revealed symbols (s 2) which come to rule the imagination of believers and eventually affect their action in society (s 3) ought also to find expression in the institutional reality of the church (s 4) and hence support the power of these symbols in the Christian community.

Since the several meanings of symbol (s 1, s 2, s 3, s 4) are interrelated and affect one another, it is possible to summarize them in a single notion of symbol used in the widest sense. This allows us to say without further qualifications that symbols find expression in stories and visible images, that they reveal the structure of reality, that they operate in the imagination, and that they enter into the creation of the social reality. Social science considerations have enabled us to say the kind of things that the great philosophers of religion—Cassirer, Voegelin, Ricoeur, Eliade—have said about symbols and assign a concrete meaning to many propositions about symbols which at first glance sound vague and poetic and sometimes even contradictory. Symbols give meaning to life, symbols constitute the human world, symbols create the concrete human mind, symbols raise questions about the world and make people critical of their environment, symbols initiate people into the divine reality, symbols mediate divine salvation, symbols are the substance of religion, etc. Since it is hard to find a bridge from traditional Catholic theology with its weak meaning of symbol to the great philosophers of the symbolic, we have used social science considerations to provide an analytical understanding of symbol that enables us to assign a more precise meaning (in terms of s 1, s 2, s 3, s 4) to the above-mentioned propositions on symbols. Symbol in the wide sense, then, is a rich and complex notion, yet not vague and undefined. It does not make sense to say that something is "only" symbolic as if calling something symbolic meant that it was not real. No, used in the widest sense, the symbol is part of present historical reality and, in fact, transcends it.

* * *

Using the word in this wide sense, we affirm that religious truth and in particular divine revelation is symbolic. And by calling it symbolic rather than conceptual we attribute more rather than less power to it. From several preceding observations we have noted that dogma or doctrine is derived from symbols and intends to lead back to symbols. It is inevitable that intelligent human beings reflect on the symbols in which they look at the world and in which they celebrate their vision of reality, and try as best they can to project these symbols in conceptual forms. Men do this to clarify the symbols, to protect them against falsification, and to derive from them a philosophy of life or *Weltanschauung*. The more rational the culture, the greater the need to translate the symbols into conceptual terms and to relate them to knowledge of the world and its history, coming from scientific and philosophical investigations. What is important, however, is that dogma or doctrine will eventually be translated back into symbolic form and nourish the religion as a lived, personal and social reality. For by itself dogma or doctrine has no power. The cognitive element by itself does not mediate salvation. If dogma becomes severed from the symbols it was intended to clarify and protect, it generates a purely conceptual understanding of reality and sets itself up as an obstacle to the Christian religion. If doctrine is regarded as independent from the symbolic order and understood simply in conceptual terms—and who will deny that this happens often—then religion is turned into a closed system of ideas, an unbelievable superstructure, and loses its power to illumine and transform human existence. Robert Bellah has called this trend "the objectivist fallacy."[4] In order to secure for religion an objective place in a highly rational culture, Christians have been tempted to objectify their faith as a system of dogmas to be believed.

The great Christian theologians of the past have been aware of the objectivist fallacy, even if they have not wrestled against it strongly enough and protected the Christian community from it. But they did stress the unknowability of God and the incommensurability of doctrine and the divine mystery. The great theologians were aware of the analogous nature of dogmatic propositions, and they insisted that the doctrines of the Christian religion must be understood in their interconnectedness as proclaiming and mediating the single and undivided mystery of God's self-communication. In the 20th century, moreover, some Christian theologians have become keenly aware that doctrine is relative to culture and history and that consequently the Christian message must be reformulated again and again as the church moves from one age to another. They have recognized that dogmas designed to protect Christian truth are not definitive propositions but stand in need of an ongoing reinterpretation. Finally, modern Catholic theology has become more aware that Christian doctrine refers not to a sacred reality apart from history, but to the deepest dimension of historical reality as its matrix, élan, and horizon. Doctrines are not cognitive statements offering information about another world but religious language that mediates access to the divine ground and the divine orientation of human existence. What is being discovered is that Christian truth is salvational: doctrines communicate salvation only if they are understood as derived from symbols and leading back to symbols. Dogmas make sense only if we find the place they occupy in the telling of the Christian story and the symbols revealed in Jesus Christ.[5]

After these remarks I am ready to make a clear distinction between the objectivist and the symbolic understanding of divine revelation and plead for the adoption of the latter. The objectivist approach regards revelation as primarily cognitive and the Christian religion as a system of truths, while the symbolic approach understands revelation in symbolic terms (the word is here used in its strong sense) and the Christian religion as a set of symbols, which people assimilate and celebrate, and out of which they define their lives and create their world. In the age of science and rationalism the Christian church put an ever greater emphasis on the cognitive dimension of Christianity. Christians shared with their culture the view that the world was a finished reality, a closed background, over against which people lived their personal and social lives. Divine revelation became for them additional information about this visible world and new information about a superior, invisible world. For contemporary social thinkers however the world is not a given; the world is personally and socially constructed in a process, in which symbols play a constitutive part. The symbolic understanding of revelation, as I have indicated, does not reject the validity of dogmas, but it understands them in the context of the symbolic. Apart from this context, they are empty and unbelievable. This has been Paul Tillich's theological approach to Christian revelation,[6] and in more recent years this approach has been adopted by Andrew Greeley.[7]

This symbolic approach, in my view, does not invalidate the historical foundation of Christianity, nor—for that matter —of any other historical religion. There is no reason to regard it as intrinsically impossible that the hidden structure of reality should reveal itself in specific historical events, such as the Exodus or the Christ-event, and that the trusting encounter with these events, through stories and their ritual celebration, should introduce people to the revealed symbols and enable them to live their lives and make their world out of these symbols. For this reason I have some hesitation to follow Robert Bellah when he adds to the distinction between the objectivist and symbolic views the idea that the objectivists affirm the historical basis of their faith while the symbolists reject it.[8] This addition, as I see it, crosses a new line. The symbolic approach to Christian theology acknowledges that something marvelous and unaccountable really happened in history which, when accompanied by a new word, revealed to people the meaning of their lives and enabled them to recreate their social existence. And this happened through symbols.

* * *

In this chapter we have examined several notions of symbols, largely drawn from social science literature, and applied them in the exercise of Christian theology. Let us now return to more strictly sociological considerations. The various notions of symbols mentioned above have led sociologists to elaborate a clear and sociologically useful concept of religion. Needless to say, not all symbols are religious. Symbols are religious when they relate people to the totality of life, when they link the details of life to an ultimate destiny. Robert Bellah offered an abbreviated definition of religion as "a set of symbolic forms and acts that relate man to the ultimate conditions of his existence."[9] This is a definition of religion that does not mention the experience of the sacred nor include any reference to divinity or gods. According to this view of religion, followed by a great number of sociologists, religious symbols are patterns of world interpretation, dominating the imagination; they are celebrated in ritual and thus reinforce the imaginative conceptualization of the world; they become embodied in the religious community or even in the social institutions in which people live; they produce the coordinates of men's perception of the world and the orientation of their action. A more elaborate definition of religion, in line with this approach, is given by Clifford Geertz: "Religion is a system of symbols which act to establish powerful, pervasive and long-lasting moods and motivations in men, by formulating conceptions of a general order of existence and clothing these conceptions with such an aura of factuality that the moods and motivations seem uniquely realistic."[10] Religion here offers the total view, it integrates every detail of life into the wider picture, it invests the struggle for existence with special meaning, it is a source of action and creates a style of life. In this sense, religion deals with the ultimate.

This definition of religion is not without its problems, and it is not surprising that there are sociologists who advocate a different approach to the study of religion. In particular, as we noted, the definition mentions neither religious experience nor the sacred. The definition is so wide that it includes in the notion of religion any secular movement committed to a total world interpretation. Is dogmatic Marxism a religion? Some sociologists, following this line of thought, even regard the modern scientific world views as an invisible religion operative in society.[11] According to the above definition, one might go so far as to say that every person, and every collectivity, has a kind of religion. Every person acts out of a symbolic understanding of reality, even if this remains unarticulated. And the same may be said of a community engaged in collective decisions and a common involvement in a wider social context. Every country has its civil religion. Implicit in action is theodicy. This sounds plausible for sociologists in the Durkheimian tradition, but even Max Weber entertained the view that people's response to evil has built into it a theodicy of some kind.[12] People, either collectively or personally, are bound to make some unconditional decisions; they will base their life orientation on an ultimate.

This wide definition of religion, incidentally, has been utilized by Christian religious thinkers, by Paul Tillich[13] and in recent years by Andrew Greeley.[14] Since every person is religious, the question that preoccupies the theologian is not whether people believe in God but what kind of divinity they actually worship. The gods are universal. From a Christian point of view, however, people have only two basic choices—either they believe in the true God or they are idolaters. This, at least, is Paul Tillich's approach.[15] Either people worship the ultimate and unconditioned source and destiny of human life, the Alpha and Omega of existence, or they absolutize partial aspects of the world with devastating consequences for themselves and others. Andrew Greeley, coming from the Catholic tradition, is not as preoccupied with idolatry as a central category of sin; he takes a more lenient attitude toward the many religions of the human community. While he, too, holds that the worship of the true God, who spoke in Israel and Jesus Christ, is normative religion, he is much more ready to see the divine mystery expressing itself in one way or another in the various symbolizations created by people's responses to the problems of life. People's quest for meaning and quest for belonging are never wholly devoid of some divine graciousness. Tillich and Greeley agree that concrete religion is always ambiguous, but for Greeley, following the Catholic tradition, true and authentic religion is not exclusively the surrender to the God beyond God, nor is inauthentic religion immediately the deadly fall into idolatry.

It is my view that if a definition of religion leads to the conclusion that every person is religious, it is simply too wide. There is no religion without some acknowledged religious experience. From our discussion in the first part of this chapter it is easy to show how the encounter of the sacred is in fact related to religion defined as symbol system of world interpretation. As soon as we ask how the new symbol is produced and how it is communicated to people, we have to start speaking of religious experience. Symbols, we said earlier, include the over-powering manifestation of the hidden structure of reality. We called this symbol (s 2). The encounter with this manifestation is religious experience. Max Weber, we recall, tried to deal with religious experience in terms of charism. There are moments in people's lives when they are in touch with a reality that transcends the proportions of their day-to-day existence, moments when they are powerfully addressed, overcome in some way, and made to look at the world from a new perspective. Sociologists study religious experience to discover its effect on people's self-understanding, on their style of life and their action in the world. In other words, sociologists wonder what kind of symbolic language religious experiences produce. They recognize first of all the powerful ecstatic experiences of the founders of religions, which created the symbol systems out of which the various religious traditions define themselves. Then they recognize the important charismatic experiences of the great personalities in these religions, through which the inherited religious traditions were vivified, reformed and reoriented. Then they acknowledge the religious experience, in varying degrees of intensity, found in the ordinary followers of these religions. Religious people live out of the symbolic forms and rituals into which their religion has initiated them; their religious experiences are mediated by the inherited symbols and they usually confirm their religious faith and make them live more deeply out of their own symbolic tradition.

Religious experience, in the great personalities and in the ordinary believers, makes the world religions into vital, flexible and creative movements in history. Religious experience, out of changed social and political circumstances, points to new meaning in the inherited symbols and becomes the experiential basis for reinterpreting traditional religious teaching. Thanks to new religious experiences, the traditional religious stories and rites bring forth new meaning that enable people, living in changing conditions, to wrestle with the problems confronting them and pass from death to life or from paralysis to vitality. The great religions bear within themselves the sources for their own regeneration. The great world religions have produced countervailing trends within their own boundaries, they have produced their own tradition of self-criticism, and they have again and again been able to bring forth, from their essential symbolism, new and unexpected meaning empowering people to respond, out of their religious heritage, to changed historical conditions. In this sense, the world religions are auto-regenerative movements, for which there are no parallels in history.

* * *

The sociologists who study religion as symbols of ultimacy come to such a positive evaluation of religion that theologians find it easy to be in dialogue with them. At the same time, some of these sociologists do not acknowledge the divine presence. Emile Durkheim, for instance, was an atheist who appreciated religion as the self-symbolization of society-coming-to-be and regarded the transcendent as a reality proportionate to social life. In the last analysis, Durkheim was a reductionist. This is true of many other sociologists. But does sociology have to be reductionist? Are sociologists, by the very methods they employ, led to deny the divine presence and translate religion into purely secular categories? Must sociologists eventually look upon religion as "nothing but" something else? This raises the important question of the relationship between sociology and theology.

While the relation of sociology and theology (or sociology and faith) is a complex issue that deserves a book-length treatment, we must make a few remarks about it in this chapter. Why is this issue so complex? It is impossible to find a simple formula relating sociology and theology because neither of these branches of knowledge is a unified human science, operating out of a clearly defined set of principles and following a universally recognized methodology. Sociology, for one, is divided into many different fields of interest, such as sociology of religion, sociology of organization, sociology of knowledge, etc., each of which demands special methodologies and each of which relates to theology in a different way. More than that, sociology includes many different theoretic approaches which are at odds with one another and give rise to important controversies. Because of the conflictual nature of sociology (leaving aside the problematic unity of theology), I have defended the view that it is impossible to find a single theoretical formulation of the relationship between sociology and theology.[16]

Let me single out one famous controversy among sociologists, to which I attach great importance and without which it is impossible to examine the relationship between sociology and faith. Several times in this book I have already alluded to the distinction between a sociology that presents itself as value-free and objective, and a sociology that, following a hermeneutic approach, regards social science as inevitably dependent on the researchers' historical standpoint and social ideals. Objective sociology (sociology O) demands that researchers abandon their personal preferences, assume an attitude of detachment, seek demonstrable and universally acceptable conclusions, and —in many instances—assimilate their methods of research as much as possible to the natural sciences. Hermeneutic sociology (sociology H) also demands that researchers abandon bias and prejudice and seek demonstrations that are universally valid; yet hermeneutic sociology insists that unless researchers clarify their historical relationship to the object they study (for instance, masters studying their servants or competitors their rivals) and unless they become conscious of the ideal of society they carry in their minds, their conclusions, however objective in appearance, will inevitably be distorted. According to sociology H, value-neutral sociology is an illusion. The sighting, sifting, reading, and systematizing of data depend on a set of presuppositions that should be examined and for which researchers must assume human responsibility. In many cases it can be shown that the scholars who sincerely claim to be value-free have actually identified with the dominant values of their society. In particular, since the vision of what human life ought to be like (a view of human nature) inevitably flows into sociological research and reflection, a social science project will either promote the well-being of the human community or simply reinforce the present system with its discrepancies.[17] Sociology H is in quest of a new objectivity. From the hermeneutic point of view, objective sociological truth is not a precise conceptual replica of the social object under study, which would only help to reify this object, legitimate it in people's minds, and arrest the dynamic thrust of history; objective truth must be a conceptual grasp of the object that includes its forward movement. Sociology H relates science and commitment and holds that the search for sociological truth is at the same time an act of transforming society.

The distinction between sociology O and sociology H emerged in the 20th century with the growing impact of the natural sciences on sociological research. The classical sociologists did not raise the question of values in the same way. Emile Durkheim, for instance, thought he could combine a moderate Positivism with a passionate commitment to social values. The controversy between objective and hermeneutical human science emerged in Germany at the beginning of the 20th century, but its importance for sociology appeared only after the ideal of the natural sciences had strongly influenced sociology, severed it from history, and made it scientific, abstract, and universal. In North America sociology O, in its various forms, predominates at universities and research institutes. Hermeneutical sociology exists as an important countervailing trend, sometimes called critical sociology, which integrates a humanistic and/or Marxian perspective into sociological research and defends a positive relation between science and commitment.[18]

The distinction between these two sociological orientations undoubtedly has implications for the sociology of religion and its relation to theology. If we follow the principles of sociology O, then sociology is value-neutral, unrelated to the personal convictions of the researcher, and hence has no intrinsic relation to theology whatever. This approach rightly claims autonomy for the sociology of religion and demands non-interference from theologians committed to a particular religion; at the same time, it does not sufficiently recognize the influence of personal presuppositions on sociological research and the impossibility of presuppositionless science. We find this objective sociological approach in Peter Berger's *The Sacred Canopy*.[19] While Peter Berger is by no means an empiricist-oriented, scientific sociologist (neither Positivist nor Functionalist), he does strongly opt in favor of sociology O. For him the essential perspective of sociological theory is that religion can be understood as a human project, grounded in particular infrastructures of human history, without reference to the effects, good and bad, which religion may have on human life. The researchers recognize of course that from their point of view religion does have these diverse consequences, but they must keep their evaluation strictly apart from the theoretical analysis of religion and remain value-free and objective. The researchers, moreover, must adopt an ontological agnosticism; they must engage in a sociological study of religion as if it did not matter whether or not religion was grounded in a transcendent reality. Once the sociological analysis has been completed and stands up under criticism of fellow sociologists, theologians or the sociologists thinking as believers may then apply the sociological theory to a better understanding of the religion to which they are committed. Peter Berger recommends that theologians study sociology and make use of the approved results of the sociology of religion for a better understanding of their own religious tradition. But the theologian as theologian cannot join the strictly value-neutral and uncommitted conversation among sociologists.

Much can be said in favor of this approach to the relation of sociology and theology. It certainly has been necessary for sociologists of religion to vindicate the independence of their discipline and to defend themselves against theologians who, in the name of dogma, wanted to tell sociologists from outside their discipline how to interpret certain phenomena or where the limits of their science are. It is not so long ago that theologians were suspicious of sociologists on principle. The above approach is also reassuring to theologians since here the sociology of religion professes its own limitations and promises not to reach beyond its value-neutral scope nor to interfere with the theological task of evaluation and discernment.

At the same time, it seems to me, this theory presupposes a unity of sociological method that is not actually found in departments of sociology. It has been my experience that sociologists disagree among themselves on basic issues. In fact, the theologians who listen to sociologists discussing among themselves the theoretical foundation of their science will soon witness the emergence of issues that make sense to them, as theologians, and permit them to join in the discussion. For instance, the famous debate between sociology O and sociology H transcends the field of sociology narrowly defined and joins a discussion carried on in the human sciences, in history, philosophy and theology. It seems to me, therefore, that, seeing the breadth of sociology and the conflictual trends within it, it is impossible to stake out clearly defined boundary lines between sociology and theology. The more fundamental the issue, the closer the relation between these two branches of knowledge. This is in fact in keeping with the perspective of sociology H.

What, then, are the implications of sociology H for the sociology of religion? Here the separation between sociology and theology are not as clearly defined. Following the hermeneutical method, the sociologists do not want to make the sociology of religion the reification and legitimation of the existing religion; they will rather situate this religion and its social impact in an understanding of what human life is meant to be and analyze religion along lines that enable them to distinguish between, and evaluate, its various trends. Thus Marxian sociologists have been able to detect as no others the ideological elements in religious traditions; at the same time, their commitment to a special view of history made them insensitive, at least until recently, to the utopian trends in religion. In our entire study we have been greatly impressed by the intention of the great social thinkers to find categories for distinguishing between the diverse religious trends and for estimating the effect of these trends on human well-being and the overcoming of alienation. From my first reading of the classical sociologists I have been struck by the humanist perspective from which they wrote and the dream of humanity which gave them a passionate concern. While these authors, beginning with Tocqueville, tried to overcome prejudices and free themselves from their inherited ideas, and in this sense aspired after value-free science, they were nonetheless committed to human values and convinced that their own studies would promote the well-being of the human community. Max Weber insisted on the value-free nature of sociology to protect the social scientists at the German universities from a government making claims of loyalty on them.

Because of the link between science and commitment in the perspective of sociology H, it seems to me unlikely that faith in the substance of the great religions should make no difference at all in the sociological investigations of these religions. The faith of sociologists that a religious tradition expresses something of the divine creates a special sensitivity to this religion, a greater awareness of its hidden meanings, and above all a sense of its forward movement. I find the ontological agnosticism recommended by Peter Berger difficult to visualize. I am more persuaded by Robert Bellah's alternative attempt to take the religious conviction of sociologists seriously and estimate its effects on their analytical understanding of religion.[20] Bellah distinguishes between the "symbolic reductionism" of sociologists like Durkheim who recognize religion as an indispensable symbolic dimension of human existence but ultimately translatable into purely secular terms proportionate to society, and the "symbolic realism" of sociologists who also appreciate religion as symbols of ultimacy yet systematically refuse to reduce them to "nothing but" human projections. According to Bellah the symbolic reductionists on some level fail in their sociological grasp of religion. Only symbolic realists are able to do justice, within the limits of the discipline, to the religious phenomenon. If I understand Bellah correctly, he does not claim that symbolic realists have faith in the divine presence; he describes their commitment more modestly as the radical refusal to reduce religion to a purely secular phenomenon. This transcends ontological agnosticism. Symbolic realists, by their refusal to become reductionists, acknowledge a conception of human life, of which the deepest dimension remains hidden, lies beyond the grasp of science, manifests itself in the world religions, and finds expression in people's personal quest for self-transcendence. If sociological analysis is carried out from this perspective, it is quite possible that sociology and theology move along the same line and theology appears as the critical prolongation of sociological concepts. At several instances in this book I have used sociological insights in this way. In particular, the sociological discovery of the symbolic and the fully developed sociology of the symbol have produced a view of religion that can be fruitfully extended and applied in Christian theology.

Recommended Readings

Frederick Dillistone, edit., *Myth and Symbols*, S.P.C.K., London, 1966.

———, *Traditional Symbols and the Contemporary World*, Epworth Press, London, 1973.

Mary Douglas, *Natural Symbols*, Barrie & Rockcliff, London, 1970.

Mircea Eliade, *Images and Symbols*, Sheed & Ward, New York, 1969.

Thomas Fawcett, *The Symbolic Language of Religion*, S.C.M., London, 1970.

Clifford Geertz, *Islam Observed*, Yale University Press, New Haven, 1968.

Andrew Greeley, *The New Agenda*, Doubleday, New York, 1973.

Paul Ricoeur, *The Symbolism of Evil*, Harper & Row, New York, 1967.

Notes

1. Cf. above, p. 119.
2. John Henry Newman, *The Grammar of Assent*, Doubleday, New York, 1955, pp. 86-92.

3. Talcott Parsons, *The Structure of Social Action*, Free Press, New York, 1968, p. 158.

4. Robert Bellah, *Beyond Belief*, Harper & Row, New York, 1970, p. 220.

5. Cf. John Kirby, "Symbols and Dogmatism: Voeglin's Distinction," *The Ecumenist*, 13, Jan.-Feb. 1975, pp. 26-31.

6. Paul Tillich, *Systematic Theology*, Vol. I, University of Chicago Press, Chicago, 1951, pp. 131, 240-244.

7. Andrew Greeley, *What a Modern Catholic Believes about God*, Thomas More Press, Chicago, 1971, pp. 37-54. Cf. G. Baum's Foreword to A. Greeley's *The New Agenda*, Doubleday, New York, 1973, especially pp. 22-32.

8. Robert Bellah, *Beyond Belief*, pp. 220-221.

9. *Ibid.*, p. 21.

10. Clifford Geertz, "Religion as a Cultural System," *The Religious Situation 1968*, edit. D. C. Cutler, Beacon Press, Boston, 1968, p. 643.

11. Cf. Thomas Luckmann, *The Invisible Religion*, Macmillan, London, 1967.

12. "The problem of theodicy has been solved in various ways. These solutions stand in the closest relationship both to the forms assumed by the god-concept and to the conception of sin and salvation crystallized in particular social groups": Max Weber, *The Sociology of Religion*, p. 139.

13. Paul Tillich, *Theology of Culture*, Oxford University Press, New York, 1964, pp. 5-9; *Systematic Theology*, Vol. III, University of Chicago Press, Chicago, 1963, pp. 157-161.

14. Cf. Andrew Greeley, *What a Modern Catholic Believes about God*, pp. 18-36; also *The Jesus Myth*, Doubleday, New York, 1971, and *The Sinai Myth*, Doubleday, New York, 1972.

15. Cf. Paul Tillich, *Systematic Theology*, Vol. I, University of Chicago Press, Chicago, 1951, p. 13.

16. Gregory Baum, "Sociology and Theology," *Concilium*, Vol. 91, pp. 22-31.

17. Cf. Gregory Baum, "Science and Commitment: Historical Truth According to Ernst Troeltsch," *Journal of Philosophy of the Social Sciences*, Vol. 1, 1971, pp. 259-277.

18. Cf. Alvin Gouldner, *The Coming Crisis of Western Sociology*, Basic Books, New York, 1970; Irving Horowitz, edit., *The New Sociology*, Oxford University Press, New York, 1964; Robert Friedrichs, *A Sociology of Sociology*, Free Press, New York, 1970; Trent Schroyer, *The Critique of Domination*, George Braziller, New York,

1973; John O'Neil, *Making Sense Together: An Introduction to Wild Sociology*, Harper & Row, New York, 1974; cf. also Martin Jay's influential *The Dialectical Imagination*, Little, Brown and Company, Boston, 1973, which introduced the social thought of the original Frankfort School to North American audiences.

19. Peter Berger, *The Sacred Canopy*, pp. 179-188.

20. Robert Bellah, *Beyond Belief*, pp. 246-257.

XII
Heaven as
Revealed Utopia

The great critics of religion have looked upon the Christian teaching on the kingdom of God and the expectation of eternal life as principal causes of human alienation. Otherworldliness, according to these critics, leads to the contempt of this world. The hope for an eternal life of happiness makes people shrug their shoulders in regard to their earthly existence and prevents them from becoming concerned enough about their situation to change the conditions of social life. The doctrine of eternal life trivializes history. A religion that promises heaven consoles people in their misery, makes them patient and meek, and protects the existing social and political orders. Otherworldly religion, according to this analysis, is inevitably ideological.

Since critical theology intends to make the church assume theological responsibility for the unintended, social consequences of its religion and free the proclamation of the gospel from the alienating trends associated with it, contemporary theologians regard the Christian teaching on the last things as a topic of special challenge. Is it possible to understand Christ's preaching of the kingdom as utopian rather than ideological religion? The great critics of religion have measured Christian teaching in the light of the common understanding held by the church over the last centuries, with its almost exclusive concentration on individual destiny. The message of the kingdom has been reduced, in the church's preaching and in the minds of the faithful, to an assurance of personal survival after death and entry into the happiness of heaven. Hell was preached as a possibility for the unrepentant sinner, and in the

Catholic Church purgatory was presented as the realm where the faithful departed of good will undergo the painful transformation that enables them to enter into eternal bliss. What we find in this common understanding is an almost complete privatization of the gospel promises. The first task of critical theology then, here as in connection with other doctrines, is the deprivatization of the church's teaching.

We have already stressed that according to the New Testament the center of Christ's preaching was the kingdom of God. Jesus was the servant and instrument of God's reign in the lives of men, promised to Israel in the ancient days, inaugurated in his person, and about to be made manifest in all its power. This kingdom was no "otherworldy reality"; it was God's reign, promised from the beginning, anticipated in the covenanted people and the sacramental church, and finally coming upon history as judgment and new creation. This kingdom was not conceived as a realm parallel to history; it was not a heavenly dominion above the realms of the earth; the kingdom was, rather, the divine reign that emerged in history as the longing of the cosmos and the fulfillment of the people's hopes. The kingdom was preached as the new age. It will destroy the sin in the hearts of men and the injustices present in their institutions, it will rectify the inequalities in the world and give people access to the sources of life. It was this kingdom that was to have no end. The promises made in the New Testament, then, affect individual people as well as society, the heart as well as the world, the body as well as the soul, present history as well as the world to come. The Christian promises are offered globally; they are not sorted out in detail. We admit, of course, that the New Testament language regarding the kingdom is dualistic, but this refers not to a dualism between mind and body, or between person and society, but to the contrast between the old age and the new. Christ ushered in a new age. The New Testament records the different ways in which the early Christians understood God's promises, from the eager expectation of the final judgment and the end of the world, to the patient confidence that the kingdom present in Christ and his church would be a source of a gradual humanization in history.

In the patristic age the message of eternal life remained focused on the community. It is true that the eschatological tension of the early church was lost very soon, but if we are to believe Henri de Lubac's famous study, *Catholicisme*,[1] in the age of the fathers the thrust of the church's teaching, including the doctrine of eternal life, focused on the redemption and destiny of the whole community. Lubac developed the thesis of his book in the thirties, after prolonged conversation with Marxist thought; he tried to demonstrate that the individualism implicit in modern Christianity was due to the privatization of religion which had distorted, against the genius of Catholicism, the collectivist understanding of sin, grace and glory proclaimed and celebrated by the church of the fathers. The church as God's people was the bearer of the divine promises, and it was this people that was to live eternally. The church was the sign and symbol of the whole human race, the one human family, whose destiny was disclosed and made visible in the fellowship of the faithful. The doctrine of eternal life revealed first and foremost the divine end and purpose of history. It directed people's imagination toward the last days of God's ultimate victory of evil and the creation of a new heaven and a new earth. The question of personal survival after death was not in the foreground. The liturgy of Christian burial confined itself to the simple words of *requies, lux* and *pax.* Dominant in the Christian imagination and the church's liturgy was the hope for the final accomplishment, the completion of history, and the resurrection of the entire people.

For the first thousand years the Christian people looked forward to the resurrection of the last day as the complete fulfillment of the divine promises and showed comparatively little interest in the state of the soul after the death of the body. This changed gradually. When the theologians in the 14th century, responding to the religion of the faithful, taught that after death the soul encounters the living God, undergoes the particular judgment, and if approved is admitted to eternal bliss in the *visio beatifica*, Pope John XXII, relying on the more ancient tradition, condemned this new trend. "The soul separated from the body," he taught, "does not enjoy the vision of God which is its total reward and will not enjoy it prior to the resurrection."² Pope John XXII was the last witness of the ancient church's collectivist imagination, which saw salvation primarily as the entry of the entire people into grace and glory. However individualistic culture had superseded the Pope. He himself changed his mind; and the next pontiff, Pope Benedict XII, revoked the position of his predecessor, solemnly proposed the new teaching, and confirmed the shift of the church's religious longing from the crowning of history in the new creation to the soul's eternal happiness after death. Until recently, this has been the common stance of modern Christianity.

In the modern period the church's teaching of eternal life was understood almost exclusively in terms of the fate that awaited the individual after his or her death. The eschatological framework of the gospel was largely abandoned. Christians no longer experienced themselves as a people on pilgrimage, as a people with an historical destiny; instead they regarded the society to which they belonged, and the church within it, as abiding elements of the divine plan and reduced the great Christian adventure to the personal journey from birth to death. Church and society were the unchanging stage on which people worked out their personal salvation. The Church's liturgy, on the whole, retained the historical vision and recalled that God had acted in Christ on behalf of all mankind and brought history to the new and final age, but the individualistic culture did not allow this ancient teaching to affect the people's piety. Death became the end of the journey and salvation the pledge of one's own personal happiness beyond the grave.

This privatizing trend in religion corresponds to the growing individualism in secular culture, which has reached its high point in modern, *Gesellschaft*-type society. Here the individual is wholly severed from the social matrix. At the same time, acting as impersonal agents in a rationalized society, people feel that they have lost the sense of self. The triumph and agony of individualism have made people focus on personal death as the great enemy which threatens the meaning of their lives in the present. Modern secularity imitates the church's concentration on death. For Heidegger, the fear of death marks a person's entire life and produces a metaphysical anguish that reveals man's authentic nature. This concentration on personal death has even found entry into sociological reflection. Alfred Schutz integrates Heidegger's view of death into his phenomenology of the social world, and Peter Berger assigns personal death a primary role in his sociology of religion and the construction of reality.[3] The fear of death overshadows the whole of a person's life; it convicts her efforts of building the world and her quest for happiness of finitude and imbues them with a peculiar anxiety. This anguish, this fear of death, the horror of chaos is, according to Berger's sociology, the generating force that makes people seek a safe and stable world, and create sacred symbols that legitimate the present order and promise future security. Religion is created as the answer to personal death and its anxiety-producing power. What we have here, it seems to me, is a psychology rather than a sociology of religion.

While it may not be surprising that such a privatizing perspective takes hold of philosophers in the modern age, it is curious to see this perspective applied in sociology. For why should a social thinker hold that death is the universal fact that has meaning apart from the social context in which it occurs? Is the reaction of people to their mortality a transcendent phenomenon, independent of their cultural world, and hence a solid ground, beyond the changing social circumstances, on which to construct a sociology of religion? The old-fashioned literature glorifying the self-sacrifice of soldiers on the battlefield is a good illustration that the attitude toward one's own death depends on social environment. Max Weber may have been only half-serious when he suggested that death has become such an absurd event only in modern, competitive, achievement-oriented society because there people daily sacrifice happiness for the sake of work, and when they finally encounter death, they feel that after having postponed happiness all their lives, they are now cheated of their reward and their entire life is being mocked and invalidated. Weber may have thought that in other cultures people were willing to live more wholeheartedly in the present with its joys and pains, and when death awaited them as the long sleep at the end of their lives, they may not have been that frightened by it. Even the attitude toward death is socially grounded. To regard the anxiety over one's mortality as a primary principle of human behavior, I conclude, corresponds not to the nature of reality but to the privatizing trend of the social world.

The attitude toward death depends on the imagination of the future, mediated throughout society by cultural or religious movements. In tribal society, the imagination of people projected the ongoing existence of the tribe and hence they found it easy to speak of life beyond the grave. They felt themselves embedded in a living reality that would perdure in the future. In the ages of nationalism and its accompanying conflicts and wars, to give another example, people's imagination of the future circled around the emergence and flowering of the nation, and when confronted with death in this struggle, they did not fear for themselves but dreamt of their nation's future. Nationalist poetry is full of accounts of such sacrificial deaths. In modern society, people's imagination of the future tends to be caught in their own personal lives. They dream of what life will be like for them in ten years, in twenty years, in thirty years. In the consumers' society of today our imagination is taught to concentrate on the rising standard of living and the ever greater personal well-being. Death, in such a context, seems utterly frightful. But already if a person is profoundly attached to her children and their families, then her imagination will circle around their future and her own personal death will not appear as the great enemy. Herbert Marcuse, the great atheistic social philosopher, has made one of the most profound remarks about death, one that one might expect to find in the great literatures of religion. "Men can die without anxiety," Marcuse wrote, "if they know that what they love is protected from misery and oblivion."[4] If the object of a person's love is protected from harm and assured of well-being, then the nothingness of her own tomorrow, threatened in death, is not a great source of anguish. But if we love ourselves, and our future imagination circles around our own well-being—this is almost inevitable in *Gesellschaft*-type society—then what we love is wholly unprotected, and death becomes the dreaded enemy. How does Marcuse's important remark apply to the Christian faith? If we yearn for the kingdom of God, if we long for God's victory over evil and all the enemies of life and believe that in Christ this victory is assured, then what we love is protected and it should not be so difficult to die.

The Christian teaching of eternal life, we conclude, rather than making the believers focus on their own death and worry about what happens to them after they die, liberates them for a greater love and makes them yearn for the reconciliation and deliverance of all peoples. The Christian message of resurrection, understood in this deprivatizing perspective, far from making Christians concentrate on their own heaven, frees them from anxiety about their own existence and directs their hope to the new creation. The doctrine of God's approaching kingdom, the central Christian symbol, summons people to forget themselves, to serve the kingdom of God coming into the lives of men and women, and to rejoice with the Christian community, gathered at worship, that in Christ God's final victory has been assured. God will have the last word. Evil will not be allowed to stand. The entry into personal salvation and future life is not prepared by concentrating on one's own life but by trusting and loving God's coming reign. The dialect of personal-and-social, which we observed when speaking of sin and grace, must also be observed when interpreting the Christian doctrine of eternal life.

This deprivatizing trend is operative in contemporary spirituality. Perhaps one of the first signs of this reorientation was given by a remarkable woman who in many ways was a conventional saint, Thérèse of Lisieux. In her oft-quoted statement, "I want to spend my heaven doing good on earth," she subtly criticized the individualism of traditional Catholic spirituality. She thought that she would not be able to rest with God as long as people were still suffering and the promised kingdom had not been established. This was then a startling innovation. In contemporary spiritual writers, such as Thomas Merton, Daniel Berrigan, Ernesto Cardinale, and James Douglas, the passage to a more collective understanding of divine salvation has been completed. While these authors attach much importance to personal life and one's personal union with God as the ground for a life that will never die, they understand this personal life as participation in the human community and a share in the salvation which is meant for all. Here each person is damaged by the misery inflicted on others. In this new spirituality there is no communion with God unless mediated by Jesus, that is, by a total solidarity with humanity, especially the underprivileged and dispossessed. Here entry into eternal life is again understood, following the New Testament, as repentance and identification with God's coming reign. Anguish about one's death and concern about one's personal heaven are not the entry into the Christian life. Nor is the question of personal survival after death the best way to approach the Christian teaching on eternal life.

The common theological approach to death and dying has also been privatized from another point of view. Usually, in sermons and books on pastoral theology, we speak of death as if people normally die peacefully in their beds. Death is here looked upon as the startling end of a person's life in a settled context of friendly faces. Yet by thinking of death in this way, we forget that vast numbers of people die very differently as victims of society. A glance at a statistics of people killed by wars, acts of genocide, unrelieved famines, and other forms of collective violence reminds us that a peaceful death in bed is by no means the normal way for people to die in the 20th century. A certain, highly private theology of dying, it seems to me, disguises from consciousness the cruel world to which we belong. We tend to think that the terms which make sense to us in our protected context apply to people everywhere. But death in bed, after a life well spent, is for many people the object of great hope. To focus on this kind of death as if it were the great enemy overlooks the political realities of the 20th century. Asking the reader's permission for a very personal remark, I recall that my own mother, hiding in Berlin from Nazi persecution of the Jews and deportation to the death camps, became overwhelmed with exhaustion, fell gravely ill, and still died in a bed surrounded by friendly faces, not by enemies. This was a grace. A Christian theology of death ought to take the political dimension seriously. To die in bed, after a long, affirmative life, is not so bad, and we can't really wish anything better for ourselves. At the same time, we do not want an imagination of the future that circles around our own personal fate. The Christian message of the coming kingdom promises deliverance from evil on a universal scale including all the peoples of the earth, and thanks to this message we want to think of our personal lives as situated in this holy, dread and universal drama.

* * *

After reflecting on the privatization imposed on the concept of death and the Christian message of eternal life, we return to the eschatological framework of the New Testament and the thrust of Christ's own preaching on the approaching reign of God. By a convergence of several intellectual trends this eschatological aspect of the gospel has received sustained attention in modern Christian theology and become a focal point in the renewal of Christian teaching. At one time, liberal theologians were almost embarrassed to speak of the apocalyptical passages of the New Testament. To preach on the end of the world and the return of Christ on the clouds of heaven had become the privilege of evangelical Christians engaged in a literalistic reading of the Bible. Yet 20th-century biblical scholarship recovered the eschatological perspective of the New Testament, and various philosophical schools of process thought taught Christian theologians to make the vision of the end a principle for understanding the present.[5] It is more especially dialogue with sociology that enables Christian theologians to regain an understanding of eschatology which preserves the personal-and-social dialectic and gives Christian preaching a utopian or transformist thrust.[6]

The gospel as utopia! From Karl Mannheim's sociology of knowledge we have derived the distinction between ideology and utopia and learned to detect the utopian trends in the Christian religion.[7] Here we find the conceptual tools for evaluating the religious imagination of man's future and for deprivatizing the church's teaching of eternal life. Mannheim was not the first social philosopher who used the concept of utopia to analyze religious language and the imagination of the future. Immediately after World War I, the young Ernst Bloch had published two studies on the spirit of utopia, one in particular dealing with the Christian doctrine of God's kingdom. In his brilliant book, *Thomas Muenzer*, with the subtitle "Theologian of Revolution,"[8] the great social philosopher examined from a non-dogmatic Marxian position the relation of eschatology and politics and showed that the Christian teaching on eternal life, in whatever form, has political meaning and in some cases even political effect.

Bloch's *Thomas Muenzer* could be compared with Weber's *The Protestant Ethic and the Spirit of Capitalism.* Weber's book, as we discussed earlier, tried to show that Calvinism, or a special development within Calvinism, provided the religious inspiration to the rising class of merchants and entrepreneurs, that made them the successful creators of a new civilization. Weber tried to demonstrate—not against Marx, but as a complement to the Marxian analysis—that present in religious inspiration was power *sui generis*, irreducible to other interests, which actually affected man's creation of culture and society. It is impossible to render an account of the origin of modern, rational society without including the religious factor. Ernst Bloch made the same kind of analysis for the revolutionary movements in Germany during the 16th century. Bloch shows that a political and economic analysis alone cannot account for the course of these events, unless accompanied by a study of radical religion, in particular the preaching of Thomas Muenzer.

Bloch here corrects the earlier studies by Marxist thinkers who saw in the radical religious movements of the past only a disguised form of political protest. Friedrich Engels, in his "The Peasant War in Germany,"[9] analyzed the oppression inflicted on peasants and laborers in 16th-century feudal society, studied the identification of the Lutheran movement with the princes and landowners, and came to the conclusion that "the chiliastic dream-visions of early Christianity offered a very convenient starting-point"[10] to the Christian radicals for mounting a revolutionary attack on the social order. For Engels, then, the religious aspirations of Muenzer and the radicals were simply a screen or a cloak for political goals. "Although the class struggles of that day were carried on under religious shibboleths, and though the interests, requirements and demands of the various classes were concealed behind a religious screen, this changed nothing in the matter and is easily explained by the conditions of the time."[11] Engels even suggests that toward the end of his life Muenzer "cloaked" his revolutionary philosophy in Christian phrases to make it more acceptable to his age. Against this reductionist view, Ernst Bloch shows in his book-length analysis of Muenzer's life and preaching that his eschatological vision of the future was a genuine religious passion, not a cloak for political revolution, and, moreover, that the spreading of social unrest and the outbreak of the peasant revolt are unaccountable without taking into consideration this radical religion. Ernst Bloch, very much like Weber, except with greater literary brilliance and poetic flair, has demonstrated the creativity of the symbolic sphere and the world-producing power of religion. In fact, he complements the research of Weber, in line with Troeltsch's important work, by analyzing the socio-political implications of the spiritual compromise with the world of the Calvinist, Lutheran and Catholic church establishments. Bloch belongs to those remarkable thinkers, following upon the success of the scientific consciousness, who rediscovered the sense and power of the symbolic.

In Muenzer's personal life and public preaching the religious imagination and the political intention were so inseparably interwoven that the attempts of his interpreters to understand him as a spiritual ecstatic who at times betrayed his vision and moved into the political arena have been unsuccessful. Muenzer was neither a spiritual visionary who occasionally fanned the revolutionary fire of his listeners, nor a secular rebel who used eschatological language to convict the privileged and the powerful and to stir people's hopes for a new society. Muenzer is inseparably both, a religious figure and a political rebel. He remained mindful of social justice when he was most concerned with God's glory, and he remained religious when he gave vent to his hatred of the ruling class in church and society. Bloch is well aware that there have been religious leaders who, inspired by their religious ideals, became dedicated to political goals and who, after the involvement with the world of politics, lost their specifically religious fervor and became purely secular in their concern. But this did not happen to Muenzer. His was a truly utopian religion. Muenzer had his odd sides, Bloch does not deny this; still, Bloch's study comes to the conclusion that the theologian of revolution was a great and tragic figure, not an angry fanatic crazed by his visions, but a courageous witness to a hope that does not die.[12]

Bloch shows that the entire preaching of Muenzer, on sin, on conversion, on inwardness, on asceticism, on poverty and the cross of Christ, was formulated with a critical conscious-ness of its political implications and defined over against Cath-olic and Protestant preaching on these topics, which unbe-knownst to these preachers, actually protected the powerful and the rich. Muenzer saw the world divided, beyond the customary boundary lines, into the friends of God, chosen by him, and the enemies of justice intent on their own advantage. These friends, Muenzer held, were dispersed through all peoples, religions, churches and traditions. Their faith, created by God even if they never heard of Jesus, consisted—as does the Christian faith—in the conversion away from egotism, domination and the alliance with the ruling class, and in the trusting identifica-tion with the poor, the exploited, the oppressed in whom God's reign will appear. But the center of Muenzer's preaching was the impatient, eschatological hope that the Lord was near, that the divine judgment had already been pronounced on the sinful society, and that God was about to manifest his victory in the liberation of his people from injustice and oppression. For Muenzer the biblical doctrine of eternal life became a harsh and fervent utopia, magnificent yet blind and misguided, sum-moning people to a struggle they were bound to lose.

The study of utopian religion in a concrete case leads Bloch to the topic that remained central in his philosophical work, namely the creative role played by day-dreams, poetry and religious expectations in the making of history. In Bloch's early books he writes about the power of day-dreams with an almost romantic enthusiasm; in his later writings, especially in his *Prinzip der Hoffnung*,[13] he becomes more measured, con-tained and qualified yet retains the same basic inspiration that the new in history has its origin in the human imagination.

Reality is unfinished, it is still in the making. This is

Bloch's metaphysics.[14] The future is hidden in the past, and yet the future must be created out of freedom. The future is grounded in the past and yet remains undetermined. Reality is purposeful for Bloch; as a Marxian thinker he recognizes a direction of human striving. Yet the future is never created according to fixed laws; the future remains open, it is produced by a process that involves people's freedom and their imagination. Bloch distinguished between the *cold* current in Marxism which stresses the scientific, determinist aspect in the making of history and the *warm* current which recognizes the element of phantasy and human longing in the creation of tomorrow. And while these currents should remain together and stimulate and limit one another, Bloch regards it as his special task to emphasize the warm current of utopia that official Marxism has neglected. With poetic power and sociological sensitivity Bloch writes about the unfinished world that gives birth to the future, about the process by which the hidden powers present in today's reality are projected into the future, and about the role of expectancy and hope in directing the creation of the new.

Bloch is a dialectical materialist in the Marxian sense of the word. Matter is primary. Matter is where it all comes from. Located in the dynamic potential of matter is the objective basis for the unfinished world, for not-yet-being. Bloch claims that theologians, "the Jacobs of theology, have robbed matter of its birthright as firstborn."[15] Matter, for Bloch, is not a substratum that receives its vitality from another principle; matter is pregnant, matter possesses its own potential, its own dynamics of self-transformation. Seen from this perspective, the spirit is not "the trump card" held over matter, but "its own blood," that is, its own vitality that cannot be separated from its substrate.[16]

Bloch carries this thinking over into his anthropology. Human beings, too, are unfinished, yet alive and self-creating out of the thrust of their materiality. This basic drive is what Bloch calls hunger. We have to eat to survive; we are basically dependent on matter and at the same time we constantly transform matter into new energies and release its hidden potentialities. Hunger, in a wider sense, reveals man's sense of unfulfillment which makes her reach out for new life and contemplate the many possibilities of as yet untried conditions of existence. By defining man in terms of her hunger, man is both open to the future and directed toward it by something within herself. Hunger gives rise to dreams, to day-dreams, to the longing for the new, yet the very same hunger also keeps this imagination in line with man's actual needs and the possibilities of her material reality. In Bloch's uncommon materialism, the new would never come to exist in history unless it existed first in man's imagination and haunted her in her day-dreams.

We have here a curious inversion of materialism into its apparent opposite, into what to many appears as idealism. Yet this inversion is characteristic of much of German thought. We remarked earlier that Hegel's idealism could be read as sociological theory rendering an account of how the symbols operative in the mind are translated into the concrete institutions of society and how dialectical reason, operative in the forward movement of society, expresses itself in the practical reactions of people to the alienating trends hidden, and eventually manifest, in the concrete condition of their lives. Ernst Bloch also provides a philosophy that shows how the subjective is translated into objectivity, how the dream is the parent of tomorrow's world, and how human hope is the source of history which man creates—all conjoined to a material logic from below. This trend of thought is not startling to the readers of this book. For when we spoke of symbols in the preceding chapter, we saw that symbols bridge the gap between subject and object in the two directions: symbols are both the reflection of society in the human mind and the objective structure of the social world which men have created according to their imagination. The symbols of the future have power in the production of society.

Bloch's anthropology of hunger ties his philosophy into the Marxian theory which assigns a special historical role to the poor and dispossessed and their ensuing class struggle against oppression. Yet while the direction of history is determined by the quest for fulfillment of human hunger, Bloch stresses the indetermination within this general direction. For the emergence of the new in history depends on the dreams of people and the power of their hope, rooted in the latency of their material conditions. History then remains open and free.

Bloch's intoxicating hope, in the face of the gigantic obstacles to man's pacification in West and East alike, is founded, curiously and lastly unconvincingly, on the dynamics of matter revealed in human hunger. Bloch is a passionate atheist; he repudiates any divine lord ruling the world from above or any supreme spiritual principle directing the world from within. Bloch opposes the divine as a dangerous factor alienating man from her material foundation. What man has to learn is to trust her material principles and create the world out of her hunger. Nonetheless, to the theological reader, Bloch's writings have a powerful religious quality: they witness an extraordinary faith in the inexhaustible fecundity of the matrix of human life; they betray the paradoxical conviction that in their vigorous actions people are simultaneously being carried forward, and they reveal an imagination haunted by the irrepressible daydream of a future realm in which people shall live in justice and peace. I honor Bloch's atheism; but the temptation for a Catholic theologian after the Blondelian shift is to see in Bloch's vehement denial simply the radical refusal to pronounce the holy name.

Bloch's anthropology of hunger offers an interesting critique of the Freudian theory that attributes to sex a centrality in human life. The sexual drive is primary only in the well-fed classes; the poor and exploited are hungry first of all. According to Bloch it is out of the primary, material self-symbolization of the poor that the whole of man's history must be understood. To illustrate the Blochian perspective, allow me to tell a dramatic incident that took place at a theological conference held in the United States a few years ago. A well-known, imaginative, psychotherapeutically-oriented theologian wanted to discuss with his audience the methods used in theology, and to do this well he first tried to initiate the participants to the telling of their own private story. Only as we become familiar with our own story, beginning with childhood and the early relations to mother and father, do we discover the bent of our mind and the orientation of reason that alone will be fruitful for us. Unless we recover our own emotional past, we might adopt a method of rational reflection that actually goes counter to our basic intuitions and strengthens our defenses against the significant repressed. The lecturer then asked the participants of the conference to form groups of two; handing out large sheets of drawing paper and felt tip markers, he then asked each couple to draw the plan of the house or apartment where they were born and where they lived as children, to indicate where mother and father slept, where their own bed was situated, etc. The couples were asked to tell their childhood story to one another and, if possible, to verbalize the feelings that emerge as they tell their story. The source of people's creativity —this, I suppose, was the lecturer's presupposition—lies in their infancy dreams and wishes, and only as they are able to overcome the defenses that keep these desires hidden from them are they able to discover the bent and power of their thinking. The minority of black and Mexican Americans present vehemently objected to this procedure. "White, middle-class nonsense!" they shouted. Yet they were unable to analyze the reasons for their strong reaction. One young Mexican American priest stomped out of the hall. A fellow participant followed him and joined the angry priest on a walk around the building. After a little while the priest's anger subsided. He turned to his companion and said, "Now I'll tell you my story. When my people were conquered in 1848. . . ." The companion was amazed. If you belong to the middle class, your story begins with the infancy relations to mother and father—the Freudian perspective—but if you belong to an oppressed group, then the conditions of this oppression overshadow the childhood conflicts with mother and father and mark the structure of daily existence so strongly that even the personal story begins with the people's fall into servitude. Then the human being appears as a sufferer of hunger—the Blochian perspective. Here self-understanding is available only through the freedom history of one's own people or class. Women can use the Blochian analysis to refute the dependent image which Freud, so devastatingly, has painted for them. At the same time there is no reason why Bloch's concept of hunger should not include eros and the sexual transcendence of self-love. For the kind of hunger that Bloch describes for us does not lead to a concentration on one's own egotistic desires, but, on the contrary, to the identification with the brother and sister in fellowship and common life, and hence to a self-transcendent conversion to the other.

So far Bloch's utopia still remains too undefined. Not every dream of future happiness is utopian. In modern, capitalistic society we are constantly exposed to images of an ideal future based on an ever higher standard of living and the continuing quest for the egotistic fulfillment of pleasure and comfort. This, according to Ernst Bloch, is no utopian dream. For we can speak of utopia only if the imagination introduces a qualitatively new element in the form of human life. The utopian day-dream does not prolong the present into the future but it elevates and recreates the present in keeping with man's unfulfilled potentialities. With this demand for the qualitatively new, Bloch tried to distinguish utopian from other future dreams, just as Mannheim did, after him, with the contrast between ideology and utopia.

Bloch distinguished between various kinds of hunger and their extensions into human longing. There are yearnings for objects that already exist in the world, and there are yearnings for objects that do not yet exist. The first yearning produces inauthentic feelings such as envy, greed, and veneration. Envy and greed do not unfold but disguise the as yet unfulfilled powers of human life. But even the veneration of people who possess what one desires, relates one inauthentically to the object of desire: for veneration leads to passivity and a person's ready submission to inequality. The yearning for objects that do not yet exist, that is, the strong feelings of expectancy in regard to the future, include anxiety, fear, hope and faith. Of these only hope is authentically human.[17] For anxiety and fear are born of alienation; and even faith makes people dependent on another, fosters their inaction, and eventually results in alienation. In hope alone do people authentically relate their yearning to the future. Only if the day-dream is accompanied by hope does it release the potentialities of matter, direct action, and enable people to create the new. These critical reflections greatly limit the day-dreams that may be rightly called utopia. Excluded are the narcissistic dreams that possess us so often, excluded the dreams of revenge and the phantasies of resentment, excluded the longings for self-aggrandizement and the contemplation of future victory over others. The philosopher of the day-dream develops here a strict asceticism of the imagination. He here excludes even religious faith in promises made by another. The only authentically human day-dream of the impossible is one that is rooted in the possibilities of man's material nature.

Bloch moves one step further in distinguishing utopia from other imaginations of the future. He contrasts "concrete" with "abstract" utopias.[18] Concrete utopias are imaginations of future fulfillment which are sufficiently close to the possibilities of the present that they give rise to practical ideas of what to do and summon forth some form of action; abstract utopias, on the other hand, present the imagination of the new future in such a remote way, wholly unrealizable in terms of present possibilities, that it paralyzes the practical intelligence, leads to inaction, and makes people into empty dreamers. In the language of Mannheim, abstract utopias are really ideological. The ordinary use of the word "utopian" has come to refer precisely to the unrealizable dream of the perfect life, which makes no contribution to changing the world. What is regrettable in this common usage, however, is that it denigrates all utopias, even concrete utopias; and when the utopias die, as Mannheim told us, society will be caught in an inflexible cage. Concrete utopias alone, according to Bloch, can generate hope and become the entry of man into a new future.

* * *

Let us return to theology. Making use of the preceding analysis of future images, we claim that the church's teaching on eternal life is a revealed utopia. The message of the kingdom which is partially present among us and yet still approaching in all its power, proposes a vision of the future in which people live in justice and peace, conjoined in friendship and the common worship of the divine mystery. This eschatological reign of God, situated at the horizon of history, is not envisaged as a conquest by a superior world but as the completion of liberation already begun, as the visible manifestation of

divine grace now operative in people's efforts to create a fraternal (sisterly) society. The glory of the future is the unfolding of
present grace.

This message of the God's reign is utopian (not ideological) because it reveals the structure of sin in the present world.
The promised realm of justice and peace is the measure by
which Christians evaluate and judge present society. "Thy will
be done on *earth* as it is in heaven." The heavenly city expresses a mandate for life in present society. The Christian
message of eternal life, then, makes people critical of present
institutions and elicits in them a longing for a more just and
more equal social order. The message of eternal life is a concrete utopia (not an abstract dream) because the promises
made for the heavenly city constantly give rise to ideas of what
should be done at this time to make society more truly human.
The eschatological message leads to social action. In this book
we have developed the theme of Christ the transformer of the
world. Indeed, the Christian message of eternal life exercises its
utopian function, despite the setbacks and cruel disappointments people have suffered, and are at this time suffering, in
history. Still, after crucifixion, the Christian message of resurrection summons forth hope in the newness of life even on this
earth. The message of God's kingdom, finally, gives birth to
self-actualizing hope (not to passive dependence) since the God
in whom Christians believe is enabler and vivifier in history
and empowers men and women to act on their own behalf.
Faith in the divine promises does not make people inactive; it
empowers them to act.

This utopian understanding of eternal life is not the only
interpretation that has been given to the Christian doctrine of
the heavenly city! But whenever the doctrine of eternal life is
not utopian, it becomes ideological.

The message of eternal life is, of course, a very special
utopia. In the first place, Christians hold that it has been divinely revealed. The church is alive by the day-dreams of the
prophets and of Jesus Christ, in which is made known the hidden structure of reality and the destiny of the human race. The
utopia of eternal life is special, moreover, because it transcends
the order of history. The divine promises remain operative even

if we should destroy the conditions for human survival on this earth. What is promised to the human family transcends the purely earthly possibilities without, however, ever bifurcating from the forward movement of history. The Christian utopia is proclaimed in terms that overcome the harmful dichotomies between heaven and earth, soul and body, and person and society. The divine promises made known in the scriptures are utopian precisely because they do not sort out the order of their fulfillment. The fulfillment remains open, dependent on human freedom, on a freedom which in turn is the work of God's present grace. The message of God's final victory over evil announces the resurrection of all gracious life in a realm of justice and peace, in which every tear shall be wiped away.

According to our remarks in the preceding chapter, this message is lifeless (and ideological) if it is regarded simply as doctrine. It becomes alive and vivifies only when it is permitted to rule the church's imagination as symbol and thus enter into the redemption of history.

The Christian message of God's coming reign produces a view of history at odds with many views currently held in culture and society. Christians disagree with all views that regard history as determined! Christians have some sympathy for the hopeful views that regard history as directed toward human progress. Such hopeful views are found (a) among people who trust science and technology as instruments of social transformation, typified by Auguste Comte, (b) among people who adopt the scientific, historical materialism that Ernst Bloch has called the cold current of Marxism, and (c) among people who follow an evolutionist model and project the ineluctable continuity of the upward movement. Christians inquire in each case what is meant by "progress" and how "the transition" from the old to the new is understood, and test whether these are in keeping with the normative symbols of revelation. Christians, moreover, are ill at ease with the language of determinism. The only determinism is that of hope. They gladly speak of God as the forward movement in history, as the ground, orientation and horizon of all human life, but they insist at the same time that history remains ever open and hence undetermined, and that it continues to depend on human freedom and the gracious moments of God's self-communication. The Christian symbols of the future demand that we speak of history paradoxically. History is destined for redemption, yet undetermined; it is alive by a divine drift toward humanization, yet remains locus of catastrophic sins; it is ever open to the unexpected new. It seems to me that this paradoxical nature is not sufficiently guarded by Teilhard de Chardin's cosmic vision of the future; one feels that he knows too much. He easily passes out of the realm of hope to the realm of science and regards the revealed utopia of God's reign as information about the future rather than as a symbol that through faith enters into the redemption of history.

Christians have little sympathy for the despairing views of history that regard human society inevitably moving toward decline. We find these views (a) among the social scientists, such as Pitirim Sorokin, who accept the cyclical model of civilization's rise and fall, (b) among cultural pessimists, such as Max Weber, who regard today's rational society as the beginning of the iron cage and the end of utopia, and (c) among contemporary natural scientists who predict the end of human history on this globe or propose a strategic lifeboat theory of survival. None of these theories can be proven. For the demonstrations offered always presuppose that history is determined, which is precisely the issue in question. The last-named theorists of gloom,[19] who tell us that we have almost exhausted the earth's resources, tend to presuppose that the social and economic institutions will remain constant, and hence they prefer to speak of future doom rather than advocate radical political change with accompanying changes in people's lifestyles. These scientists try to measure the carrying capacity of the earth, but they do not reflect on its unrealized sharing capacity yet to be achieved. In such an intellectual climate, Christians must affirm, on the strength of the divine promises, that history remains open to human freedom and creativity, open to the unexpected. In our day the churches must preach against the loss of nerve.[20] While the churches of the past were usually the ideological guardians of the established order, today, speaking from a new perspective of faith, the churches should summon people to hope and action, to significant changes in the economic system and the power structures of the wealthy nations, and to the humane expansion of the earth's sharing capacity.

The message of God's coming reign should enable Christians to look upon the destructive eventualities of the future not simply as a fate to be accepted with patience, but as major challenges which they want to use, despite the loss entailed, as opportunities for greater humanization. Christians, out of hope, want to remain free in the face of the inevitable. We read of Christians imprisoned by the Nazis who made the concentration camps into a starting point of the ecumenical movement. This does not mean that evil is "providential." Nor do I wish to suggest that Christians have reacted this way in typical fashion. What I am concerned with here is the meaning of the Christian symbols of the future for present action and the approach toward history of those whose mind is possessed by the divine utopia.

Christians entertain a messianic view of history. They yearn and hope for the triumph of God over evil in personal and social life. This does not mean that they expect things to become better all the time, nor does it imply that they endorse an evolutionary theory of society. To express the historical messianism of the gospel it may be necessary to use paradoxical language: Christians believe that the orientation of history toward renewed life is unalterable, yet the certainty they derive from this is often only the trust that after the great catastrophes produced by human sin we shall again begin to move forward. God is the forward movement *in* history, but not necessarily the forward movement *of* history. The Christian cross, irremovably situated in human history, reveals the defeats created by human sin through which the process of redemption moves toward the newness of life. Yet we do not want to make this cross the symbol of the meaningless of history, nor interrupt our identification with an historical movement for justice, claiming in the name of the cross that all historical endeavors are fragmentary and problematic. The message of eternal life, it seems to me, makes Christians resist not only the skeptics, the careless and the egotists who do not pay attention to the making of the future, but also the tragically resigned who greatly care but regard the historical struggle as a hopeless undertaking. There are believing Christians who restrict the divine promises to the future of personal life and have no hope in God's coming into history. This, to my mind, is a privatization of the gospel that robs it of its power and distorts its social and political meaning. "How, then, do you expect history to end?" the curious always ask. "Do you predict the perfect pacification of life within human history?" Such questions break the symbol power of the Christian message. The revealed utopia is not a prediction, but a promise out of which people are to live. To transform it into information predicting the outcome of the historical process is to change its very nature.[21] The message of God's coming reign reveals the forward thrust of God's gracious presence in people's lives, directs their engagement in action, brings out the religious meaning of the struggle, and creates hope in the fulfillment of the divine promises.

The church's eschatological message implies a critique of the existing order as well as of the existing countervailing movements attempting to change this order. In particular, the message of God's coming reign offers a critique of all secular utopias. For by negating the religious dimension a purely secular utopia produces, quite apart from other possible dehumanizing effects, a repression of the Holy Spirit and thus easily creates a substitute religion, with unintended and uncontrolled social consequences. Marx himself, we recall, was quite unaware of the symbolic nature of his interpretation of history and did not foresee the powerful role which this symbol was to play in the lives of his followers. Since the church's eschatological message differs from secular utopias, the German political theologians like to oppose eschatology and utopia and hence refuse to regard the Christian hope for the kingdom as utopian. The eschaton stands equally against ideologies and utopias. For these theologians the church's prophetic role consists almost exclusively in the negative critique of the dominant order and the countervailing movements, and includes neither a positive commitment to action nor positive recommendations for strategy of social change. The church's political mission seems here confined to a prophetic distance.

Latin American theologians of liberation have objected to these German religious thinkers.[22] A church that restricts itself to negative evaluation remains abstract, aloof and uncommitted, and hence in fact remains where it has been, namely institutionally linked to the dominant order. What is demanded of the church, according to the Latin American liberation theology, is a critical stance toward the existing order and an identification with the existing movement for emancipation and justice. The church must choose the side of the exploited and the countervailing movement, for not to choose means to remain identified with the interests of the ruling class. Within the political movement for liberation, the church will have to play a critical role, examine the means that are being adopted and evaluate the ideals of human life that are being proposed. Especially if the liberation movement becomes successful and takes over the rule in a particular country, the church must remain watchful that the utopia of social justice does not turn into an ideology of the victors and defend the new establishment against the reasonable demands of the poor and the marginal. The Latin American theologians are well aware of the critical function which Christian eschatology must play within a secular political utopia. But this critical function cannot be exercised except from a position of solidarity with this movement. The Latin American theologians oppose German political theology not because it demands a critique of the secular utopia, but only because the German thinkers seem to think that such a critique can be offered apart from a political identification with it.

More than one issue is involved in this controversy. In the first place, it does seem at times that German political theologians are politically abstract and assign a purely critical function to the church's mission in society. Still, it is important to recall that for Johannes Metz, the leading Catholic political theologian, the critical reflection to which the church is summoned should begin with a critique of its own historical situation.[23] The church should come to acknowledge that it does not address itself to moral issues from a neutral position, but that it is in fact, through various institutional links, identified with the government and the interests of the dominant classes. To propose such a theology in Germany, a country where the churches, both Catholic and Lutheran, are recognized and supported by the government as ecclesiastical establishments, is much more than to offer a purely negative critique; Metz's position actually demands a positive, political act on the part of the churches which, in the context of his country, is radical. Political theologians in Germany think that an ecclesiastical act by which the churches free themselves from identification with the dominant institutions would actually release critical forces in Germany that would lead to greater social justice and wider emancipation. In the German context, then, political theology is not as abstract as it first appears.

Other issues are involved in this controversy. In Latin America, as we mentioned in a previous chapter,[24] critical theologians observe a single dominant factor of oppression, namely the capitalist system with its center in the North Atlantic community, to which all other forms of oppression in their societies are subordinated. Commitment to liberation in such a situation, they argue, implies the identification with the historical movement that fights the capitalist system. Yet we mentioned above that critical theologians in other parts of the world see their societies caught in interlocking forms of oppression, in which the economic system plays an important but not the only important role, and hence they do not think that commitment to human liberation implies a single political option. All critical theology, as we have shown, is based on an identification with the movements of the exploited for emancipation, but this identification can be lived out in several strategies. We mentioned in particular the reformist and the radical options facing Christians in North America. I suppose that similar complex situations are also found in Western Europe. In a situation where the Christian commitment to social justice remains open to a variety of strategies, one does not expect the church, the hierarchical church, to identify itself with a single political option. What the church ought here to do is to embody critical social concern, place its institutional weight on the side of emancipation, and faithfully preach the transformist gospel so that people will opt for what they regard as the responsible course of political action.

Christians who have trusted in a transformist gospel and understood the message of the kingdom as utopian have often experienced a special difficulty. They have found that with the involvement in political life and in movements for personal transformation, they experienced a waning of religious interest. While every religious expression has a built-in social and political meaning—we have amply demonstrated this—religion is not exhausted by this meaning. Religion can never be equated with its effects on personal and social life. When we study the history of the social gospel in Canada and the United States, we find that many Christians who, following the summons of faith, involved themselves in social action often found that their specifically religious interest disappeared, that they no longer felt at home in the language of the church, and that they had difficulties in distinguishing their own commitment from that of their secular friends. One of the reasons for this estrangement from the Christian community may well have been the hostility of the churches to the critical movements and their ardent advocates. Be this as it may, it is a fact that many engaged Christians experienced a loss of religious substance. While individuals may survive such a loss of interior life and remain dedicated to their task, the loss of interiority and religious experience has destructive consequences for a Christian community. A church that loses its rootedness in the saving acts of God, in their liturgical celebration and in the personal spirituality of its members eventually loses access to the Spirit that keeps it alive and sends it on its earthly mission. The loss of inwardness will in the long run undermine the solidarity with others and weaken the church's impact on society. The Christian church that at this time is trying to understand its mission in terms of solidarity and liberation must engage in contemplation of the mystery of God as matrix and enabler in human life and as forward movement in history. In the Christian perspective, action equals passion. While we see, we are being enlightened, while we act, we are being carried forward, while we love, we are being saved from selfishness, and while we embrace all people in solidarity, we are being freed inwardly to cross one boundary after another. Every step toward greater humanization is due to the expansion of new and gracious life in us. We are alive by a power that transcends us. In today's world, it has often become difficult to worship this transcendent mystery, since God is not only the life of our life but also the abiding pain we experience in the face of a suffering, oppressed and hungry humanity.

Recommended Readings

Rubem Alves, *Tomorrow's Child*, Harper & Row, New York, 1972.

Ernst Bloch, *Man on His Own*, Herder & Herder, New York, 1970.

————, *A Philosophy of the Future*, Herder & Herder, New York, 1970.

————, *Atheism in Christianity*, Herder & Herder, New York, 1972.

Carl Braaten, *The Future of God*, Harper & Row, New York, 1969.

Ewert Cousins, edit., *Hope and the Future of Man*, Fortress Press, Philadelphia, 1972.

Frederick Herzog, edit., *The Future of Hope*, Herder & Herder, New York, 1970.

Jurgen Moltmann, *Theology of Hope*, S.C.M., London, 1967.

Edward Schillebeeckx, *God the Future of Man*, Sheed & Ward, New York, 1968.

Hans Schwarz, *On the Way to the Future*, Augsburg Publ., Minneapolis, 1972.

Notes

1. Henri de Lubac, *Catholicism*, trans. L. C. Sheppard, Burns & Oates, London, 1962, especially pp. 49-62.
2. *Enchiridion Symbolorum*, edit. Denzinger-Schönmetzer, Herder, Freiburg, 1963, p. 295.
3. Peter Berger, *The Sacred Canopy*, pp. 23-28; *The Social Construction of Reality*, pp. 27, 101-102.

4. Herbert Marcuse, *Eros and Civilization*, Vintage Books, New York, 1962, p. 216.

5. For contemporary literature on eschatology, see Edward Schillebeeckx, "The Interpretation of Eschatology," *Concilium*, Vol. 41, Paulist Press, New York, 1969, pp. 42-56.

6. For a popular presentation of deprivatized eschatology, see Gregory Baum, "Eschatology," *An American Catechism, Chicago Studies*, 12, Fall 1973, pp. 304-311.

7. Cf. above, p. 171.

8. Ernst Bloch, *Thomas Münzer als Theologe der Revolution*, rev. ed., Suhrkamp Verlag, Frankfurt am Main, 1969.

9. Friedrich Engels, *Marx & Engels on Religion*, introd. by Reinhold Niebuhr, Schocken Books, New York, 1964, pp. 97-118.

10. *Ibid.*, p. 102.

11. *Ibid.*, p. 103.

12. Ernst Bloch, *op. cit.*, p. 99.

13. Ernst Bloch, *Das Prinzip der Hoffnung*, 2 vols., Suhrkamp Verlag, Frankfurt am Main, 1969.

14. For Bloch's mature thought in English, see sections of his *Prinzip der Hoffnung* published with a useful introduction by Harvey Cox in Ernst Bloch, *Man on His Own*, Herder & Herder, New York, 1970; also *A Philosophy of the Future*, Herder & Herder, New York, 1970, and *Atheism in Christianity*, Herder & Herder, New York, 1972.

15. Ernst Bloch, *Tübinger Einleitung in die Philosophie*, Suhrkamp Verlag, Frankfurt am Main, 1970, p. 230.

16. *Ibid.*, p. 234.

17. Ernst Bloch, *Prinzip der Hoffnung*, pp. 82-84.

18. *Ibid.*, pp. 178-180.

19. Cf. D. H. Meadows *et al.*, edit., *The Limits to Growth*, New American Library, New York, 1972 and the critical reply, H. S. D. Cole, edit., *Thinking about the Future: A Critique of the Limits to Growth*, Chatto & Windus for the Sussex University Press, 1973.

20. Edgar Bruns, "History, Religion and 'The Failure of Nerve' Today," *The Ecumenist*, 8, March-April 1970, pp. 37-38.

21. "Christian hope is not the attempt of reason to pierce through the future and so to rob it of its mystery. . . . Christian eschatology therefore is not an ideology of the future": John Baptist Metz, "Creative Hope," *New Theology No. 5*, edit. Martin Marty and Dean Peerman, Macmillan, London, 1969, p. 140.

22. Gustavo Gutierrez, *A Theology of Liberation*, Orbis Books, Maryknoll, N.Y., 1973, pp. 220-225.

23. John Baptist Metz, "Zur Präsenz der Kirche in der Gesellschaft, *Die Zukunft der Kirche: Concilium-Kongress 1970*, Benziger Verlag, Zurich, 1971, pp. 86-96.

24. Cf. above, p. 214.